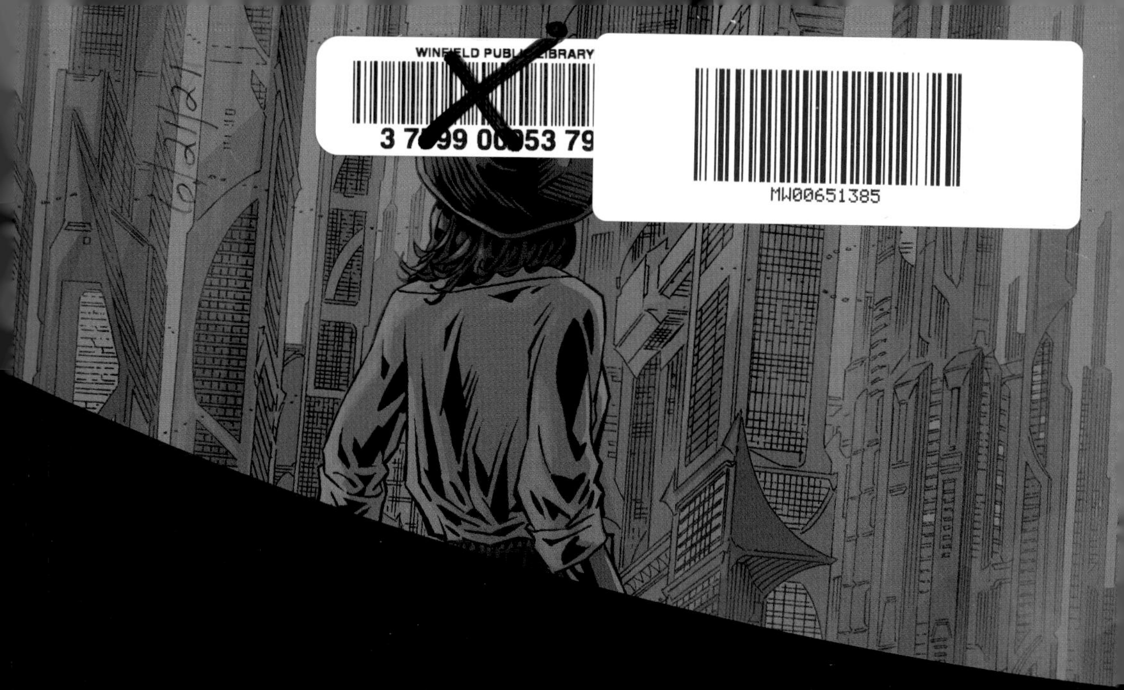

OIN THE FUTURE™

ZACK KAPLAN
PIOTR KOWALSKI
BRAD SIMPSON
HASSAN OTSMANE-ELHAOU

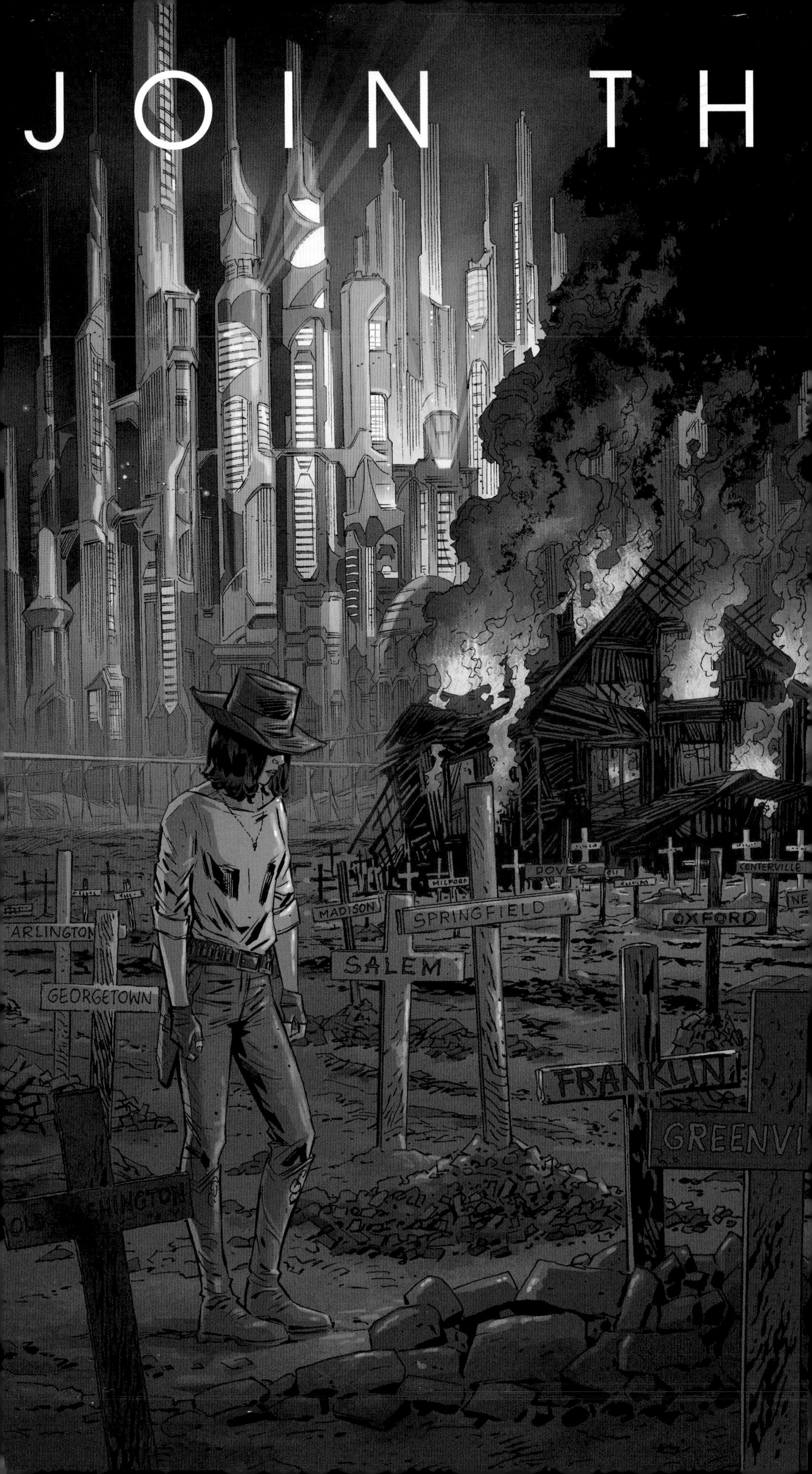
JOIN TH
ARLINGTON
GEORGETOWN
MADISON
MILFORD
SPRINGFIELD
SALEM
DOVER
CENTERVILLE
OXFORD
FRANKLIN
GREENVI

ZACK KAPLAN writer
PIOTR KOWALSKI artist

BRAD SIMPSON colorist

HASSAN OTSMANE-ELHAOU letterer

PIOTR KOWALSKI w/ BRAD SIMPSON front & original covers

NATASHA ALTERICI, TOMMY LEE EDWARDS, SOO LEE, ANDREA MUTTI, BRANDON PETERSON & DARICK ROBERTSON variant covers

CHARLES PRITCHETT logo designer

COREY BREEN book designer

MIKE MARTS editor

created by ZACK KAPLAN

MIKE MARTS - Editor-in-Chief • JOE PRUETT - Publisher/CCO • LEE KRAMER - President • JON KRAMER - Chief Executive Officer
STEVE ROTTERDAM - SVP, Sales & Marketing • DAN SHIRES - VP, Film & Television UK • CHRISTINA HARRINGTON - Managing Editor
MARC HAMMOND - Sr. Retail Sales Development Manager • RUTHANN THOMPSON - Sr. Retailer Relations Manager
KATHERINE JAMISON - Marketing Manager • KELLY DIODATI - Ambassador Outreach Manager • BLAKE STOCKER - Director of Finance
AARON MARION - Publicist • LISA MOODY - Finance • RYAN CARROLL - Development Coordinator • JAWAD QURESHI - Technology Advisor/Strategist
RACHEL PINNELAS - Social Community Manager • CHARLES PRITCHETT - Design & Production Manager • COREY BREEN - Collections Production
TEDDY LEO - Editorial Assistant • STEPHANIE CASEBIER & SARAH PRUETT - Publishing Assistants

AfterShock Logo Design by COMICRAFT
Publicity: contact AARON MARION (aaron@publichausagency.com) & RYAN CROY (ryan@publichausagency.com) at PUBLICHAUS
Special thanks to: ATOM! FREEMAN, IRA KURGAN, MARINE KSADZHIKYAN, KEITH MANZZELLA, STEPHANIE MEADOR, ANTONIA LIANOS & ED ZAREMBA

AFTERSHOCKCOMICS.COM Follow us on social media

I N T R O D U C T I O N

Dedicated to my daughter
and to all the daughters of the future.

Listen here.

That future out there? It's always changing.

Westerns and science fiction both explore a frontier that faces great change and volatility. The past changes, it always changes, and the future will change, too.

Sometimes, the future might feel as though everything is lost (and life might even feel that way right now). Every insurmountable problem feels dark and deadly, life's every adversary seems unflinching, uncaring and unstoppable, and hope slowly slips away.

Other times, the future might overwhelm us with such alluring modern prosperity and technological convenience that we lose proper connection with each another, and we blindly forget just a little of our values and our empathy in this unjust world.

One day in the future, it might feel like you've lost control of yourself and your future.

But here is the God's honest truth: You can shape the future however you believe it should be.

So be strong. Hold firm in your values, and trust your actions have merit and consequence.

Raise your voice. Respect its power, and speak up for those less fortunate than you.

Always persist. Never accept someone else's future over your own vision of hope.

Learn to do things yourself. Develop a passion for hard work and be independent.

Have grit. Get back up when you fall down, because you will fall down over and over.

Believe in who you are. Believe you can do anything if you put your mind to it.

And stand for something. And as you do, with confidence and purpose, others will see it.

And they will join you.

After all, it's your future.

ZACK KAPLAN

1

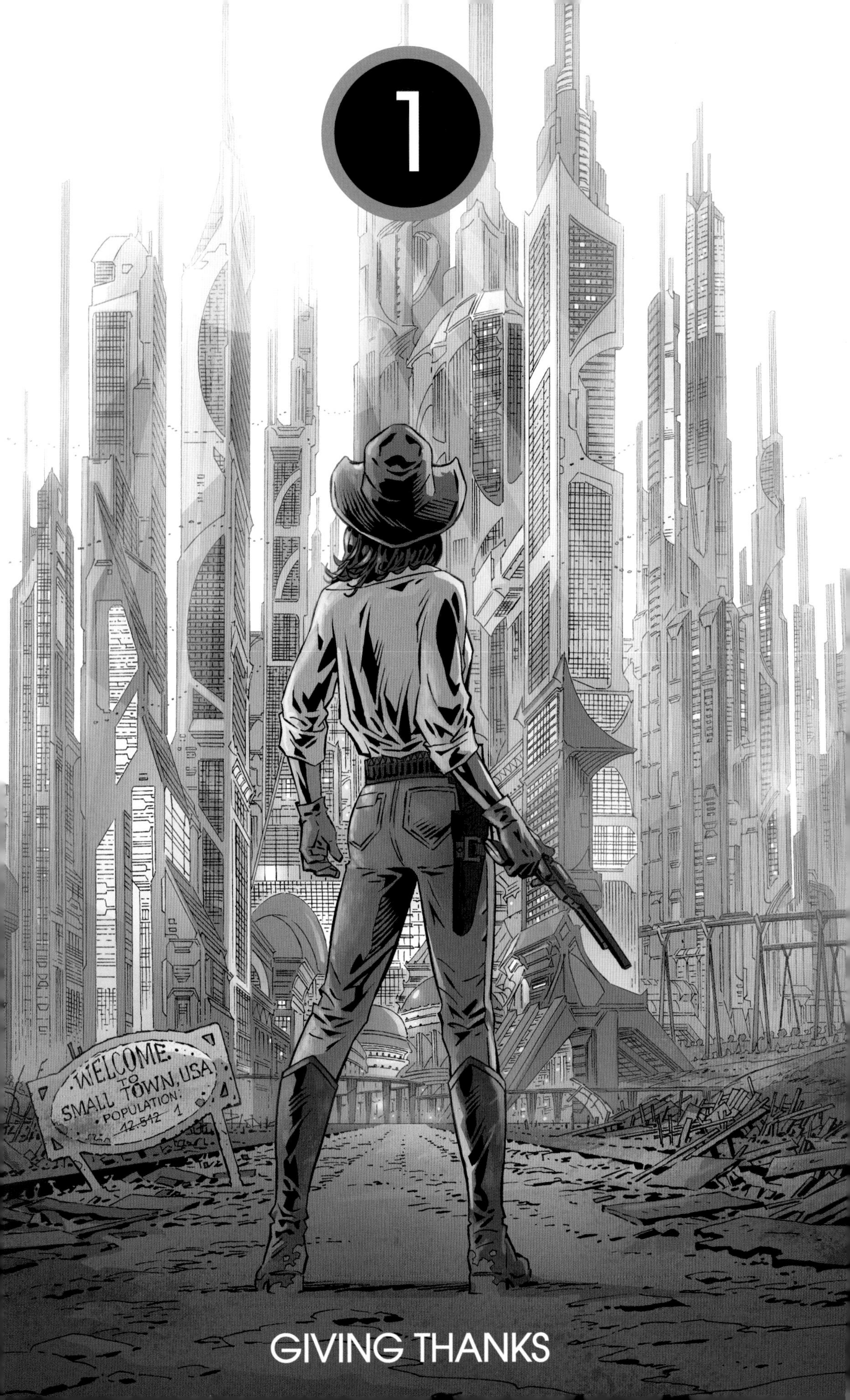
WELCOME
TO
SMALL TOWN, USA
POPULATION:
~~12,542~~ 1

GIVING THANKS

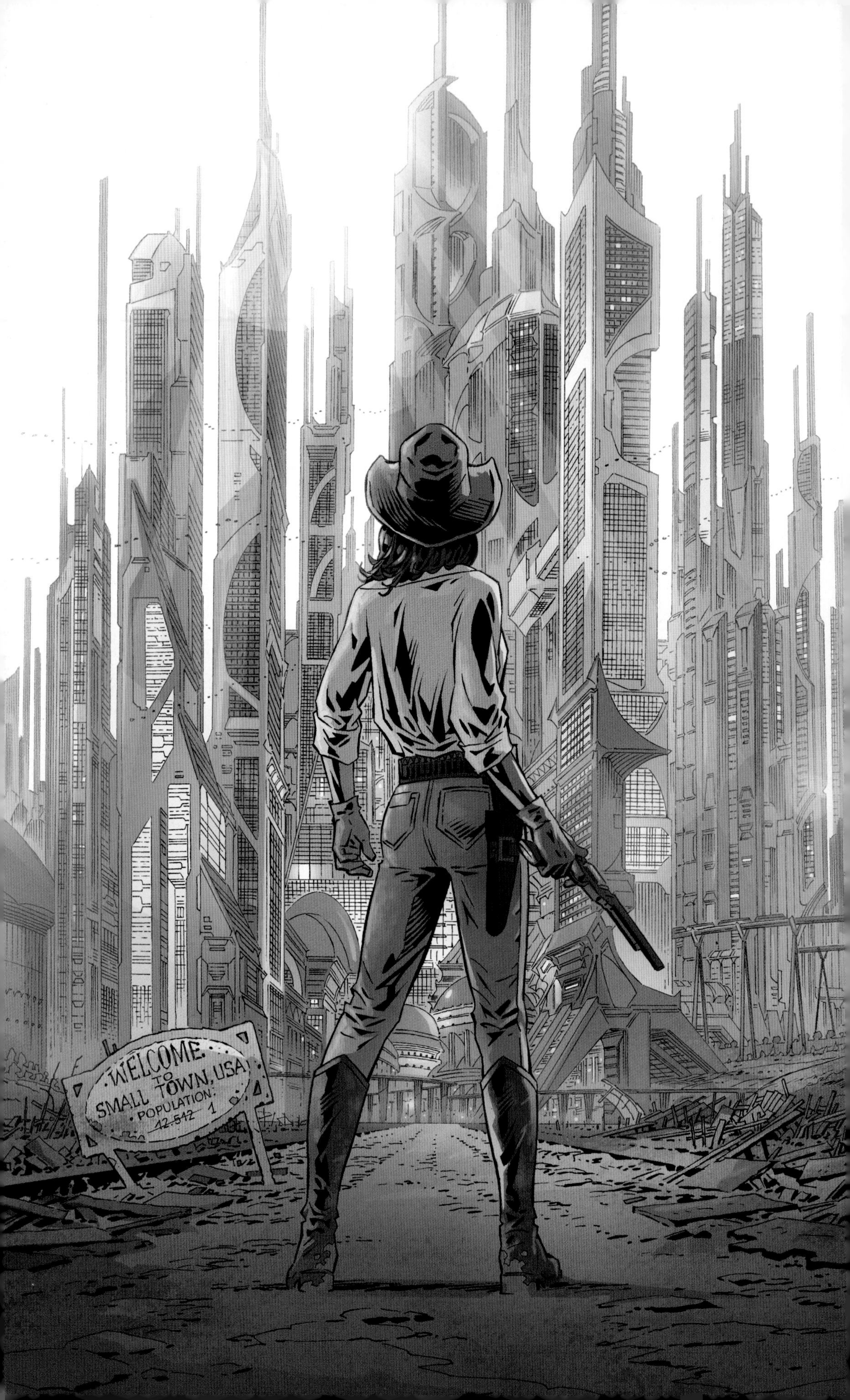
WELCOME
TO
SMALL TOWN, USA
POPULATION:
12.542 1

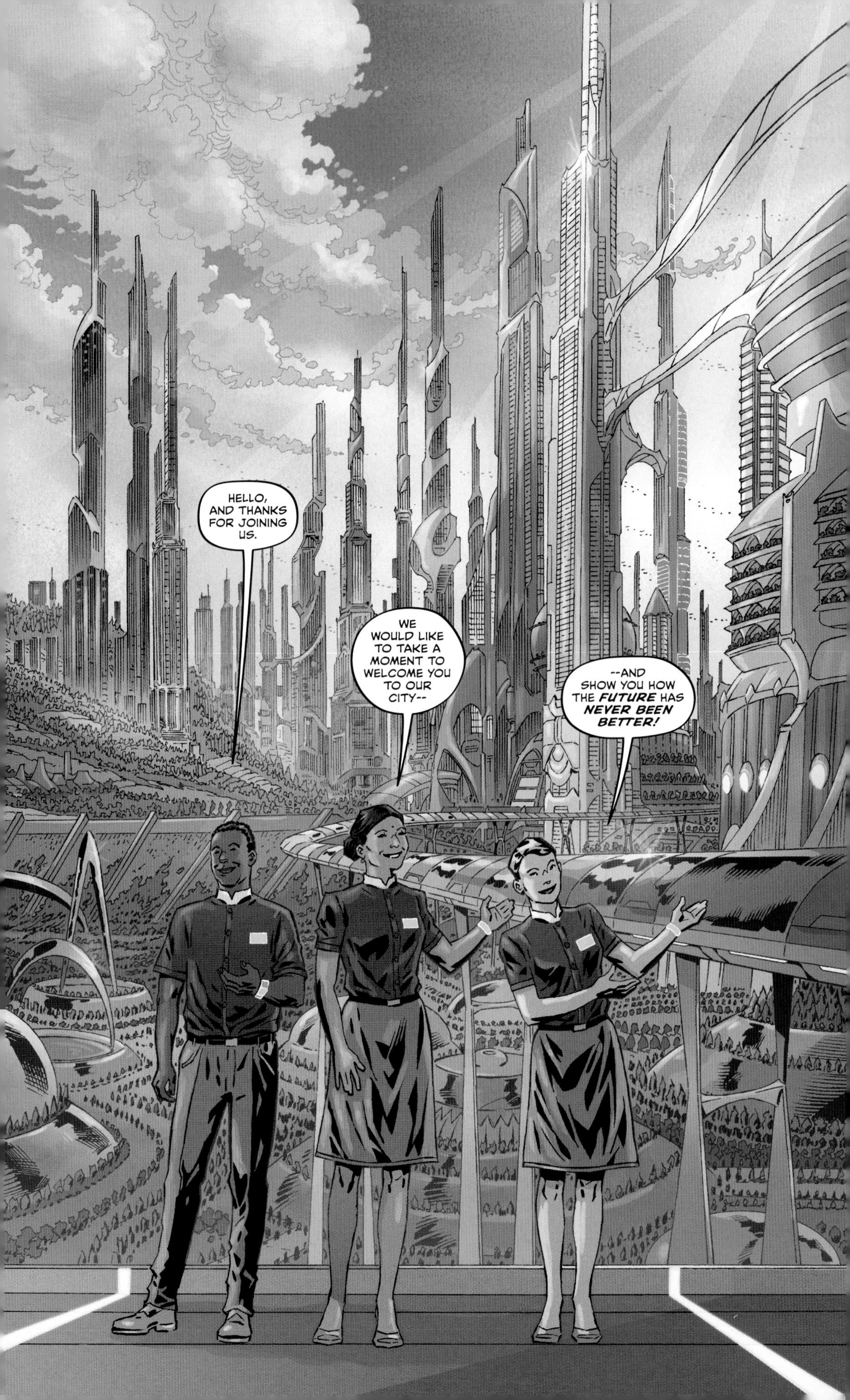
HELLO, AND THANKS FOR JOINING US.
WE WOULD LIKE TO TAKE A MOMENT TO WELCOME YOU TO OUR CITY--
--AND SHOW YOU HOW THE *FUTURE* HAS ***NEVER BEEN BETTER!***

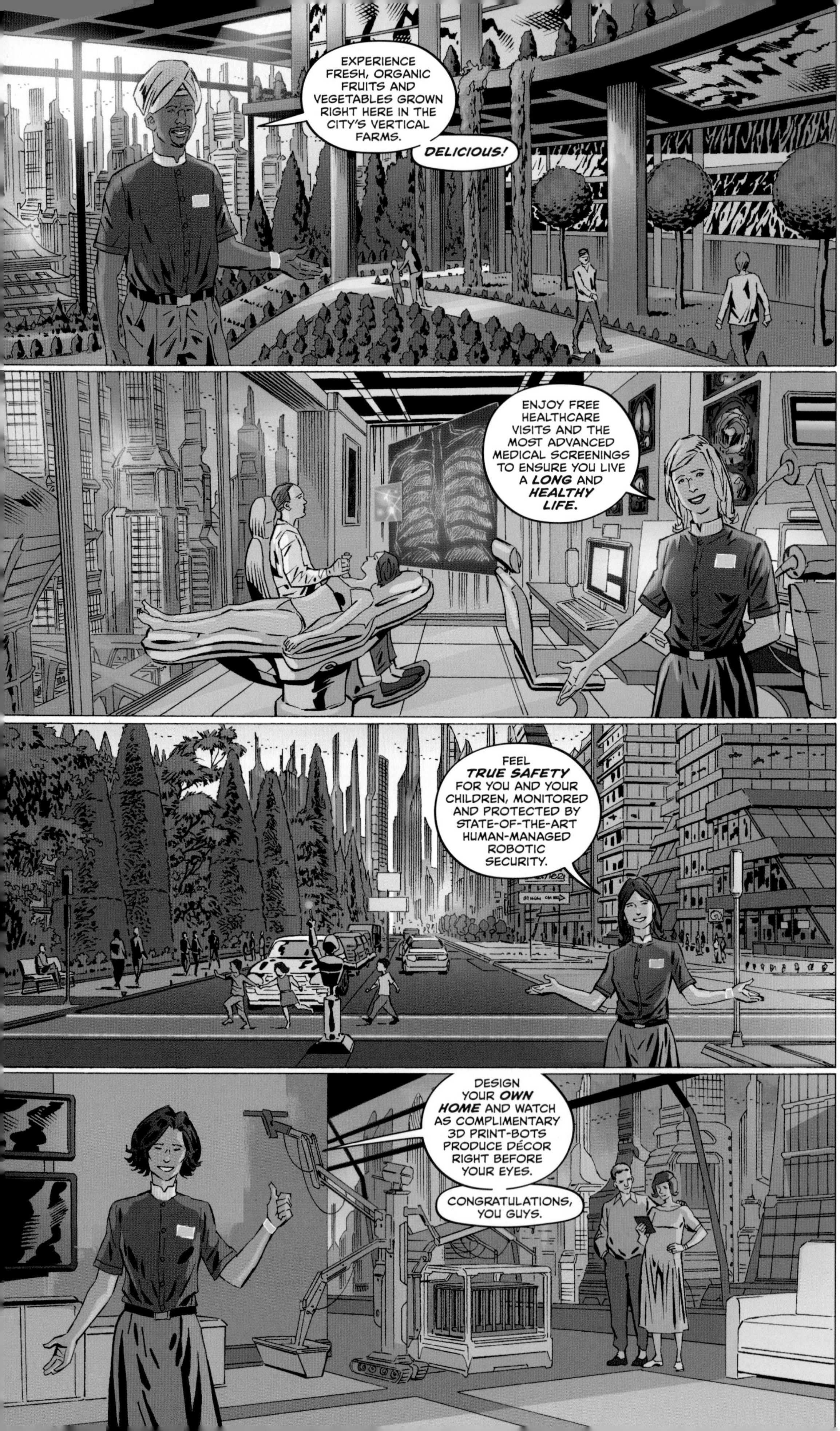
EXPERIENCE FRESH, ORGANIC FRUITS AND VEGETABLES GROWN RIGHT HERE IN THE CITY'S VERTICAL FARMS.
DELICIOUS!
ENJOY FREE HEALTHCARE VISITS AND THE MOST ADVANCED MEDICAL SCREENINGS TO ENSURE YOU LIVE A *LONG* AND *HEALTHY LIFE.*
FEEL *TRUE SAFETY* FOR YOU AND YOUR CHILDREN, MONITORED AND PROTECTED BY STATE-OF-THE-ART HUMAN-MANAGED ROBOTIC SECURITY.
DESIGN YOUR *OWN HOME* AND WATCH AS COMPLIMENTARY 3D PRINT-BOTS PRODUCE DÉCOR RIGHT BEFORE YOUR EYES.
CONGRATULATIONS, YOU GUYS.

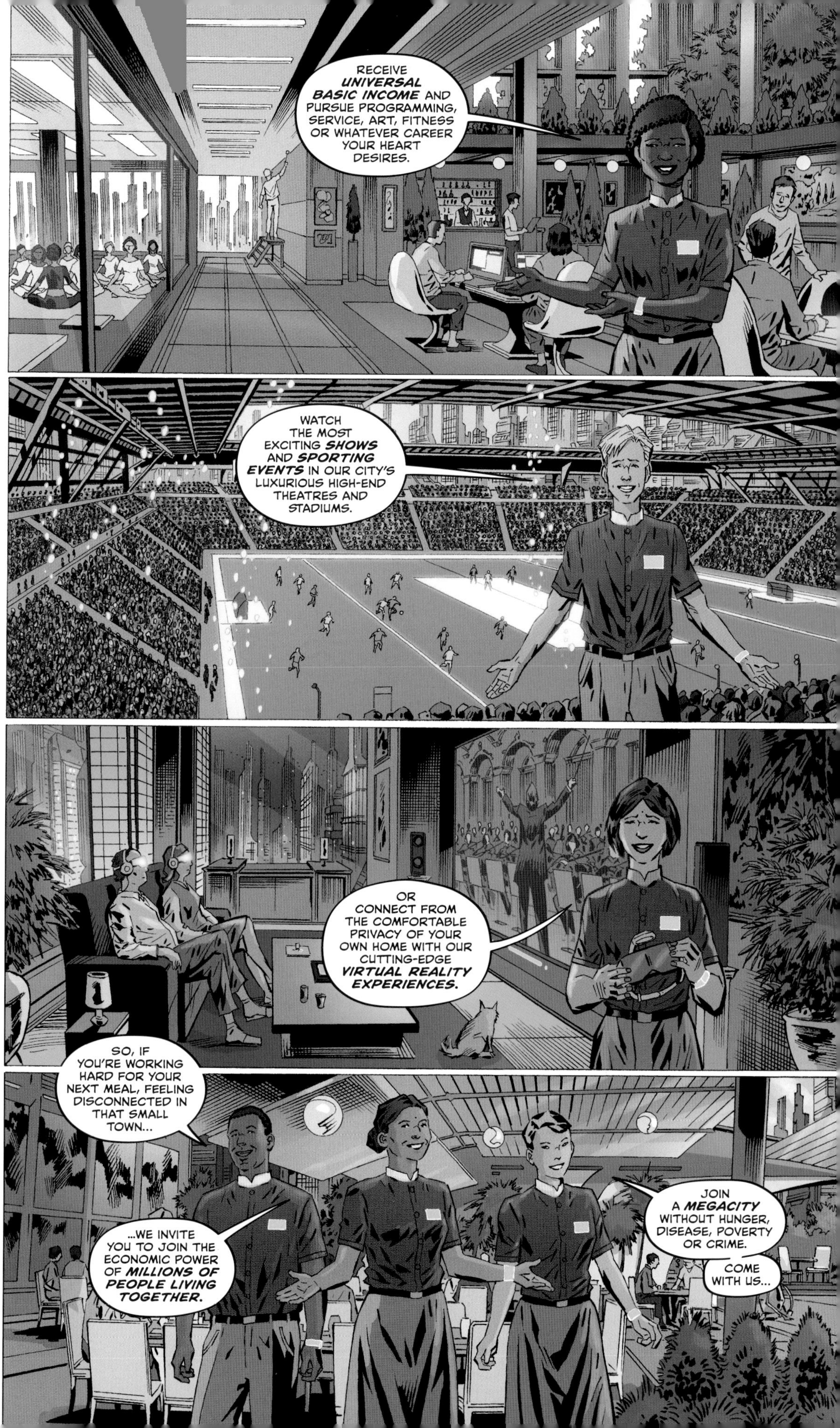
RECEIVE UNIVERSAL BASIC INCOME AND PURSUE PROGRAMMING, SERVICE, ART, FITNESS OR WHATEVER CAREER YOUR HEART DESIRES.
WATCH THE MOST EXCITING SHOWS AND SPORTING EVENTS IN OUR CITY'S LUXURIOUS HIGH-END THEATRES AND STADIUMS.
OR CONNECT FROM THE COMFORTABLE PRIVACY OF YOUR OWN HOME WITH OUR CUTTING-EDGE VIRTUAL REALITY EXPERIENCES.
SO, IF YOU'RE WORKING HARD FOR YOUR NEXT MEAL, FEELING DISCONNECTED IN THAT SMALL TOWN...
...WE INVITE YOU TO JOIN THE ECONOMIC POWER OF MILLIONS OF PEOPLE LIVING TOGETHER.
JOIN A MEGACITY WITHOUT HUNGER, DISEASE, POVERTY OR CRIME.
COME WITH US...

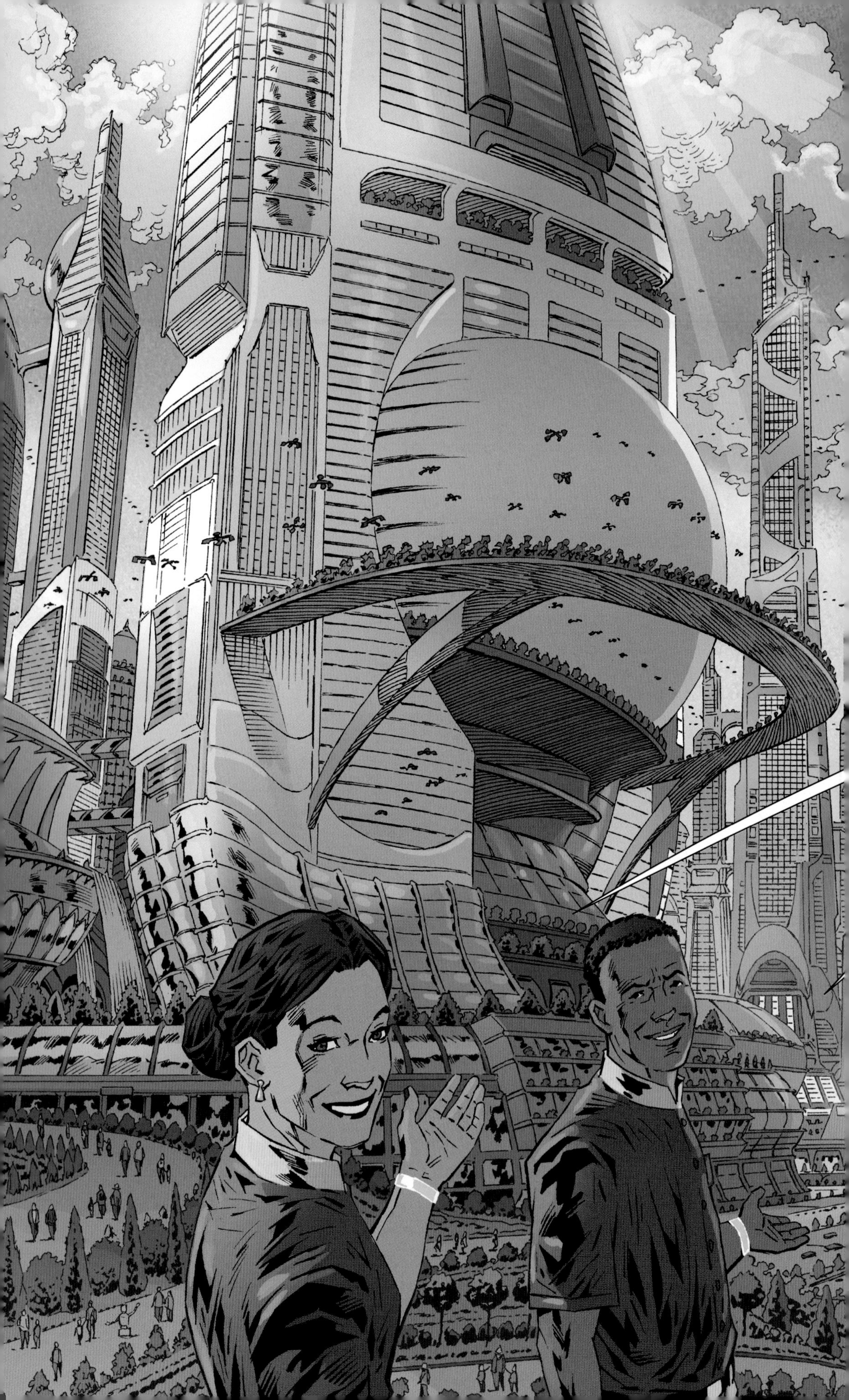

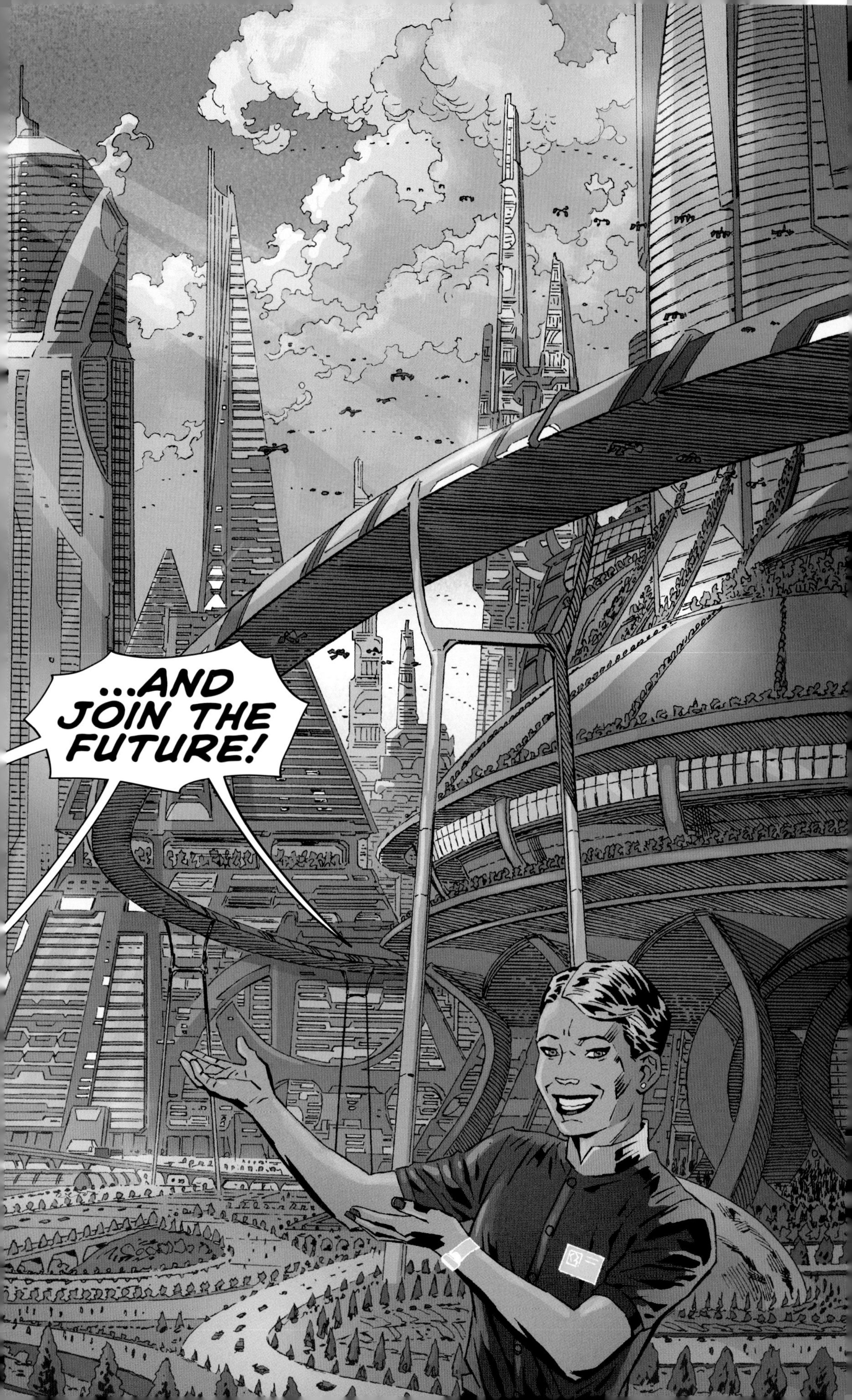
...AND JOIN THE FUTURE!

JOIN THE
FUT

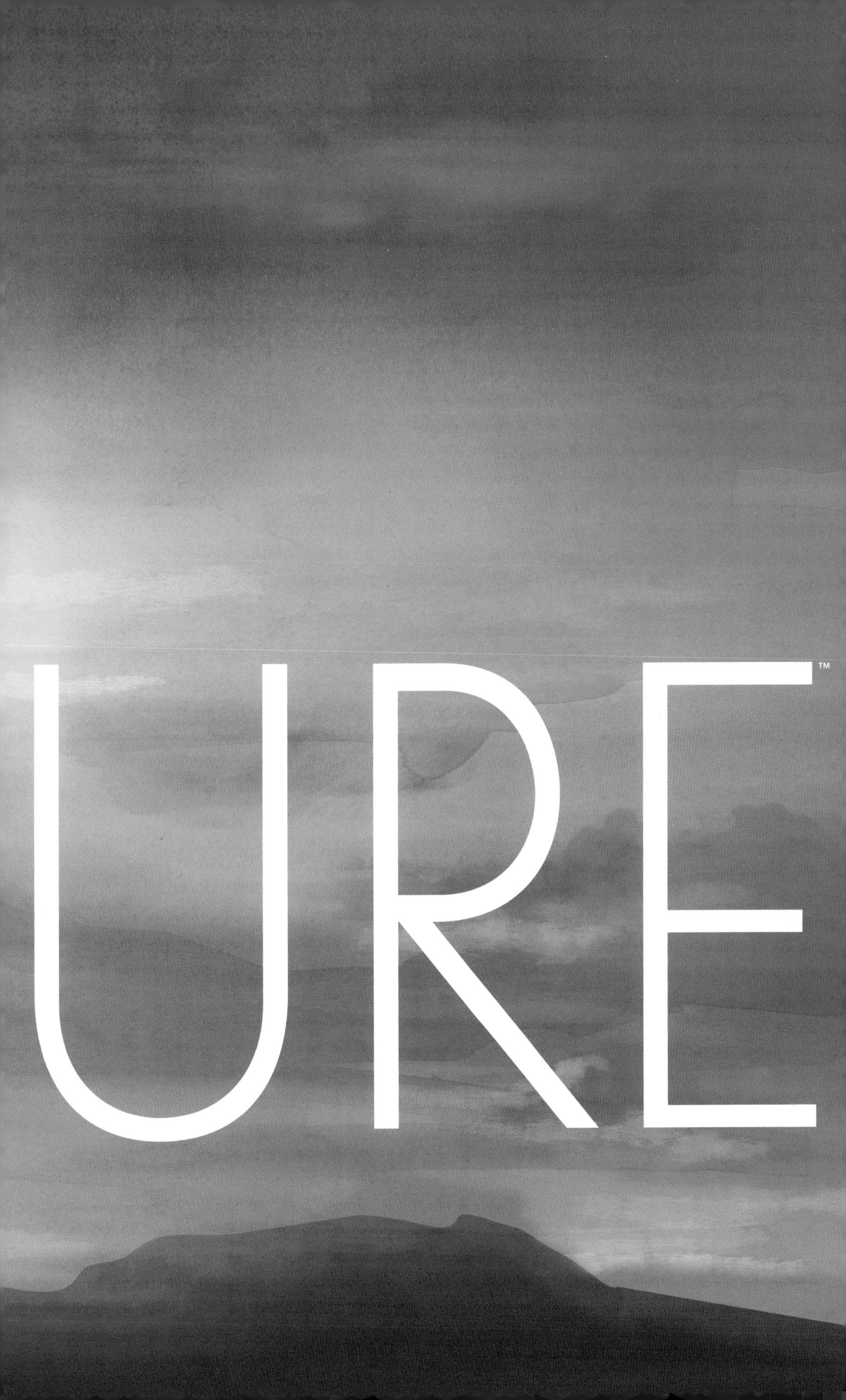
URE™

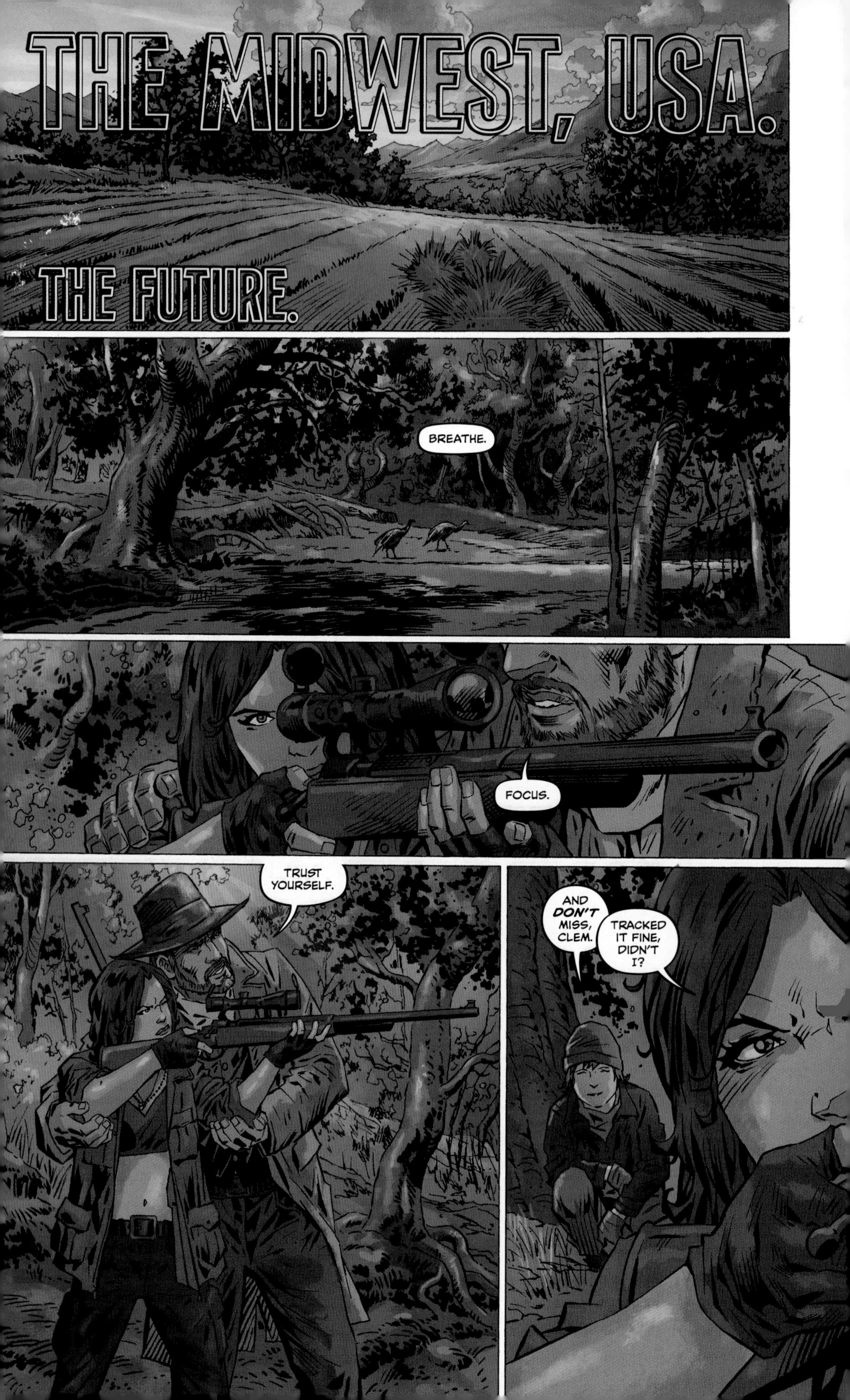
THE MIDWEST, USA.
THE FUTURE.
BREATHE.
FOCUS.
TRUST YOURSELF.
AND DON'T MISS, CLEM.
TRACKED IT FINE, DIDN'T I?

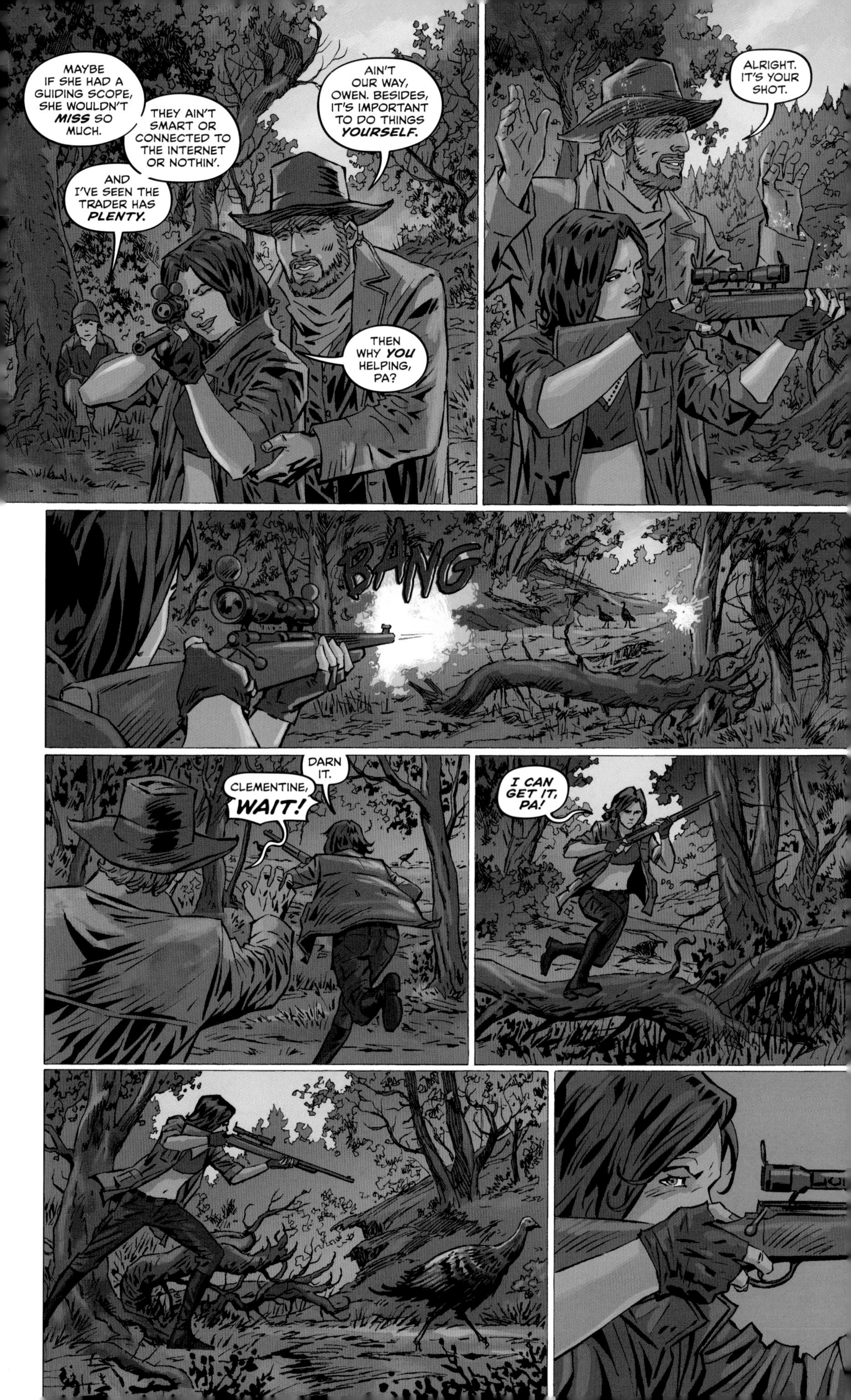

MAYBE IF SHE HAD A GUIDING SCOPE, SHE WOULDN'T MISS SO MUCH.
THEY AIN'T SMART OR CONNECTED TO THE INTERNET OR NOTHIN'.
AND I'VE SEEN THE TRADER HAS PLENTY.
AIN'T OUR WAY, OWEN. BESIDES, IT'S IMPORTANT TO DO THINGS YOURSELF.
THEN WHY YOU HELPING, PA?
ALRIGHT. IT'S YOUR SHOT.
BANG
DARN IT.
CLEMENTINE, WAIT!
I CAN GET IT, PA!

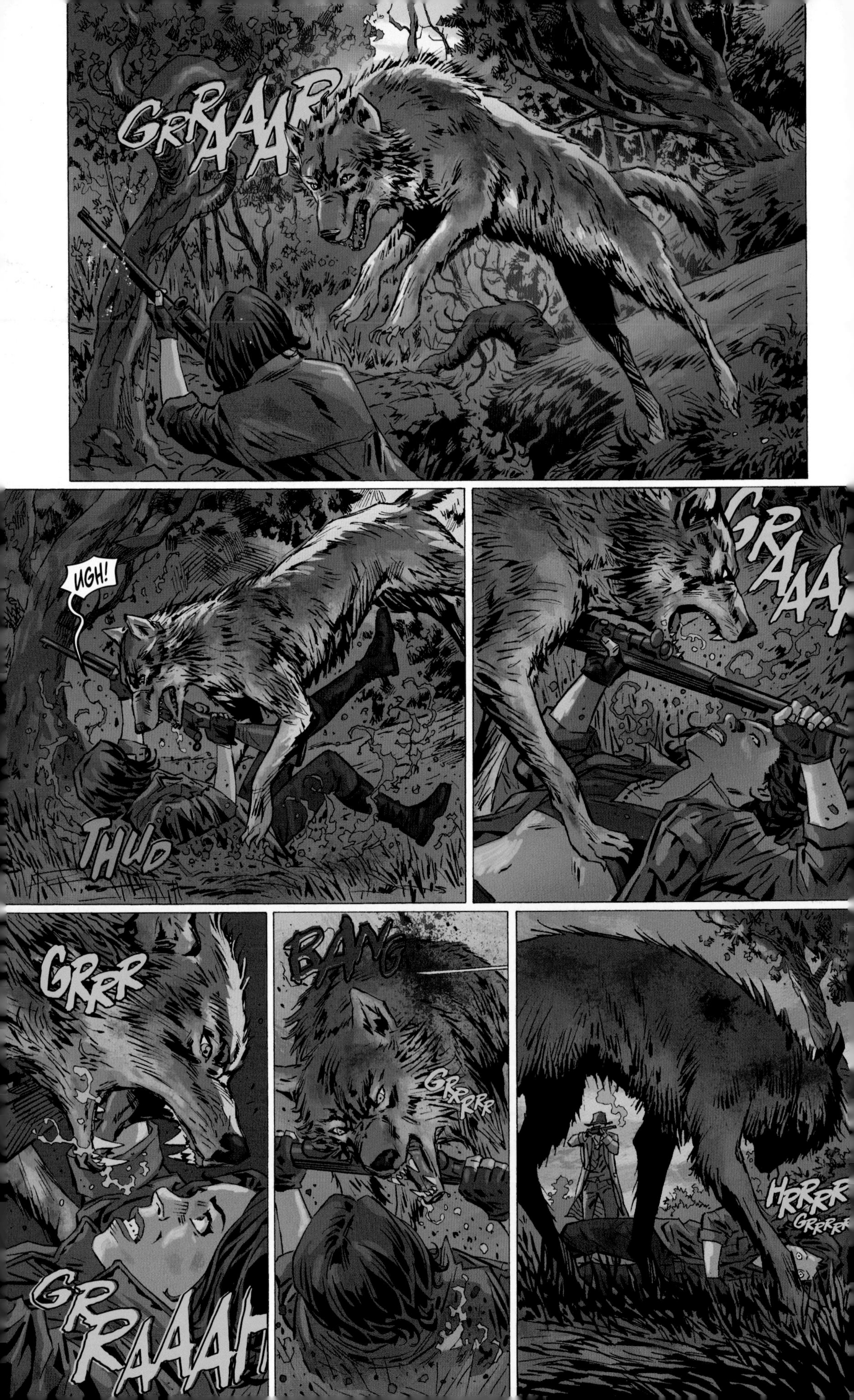
GRRAAAR
UGH!
THUD
GRAAA
GRRR
GRAAAH
BANG
GRRRRR
HRRRR
GRRRRR

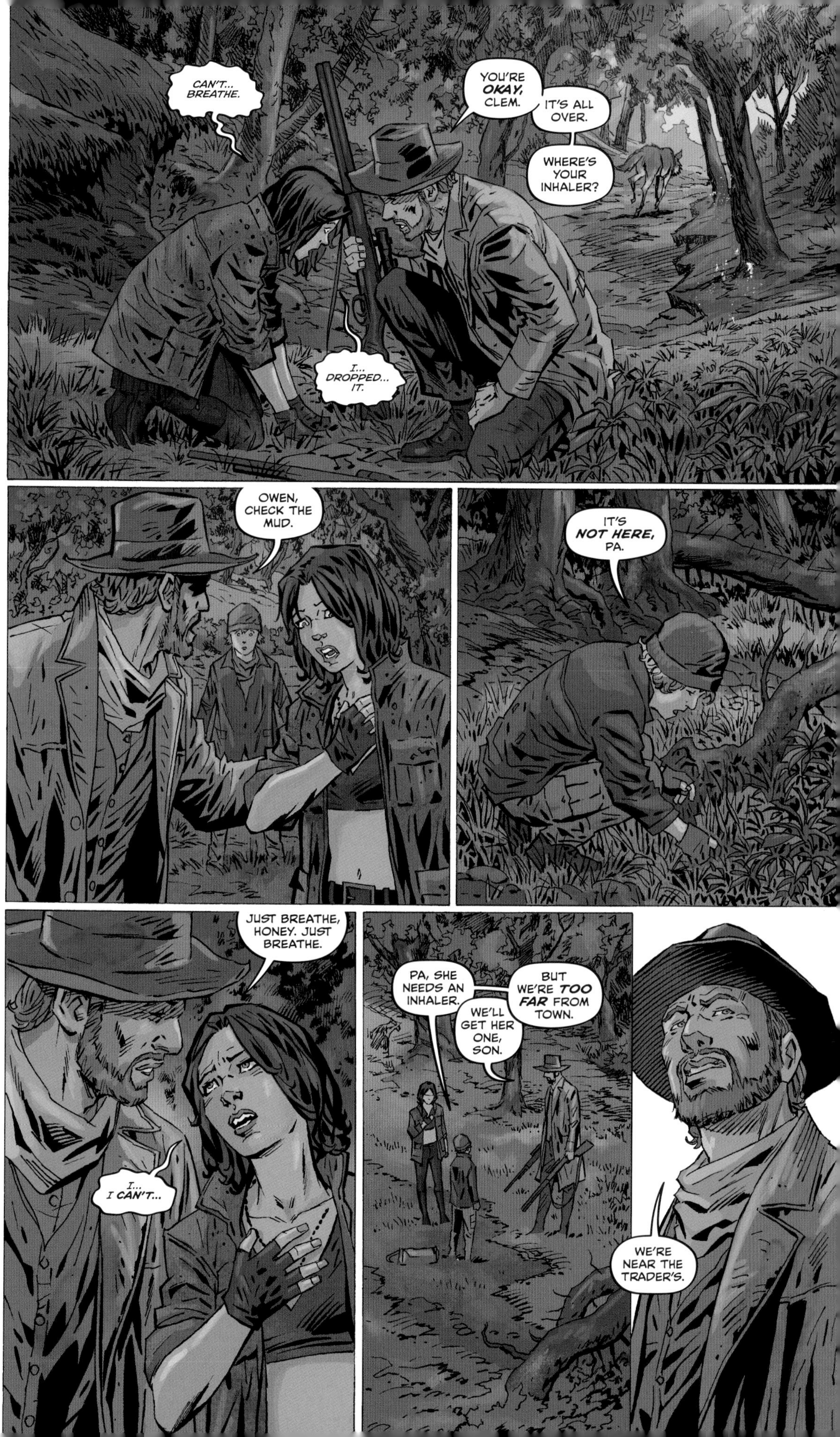

CAN'T... BREATHE.
YOU'RE OKAY, CLEM.
IT'S ALL OVER.
WHERE'S YOUR INHALER?
I... DROPPED... IT.
OWEN, CHECK THE MUD.
IT'S NOT HERE, PA.
JUST BREATHE, HONEY. JUST BREATHE.
I... I CAN'T...
PA, SHE NEEDS AN INHALER.
BUT WE'RE TOO FAR FROM TOWN.
WE'LL GET HER ONE, SON.
WE'RE NEAR THE TRADER'S.

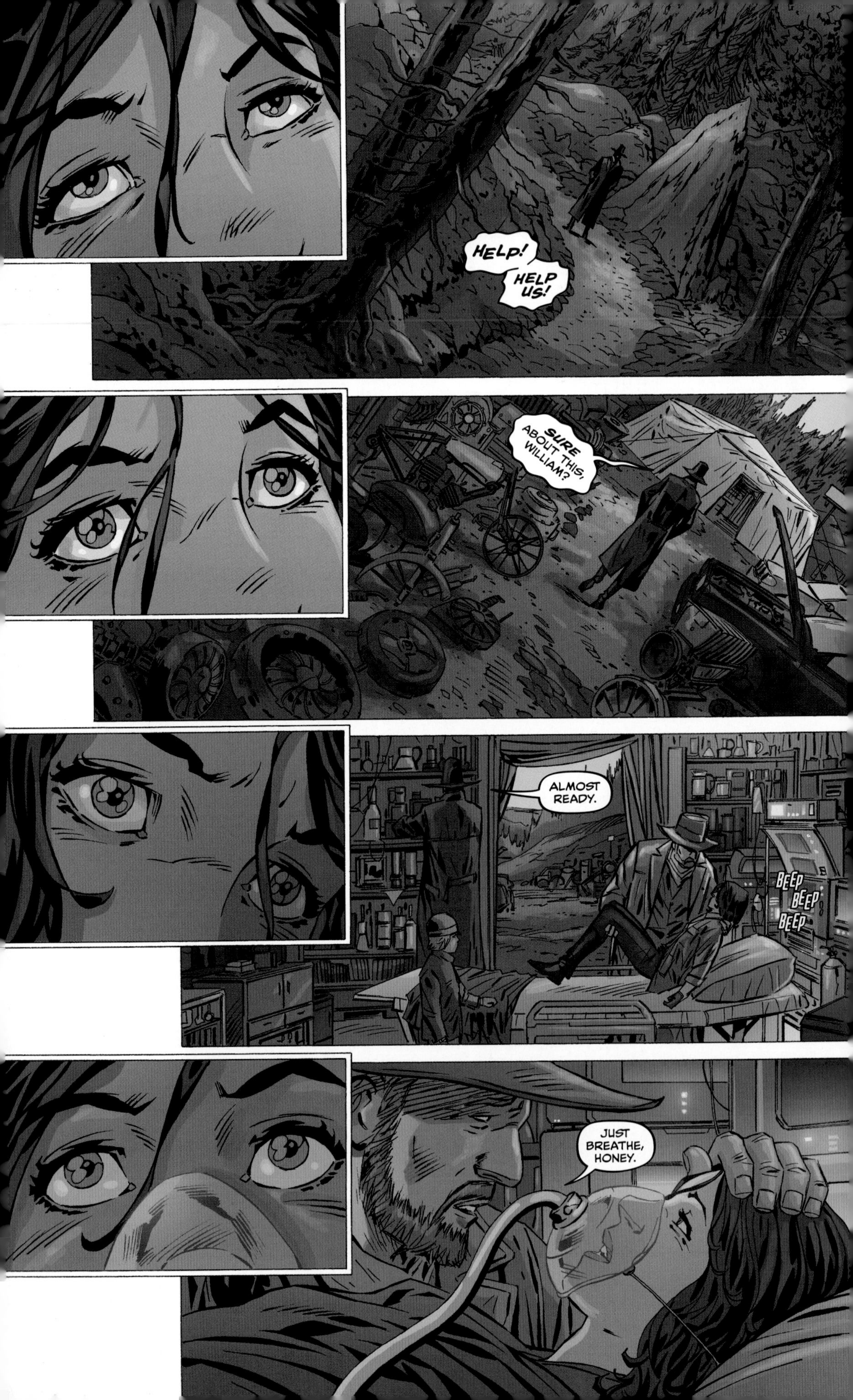
HELP!
HELP US!
SURE ABOUT THIS, WILLIAM?
ALMOST READY.
BEEP
BEEP
BEEP
JUST BREATHE, HONEY.

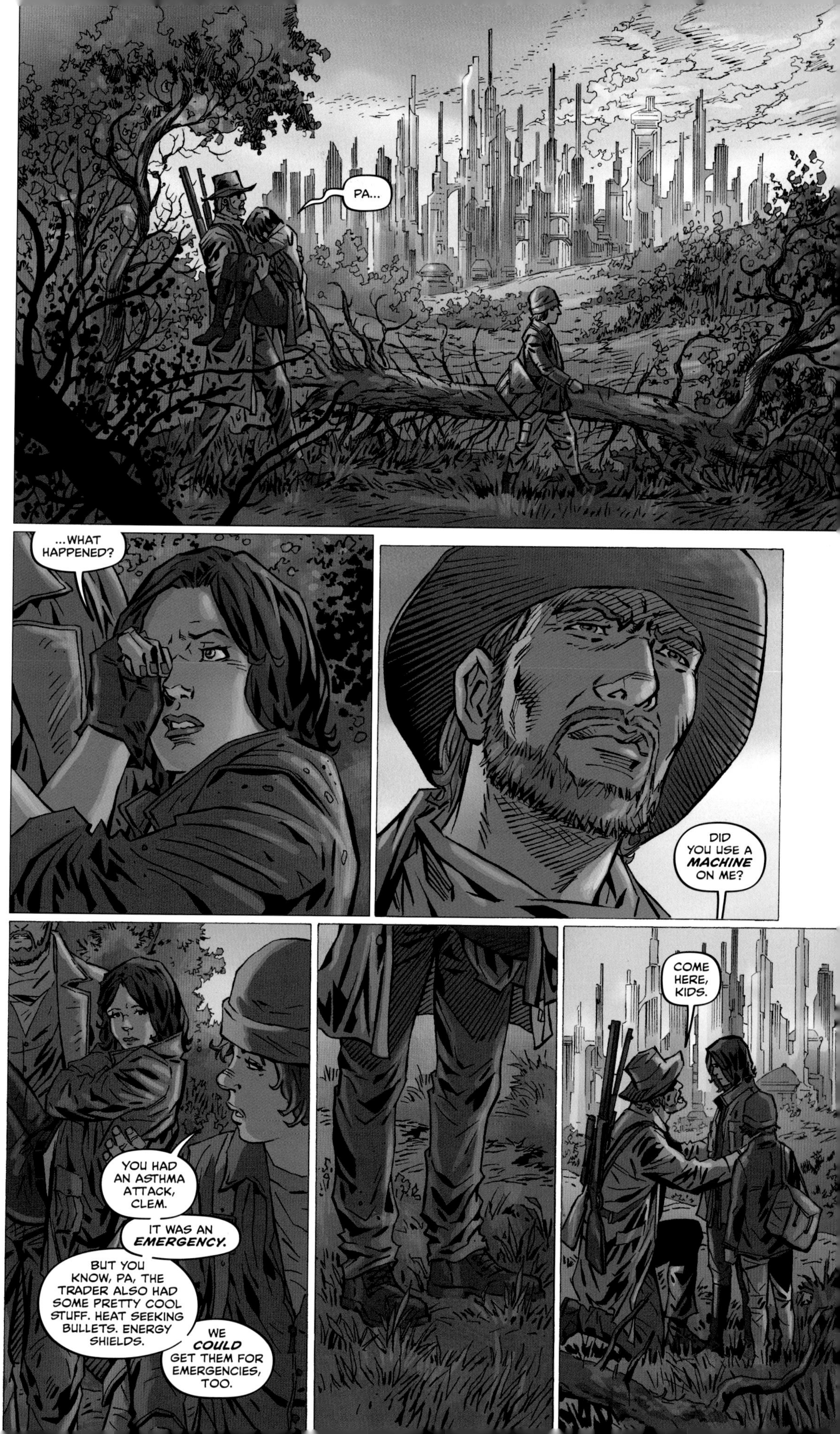

PA...
...WHAT HAPPENED?
DID YOU USE A MACHINE ON ME?
YOU HAD AN ASTHMA ATTACK, CLEM.
IT WAS AN EMERGENCY.
BUT YOU KNOW, PA, THE TRADER ALSO HAD SOME PRETTY COOL STUFF. HEAT SEEKING BULLETS. ENERGY SHIELDS.
WE COULD GET THEM FOR EMERGENCIES, TOO.
COME HERE, KIDS.

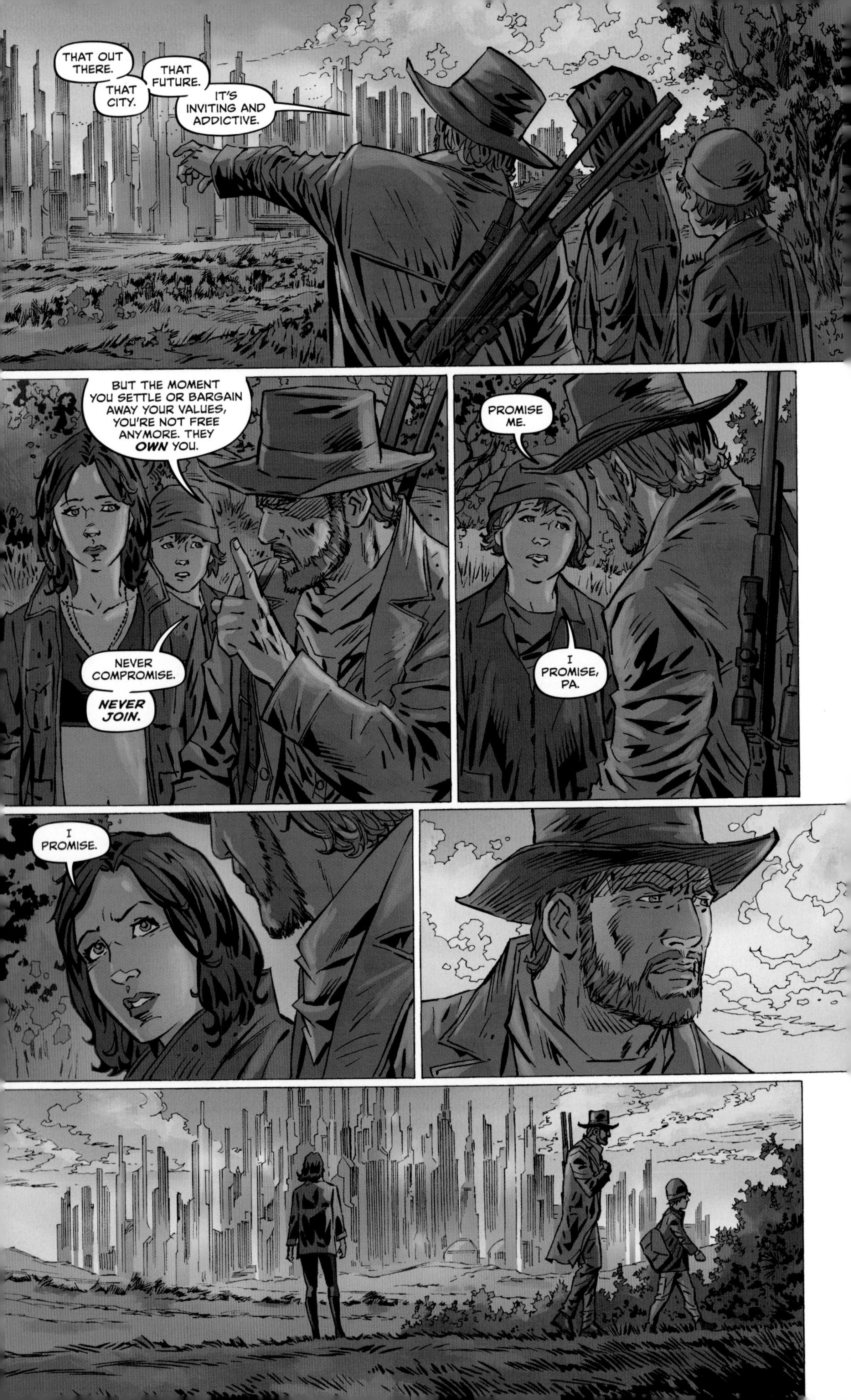
THAT OUT THERE.
THAT CITY.
THAT FUTURE.
IT'S INVITING AND ADDICTIVE.
BUT THE MOMENT YOU SETTLE OR BARGAIN AWAY YOUR VALUES, YOU'RE NOT FREE ANYMORE. THEY OWN YOU.
NEVER COMPROMISE.
NEVER JOIN.
PROMISE ME.
I PROMISE, PA.
I PROMISE.

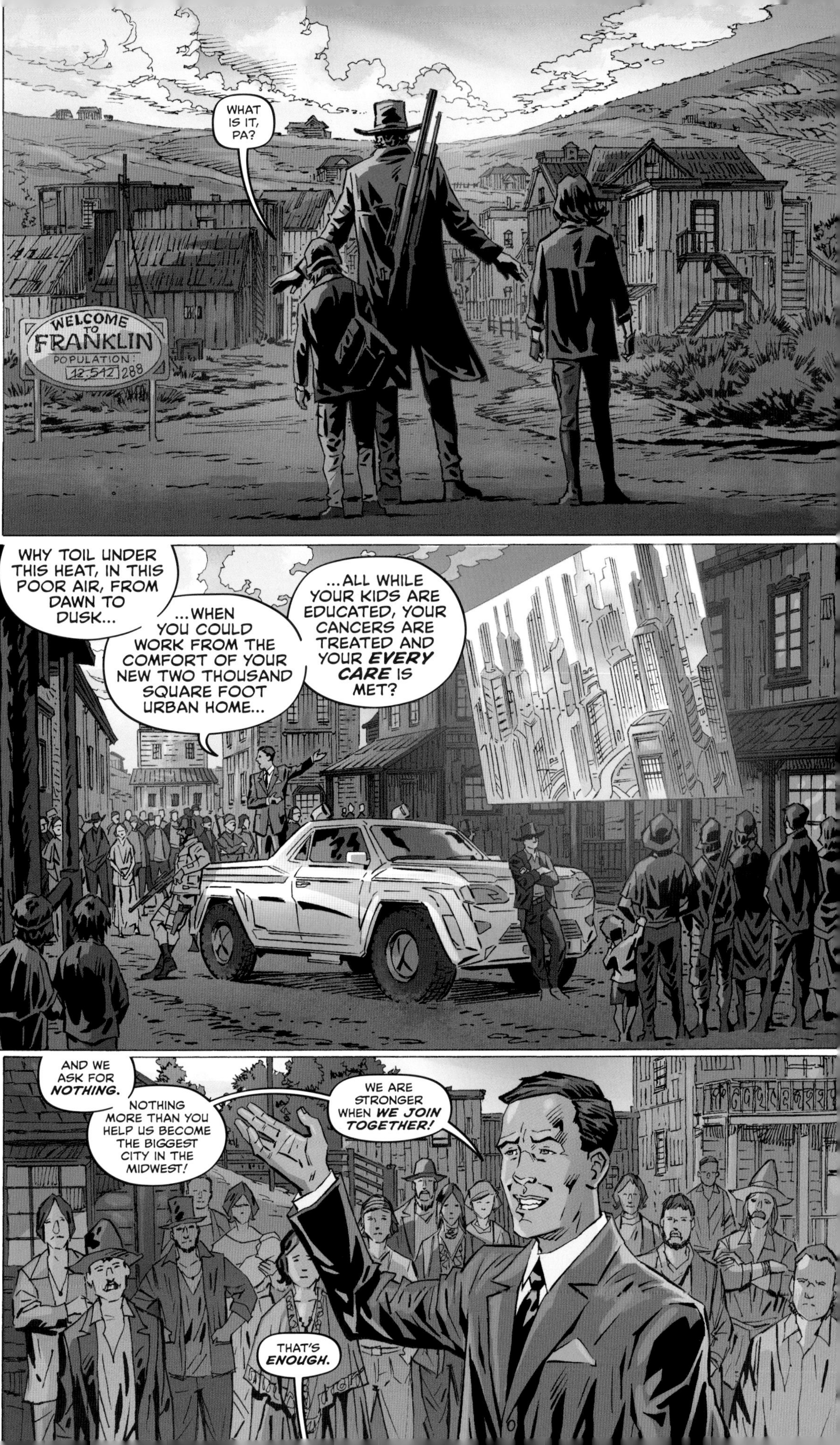
WHAT IS IT, PA?
WELCOME TO FRANKLIN
POPULATION: 12,512 288
WHY TOIL UNDER THIS HEAT, IN THIS POOR AIR, FROM DAWN TO DUSK...
...WHEN YOU COULD WORK FROM THE COMFORT OF YOUR NEW TWO THOUSAND SQUARE FOOT URBAN HOME...
...ALL WHILE YOUR KIDS ARE EDUCATED, YOUR CANCERS ARE TREATED AND YOUR **EVERY CARE** IS MET?
AND WE ASK FOR **NOTHING.**
NOTHING MORE THAN YOU HELP US BECOME THE BIGGEST CITY IN THE MIDWEST!
WE ARE STRONGER WHEN **WE JOIN TOGETHER!**
THAT'S **ENOUGH.**

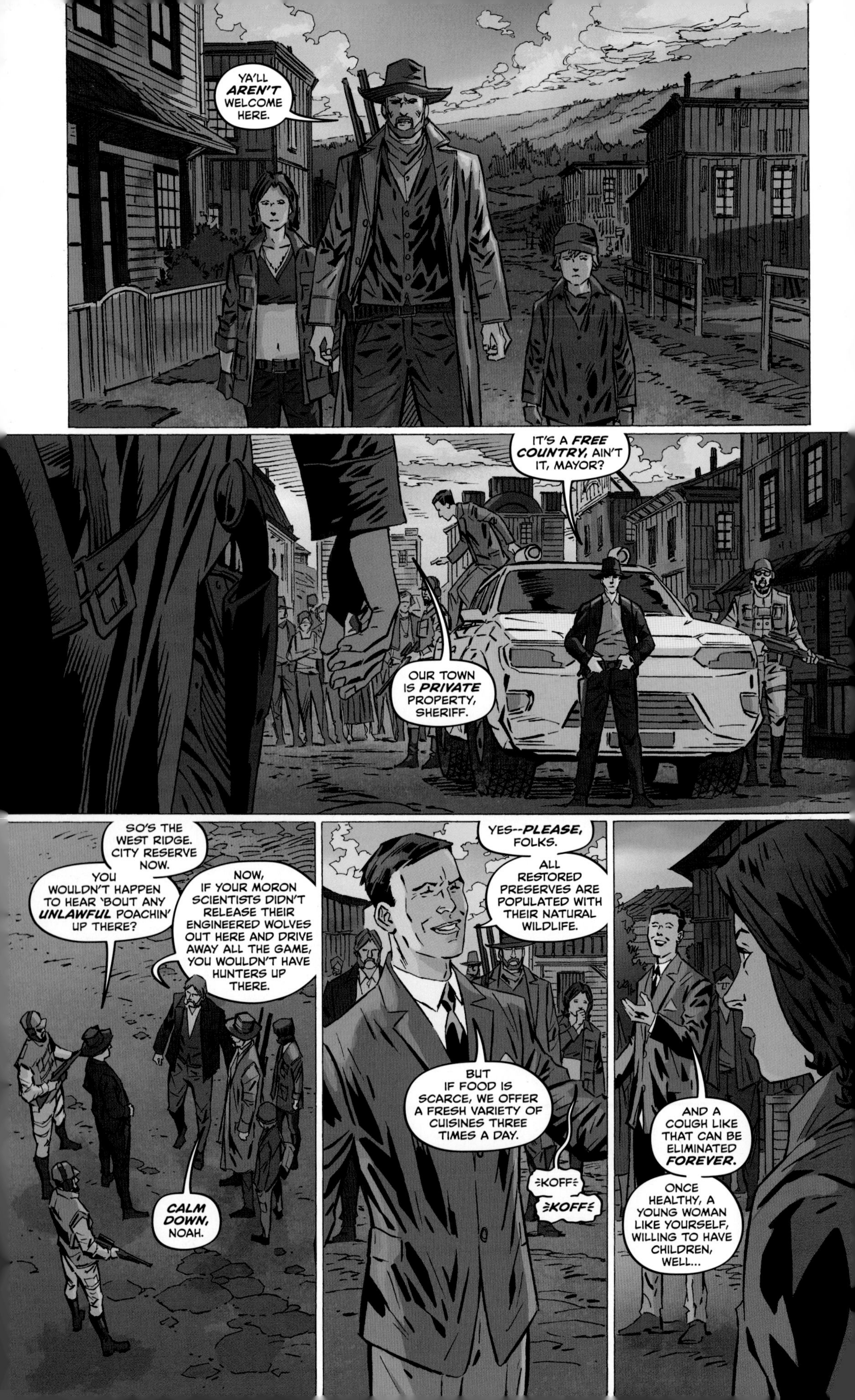
YA'LL **AREN'T** WELCOME HERE.
IT'S A **FREE COUNTRY,** AIN'T IT, MAYOR?
OUR TOWN IS **PRIVATE** PROPERTY, SHERIFF.
SO'S THE WEST RIDGE. CITY RESERVE NOW.
YOU WOULDN'T HAPPEN TO HEAR 'BOUT ANY **UNLAWFUL** POACHIN' UP THERE?
NOW, IF YOUR MORON SCIENTISTS DIDN'T RELEASE THEIR ENGINEERED WOLVES OUT HERE AND DRIVE AWAY ALL THE GAME, YOU WOULDN'T HAVE HUNTERS UP THERE.
CALM DOWN, NOAH.
YES--**PLEASE,** FOLKS.
ALL RESTORED PRESERVES ARE POPULATED WITH THEIR NATURAL WILDLIFE.
BUT IF FOOD IS SCARCE, WE OFFER A FRESH VARIETY OF CUISINES THREE TIMES A DAY.
KOFF
KOFF
AND A COUGH LIKE THAT CAN BE ELIMINATED **FOREVER.**
ONCE HEALTHY, A YOUNG WOMAN LIKE YOURSELF, WILLING TO HAVE CHILDREN, WELL...

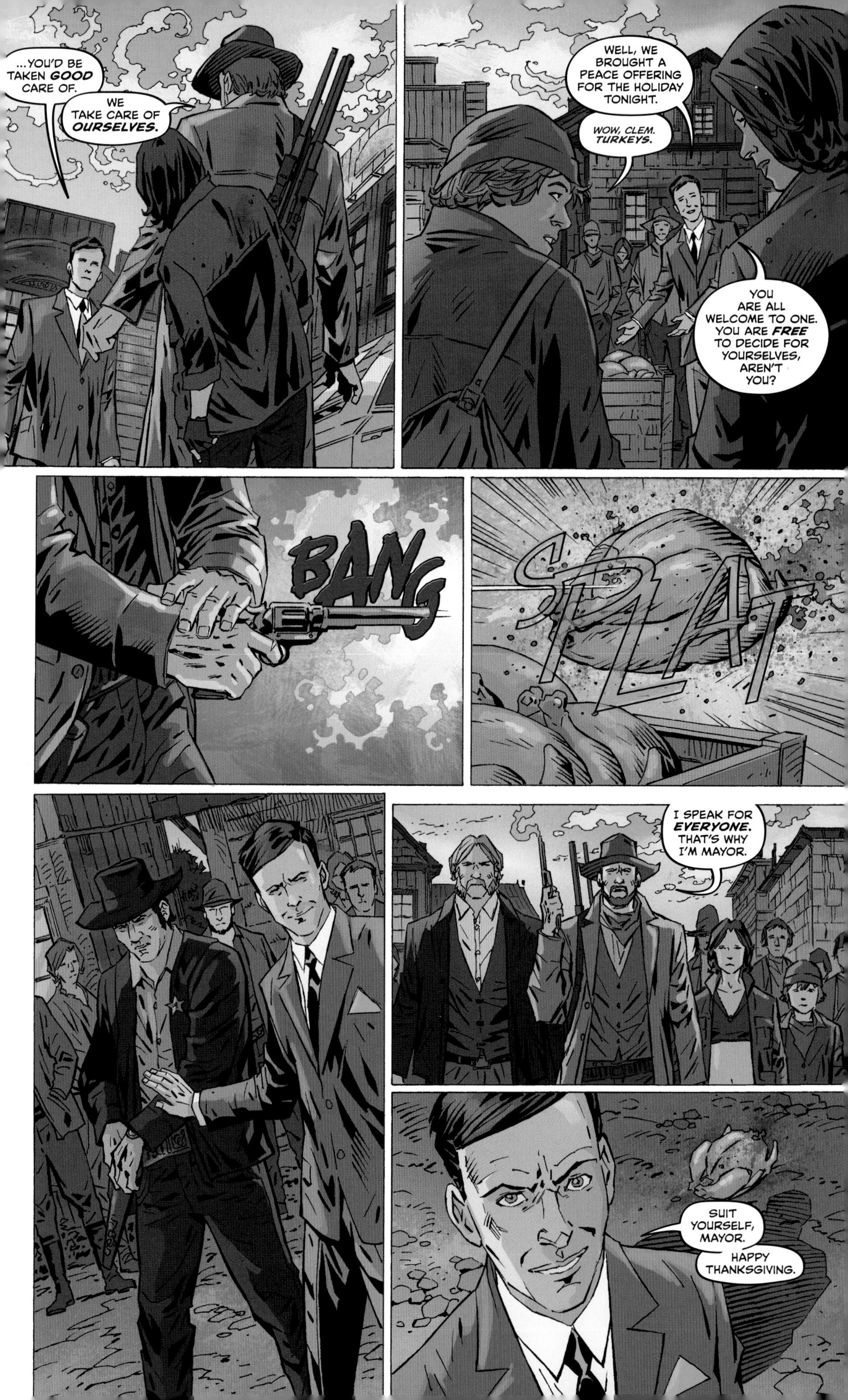
...YOU'D BE TAKEN GOOD CARE OF.
WE TAKE CARE OF OURSELVES.
WELL, WE BROUGHT A PEACE OFFERING FOR THE HOLIDAY TONIGHT.
WOW, CLEM. TURKEYS.
YOU ARE ALL WELCOME TO ONE. YOU ARE FREE TO DECIDE FOR YOURSELVES, AREN'T YOU?
BANG
SPLAT
I SPEAK FOR EVERYONE. THAT'S WHY I'M MAYOR.
SUIT YOURSELF, MAYOR.
HAPPY THANKSGIVING.

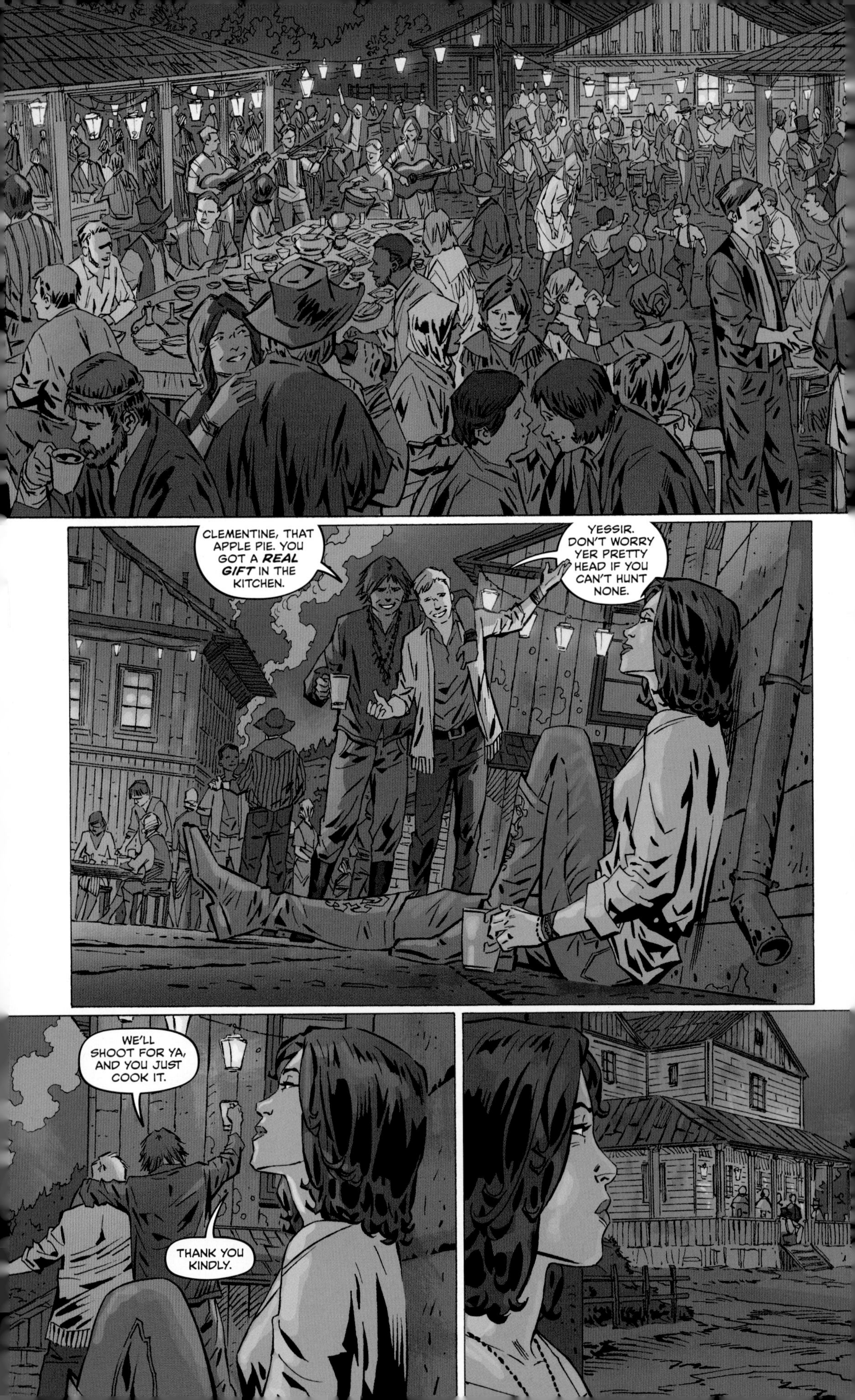
CLEMENTINE, THAT APPLE PIE. YOU GOT A ***REAL GIFT*** IN THE KITCHEN.
YESSIR. DON'T WORRY YER PRETTY HEAD IF YOU CAN'T HUNT NONE.
WE'LL SHOOT FOR YA, AND YOU JUST COOK IT.
THANK YOU KINDLY.

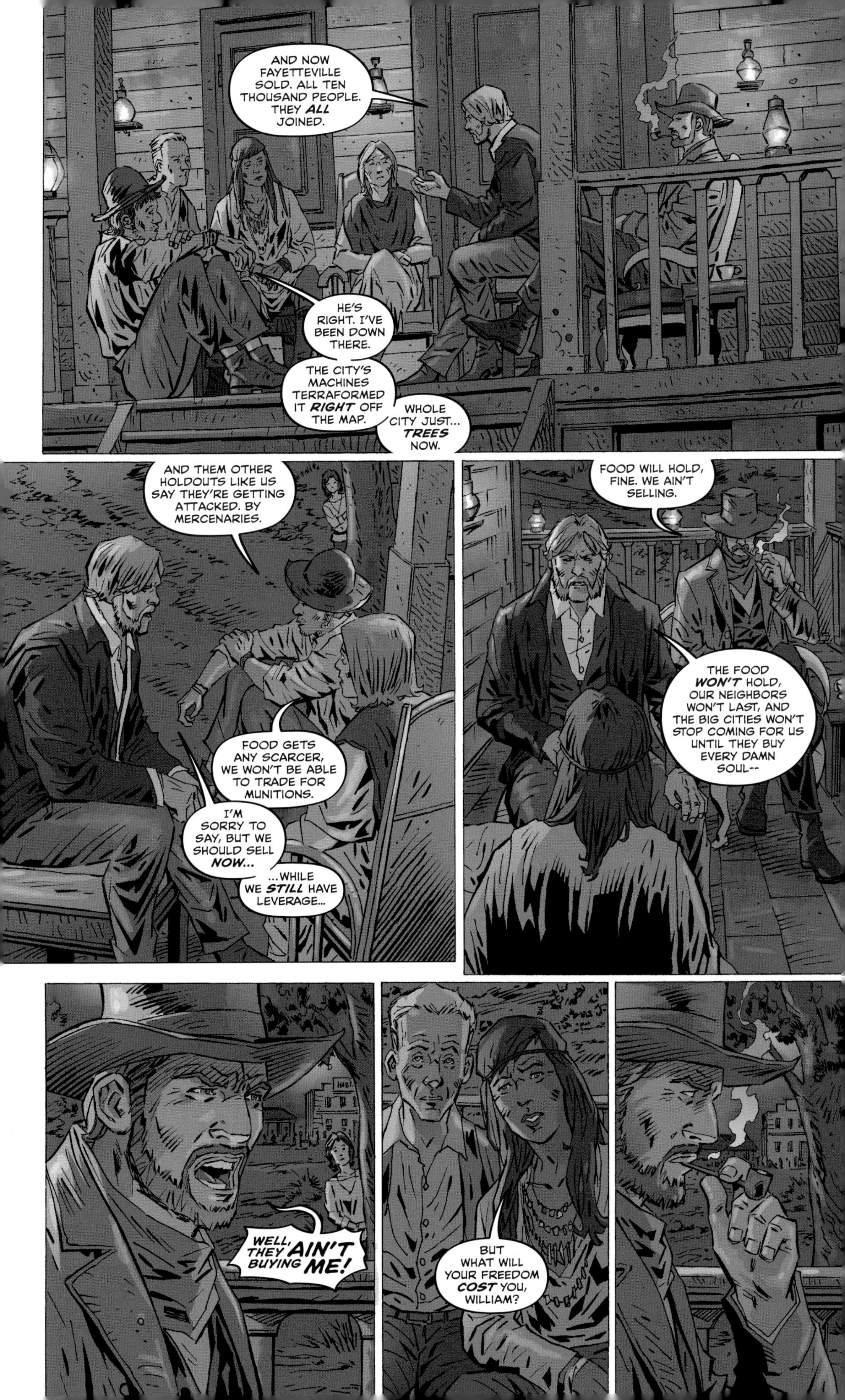

AND NOW FAYETTEVILLE SOLD. ALL TEN THOUSAND PEOPLE. THEY ALL JOINED.
HE'S RIGHT. I'VE BEEN DOWN THERE.
THE CITY'S MACHINES TERRAFORMED IT RIGHT OFF THE MAP.
WHOLE CITY JUST... TREES NOW.
AND THEM OTHER HOLDOUTS LIKE US SAY THEY'RE GETTING ATTACKED. BY MERCENARIES.
FOOD GETS ANY SCARCER, WE WON'T BE ABLE TO TRADE FOR MUNITIONS.
I'M SORRY TO SAY, BUT WE SHOULD SELL NOW...
...WHILE WE STILL HAVE LEVERAGE...
FOOD WILL HOLD, FINE. WE AIN'T SELLING.
THE FOOD WON'T HOLD, OUR NEIGHBORS WON'T LAST, AND THE BIG CITIES WON'T STOP COMING FOR US UNTIL THEY BUY EVERY DAMN SOUL--
WELL, THEY AIN'T BUYING ME!
BUT WHAT WILL YOUR FREEDOM COST YOU, WILLIAM?

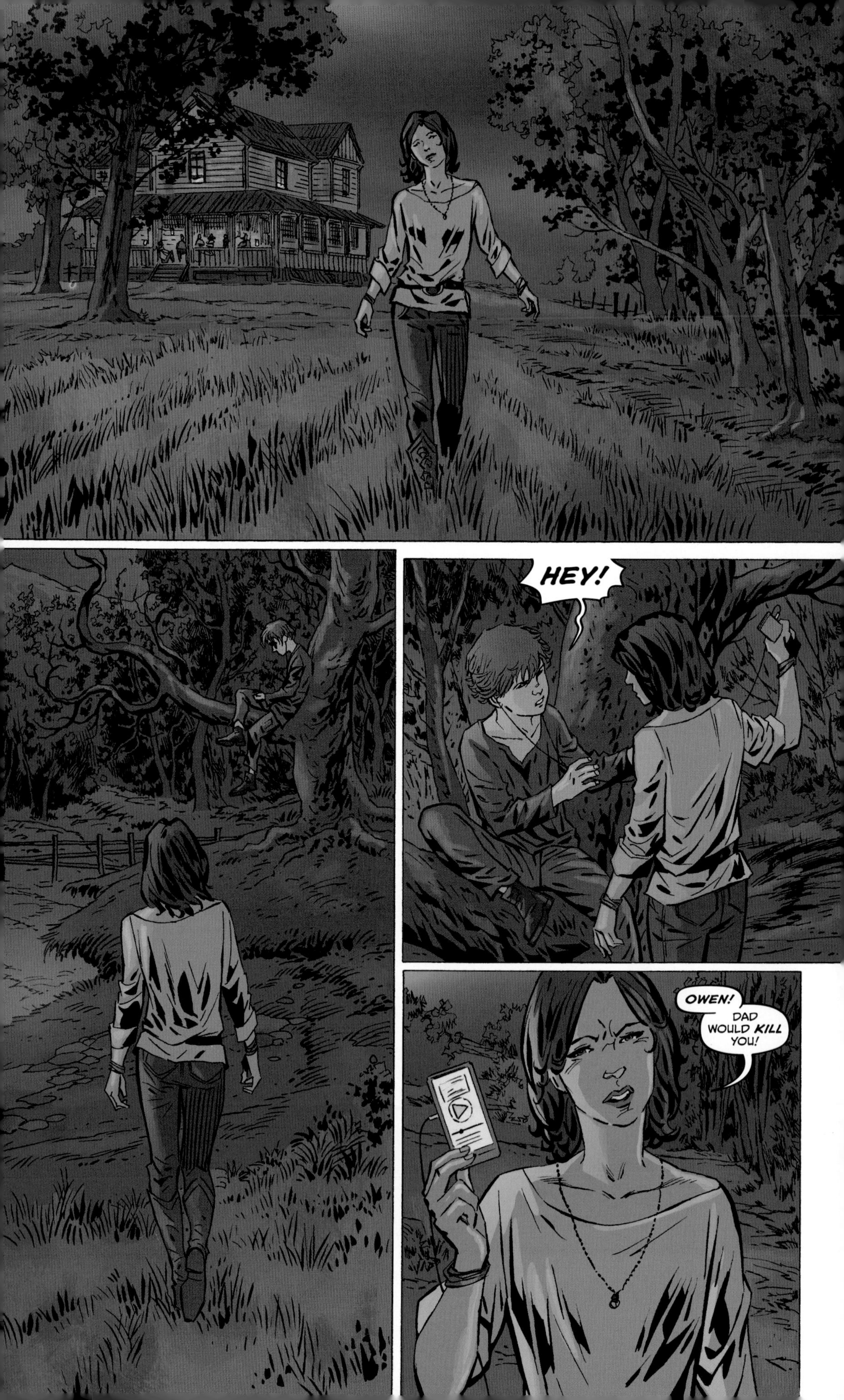
HEY!
OWEN!
DAD WOULD KILL YOU!

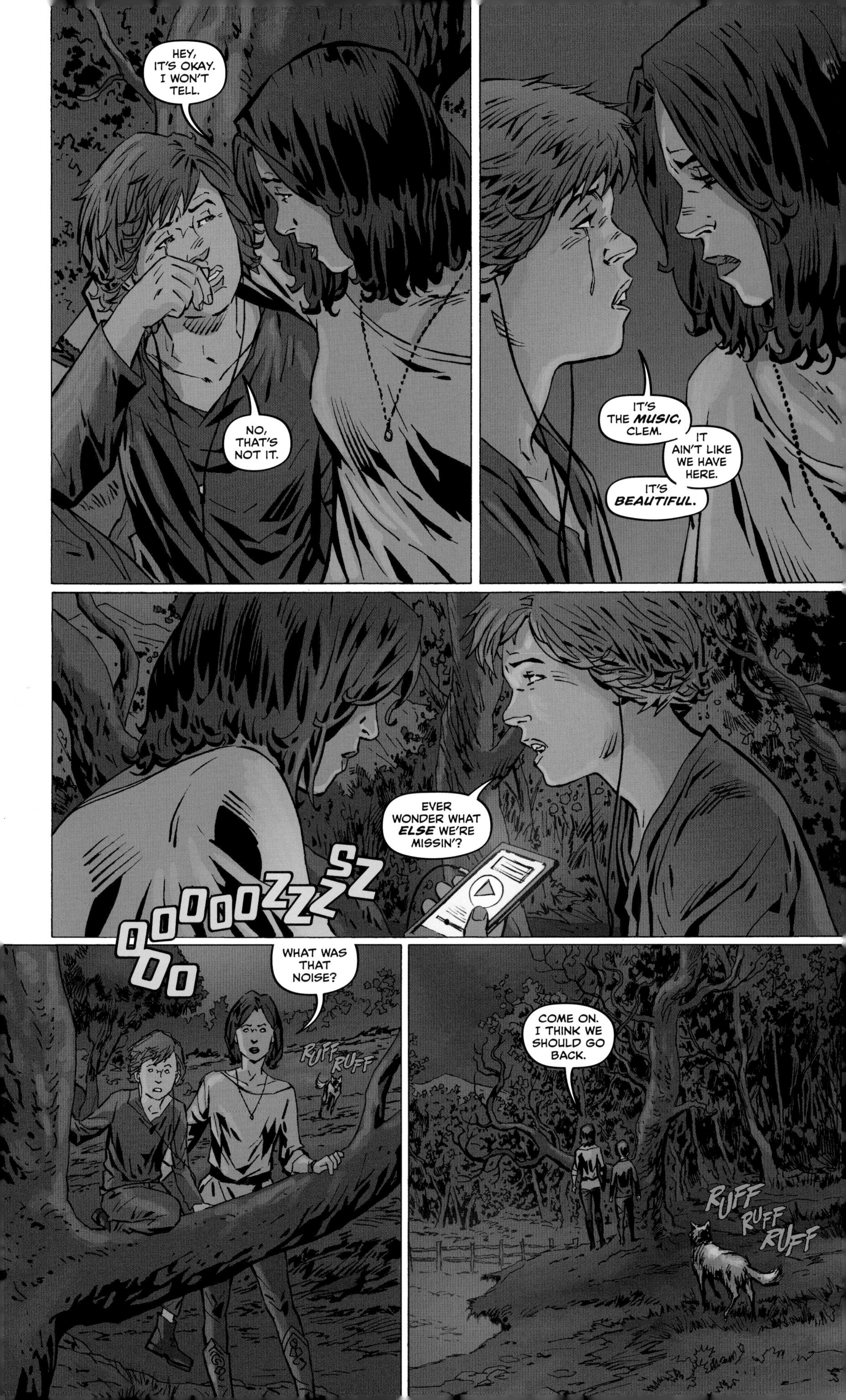
HEY, IT'S OKAY. I WON'T TELL.
NO, THAT'S NOT IT.
IT'S THE **MUSIC,** CLEM.
IT AIN'T LIKE WE HAVE HERE.
IT'S **BEAUTIFUL.**
EVER WONDER WHAT **ELSE** WE'RE MISSIN'?
OOOOOOOZZZSZ
WHAT WAS THAT NOISE?
RUFF RUFF
COME ON. I THINK WE SHOULD GO BACK.
RUFF RUFF RUFF

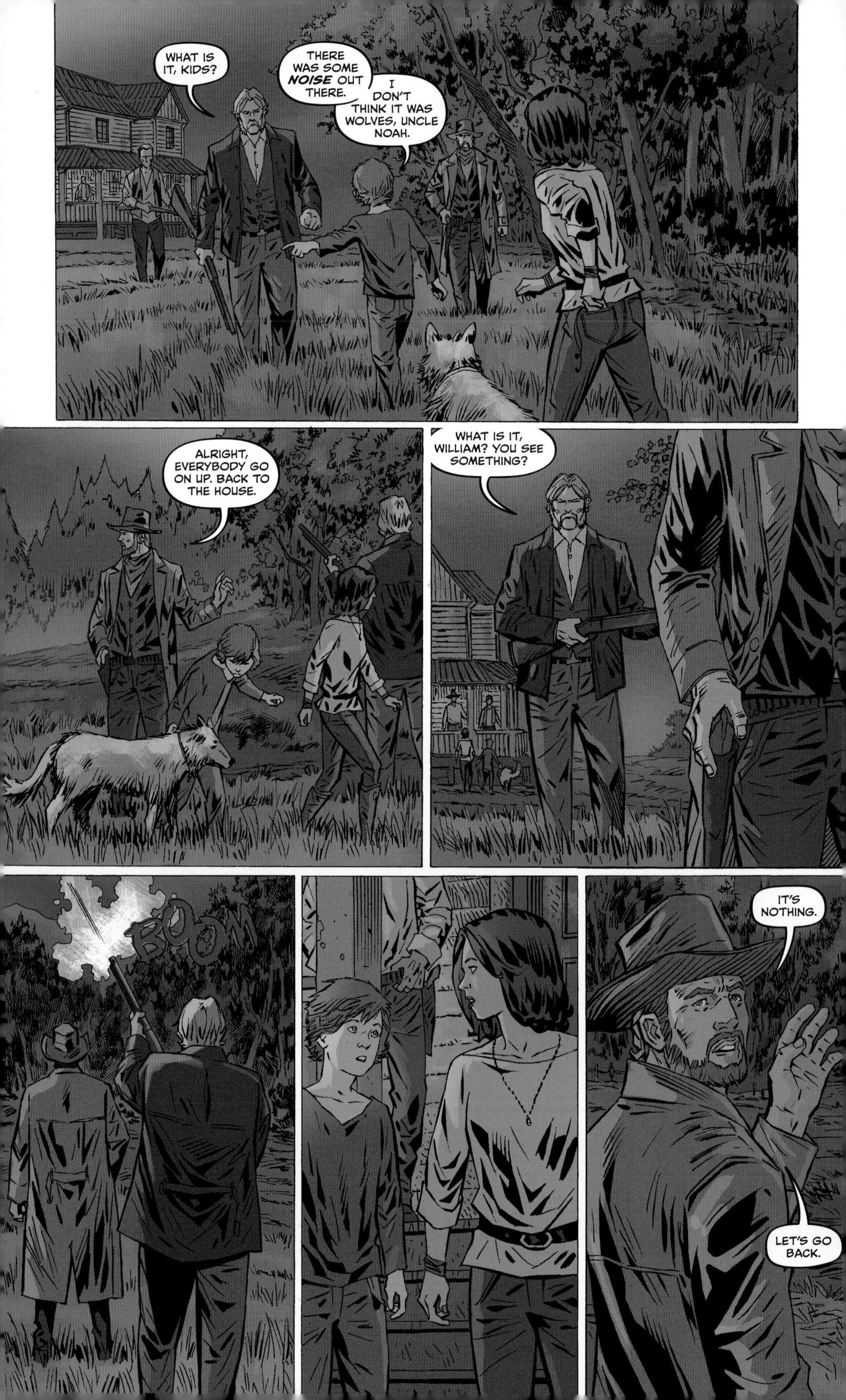
WHAT IS IT, KIDS?
THERE WAS SOME NOISE OUT THERE.
I DON'T THINK IT WAS WOLVES, UNCLE NOAH.
ALRIGHT, EVERYBODY GO ON UP. BACK TO THE HOUSE.
WHAT IS IT, WILLIAM? YOU SEE SOMETHING?
BOOM
IT'S NOTHING.
LET'S GO BACK.

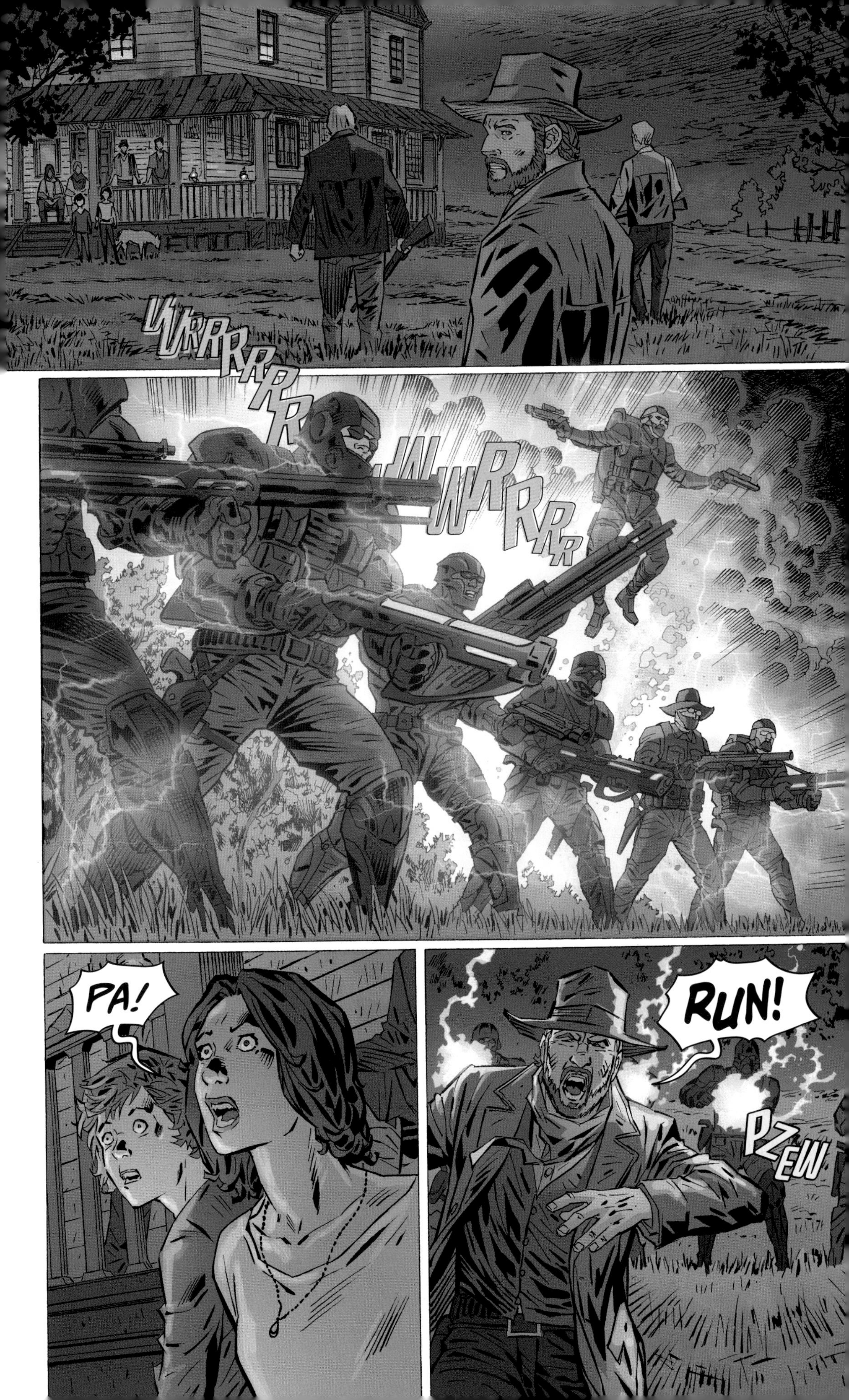
WURRRRRRR
WURRRR
PA!
RUN!
PZEW

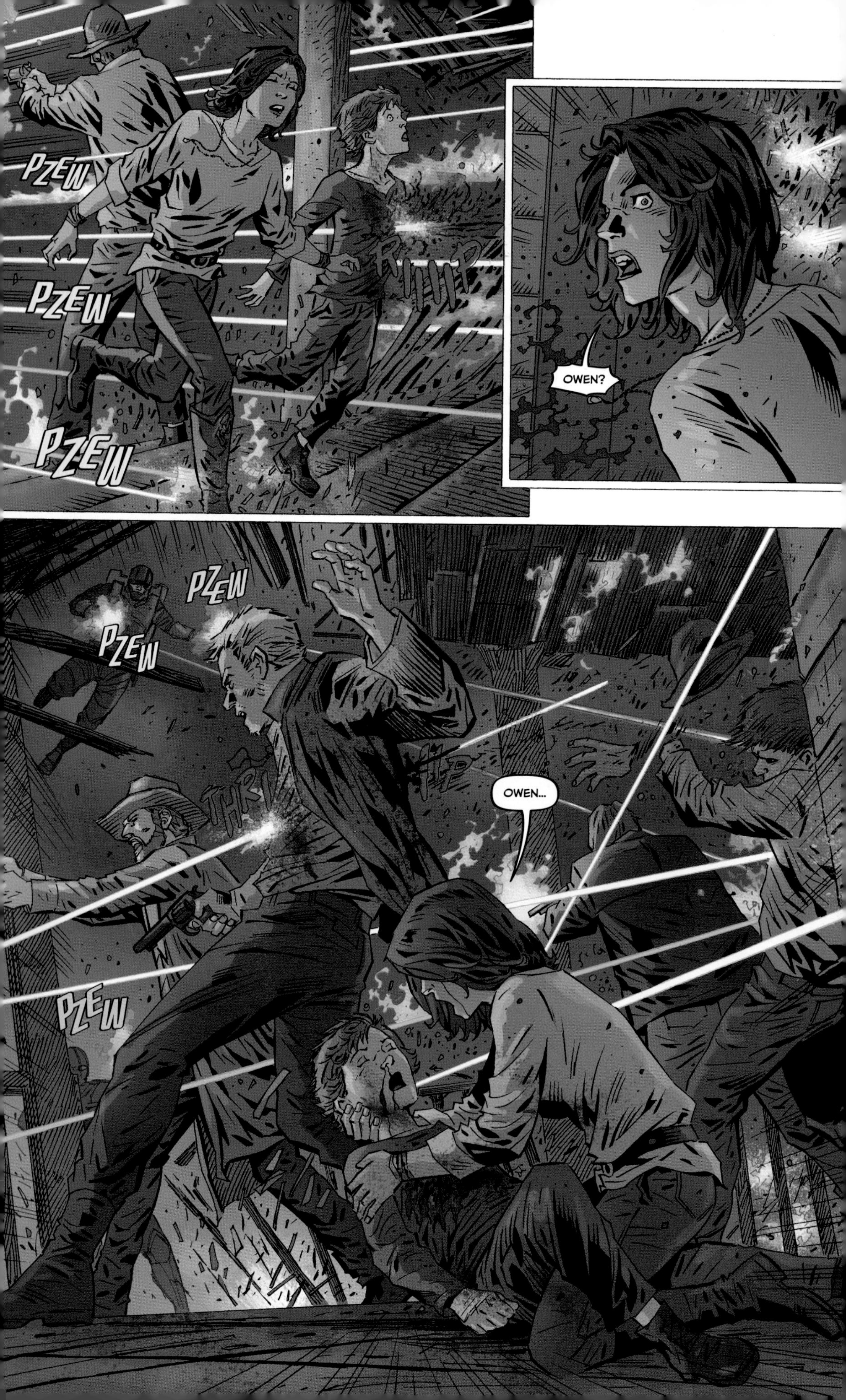
PZEW
PZEW
PZEW
RIIIIP
OWEN?
PZEW
PZEW
THRIIIP
OWEN...
PZEW

2

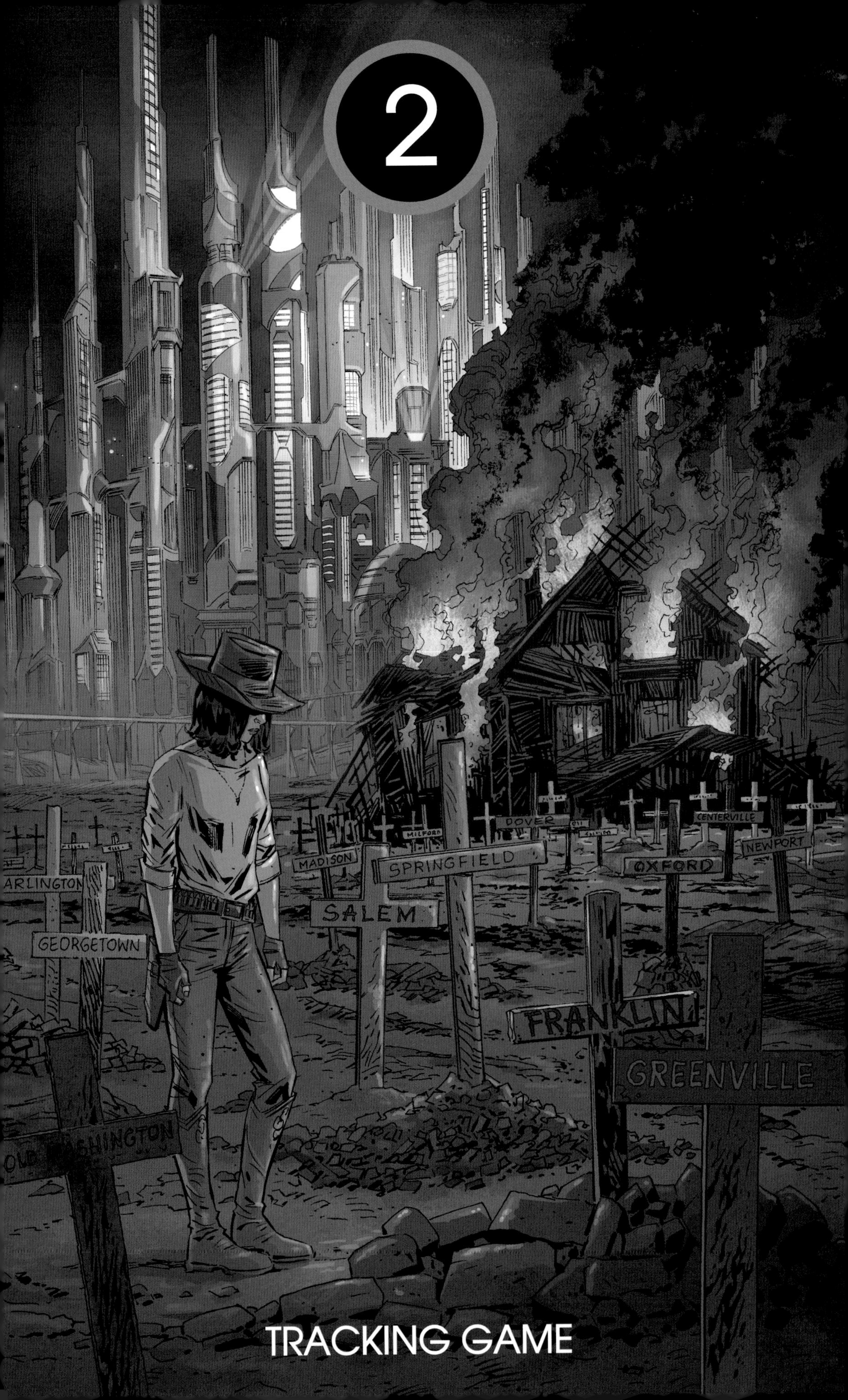
ARLINGTON
GEORGETOWN
MADISON
MILFORD
SPRINGFIELD
SALEM
DOVER
CENTERVILLE
NEWPORT
OXFORD
FRANKLIN
GREENVILLE

TRACKING GAME

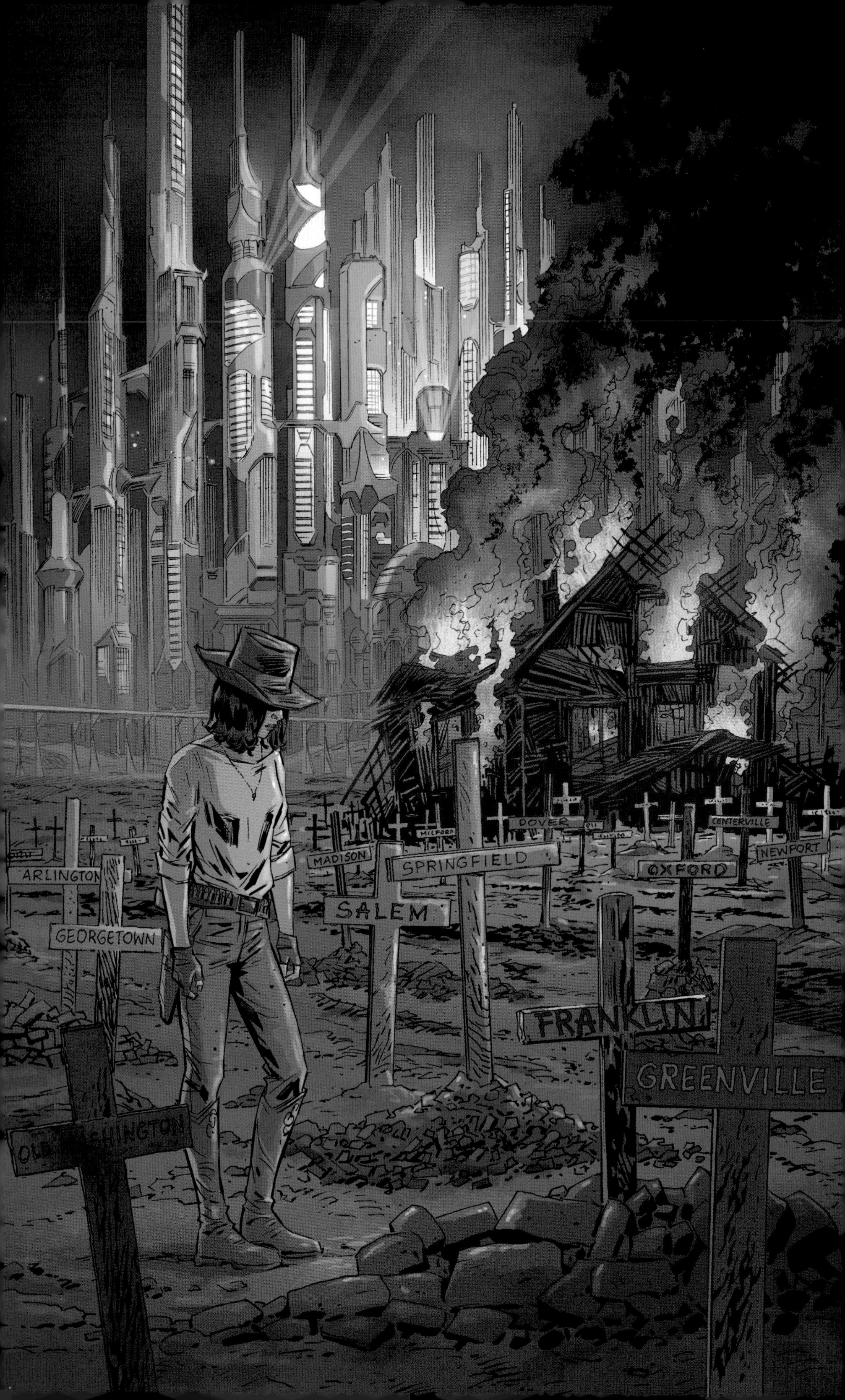
ARLINGTON
GEORGETOWN
MADISON
MILFORD
SALEM
SPRINGFIELD
DOVER
CENTERVILLE
NEWPORT
OXFORD
FRANKLIN
GREENVILLE

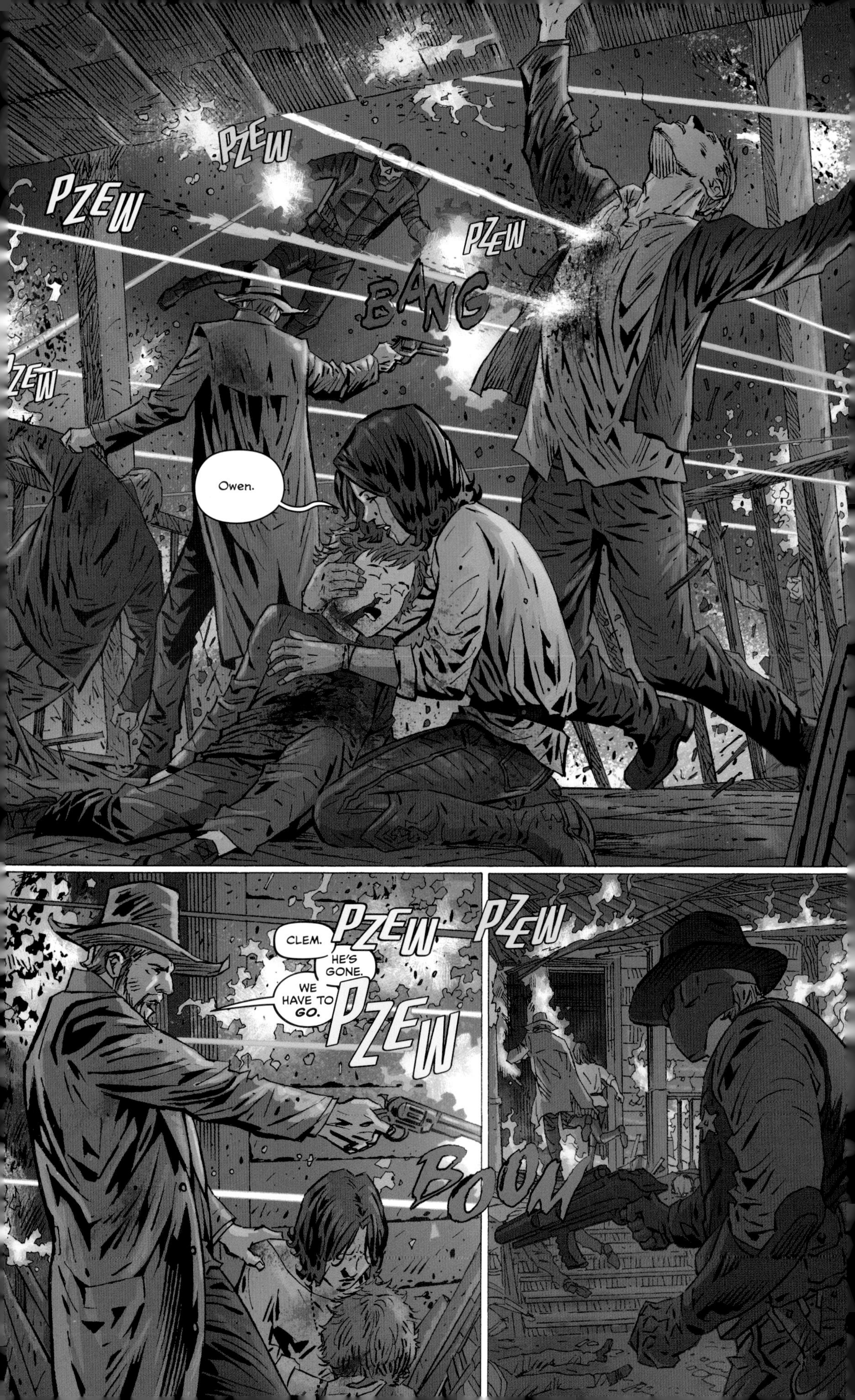
PZEW
PZEW
PZEW
BANG
PZEW
Owen.
CLEM.
PZEW
HE'S GONE.
WE HAVE TO GO.
PZEW
PZEW
BOOM

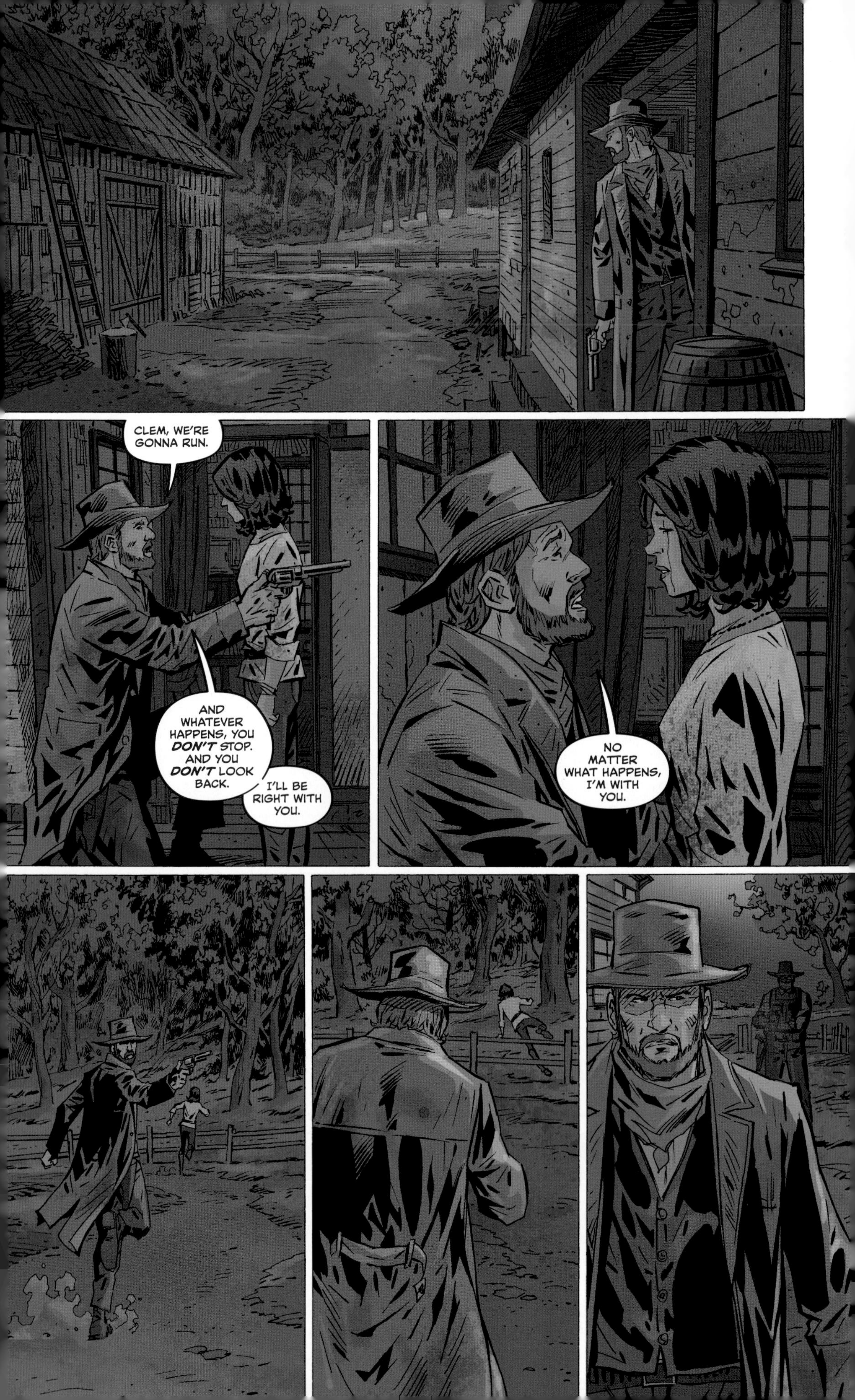

CLEM, WE'RE GONNA RUN.
AND WHATEVER HAPPENS, YOU DON'T STOP. AND YOU DON'T LOOK BACK.
I'LL BE RIGHT WITH YOU.
NO MATTER WHAT HAPPENS, I'M WITH YOU.

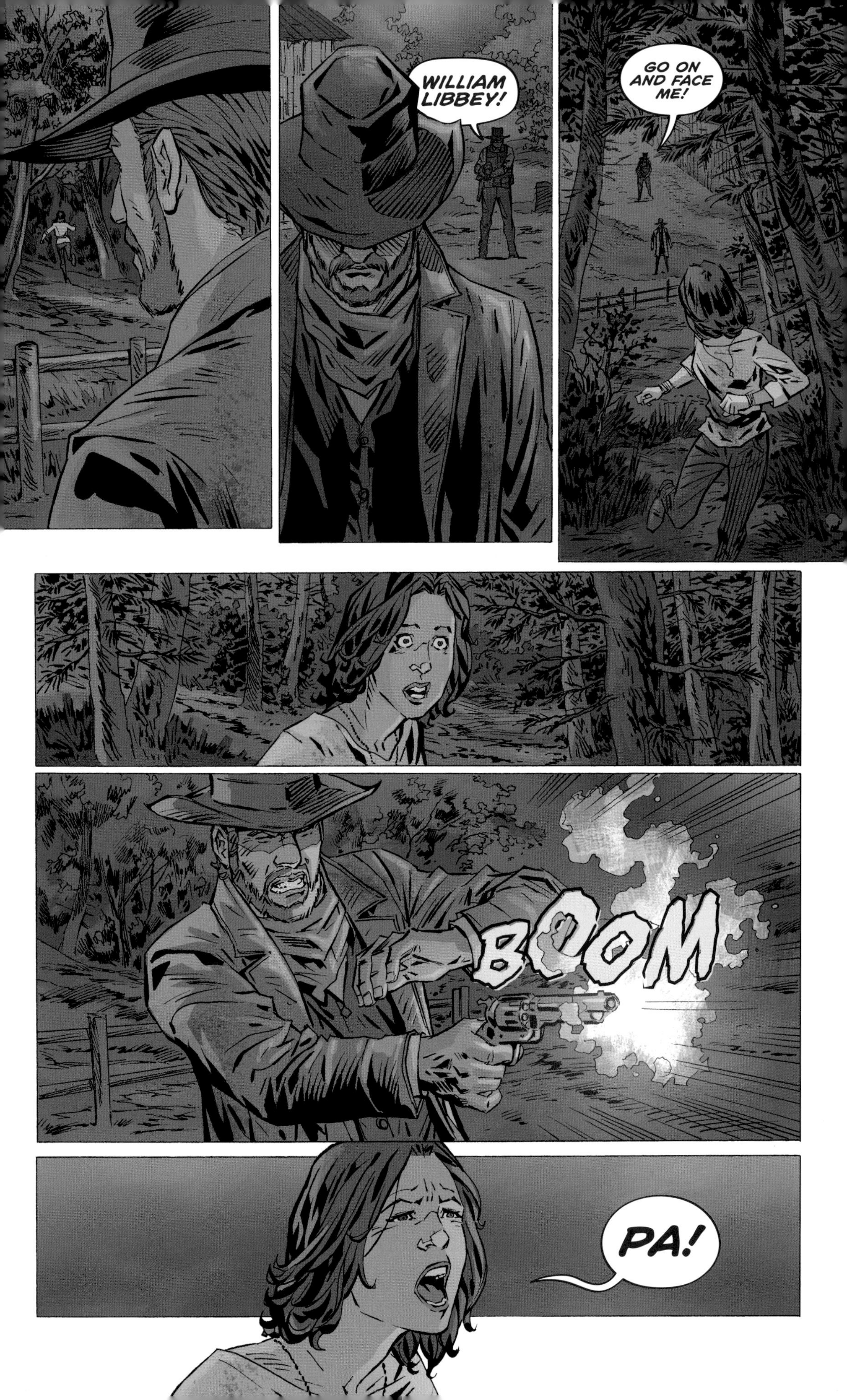
WILLIAM LIBBEY!
GO ON AND FACE ME!
BOOM
PA!

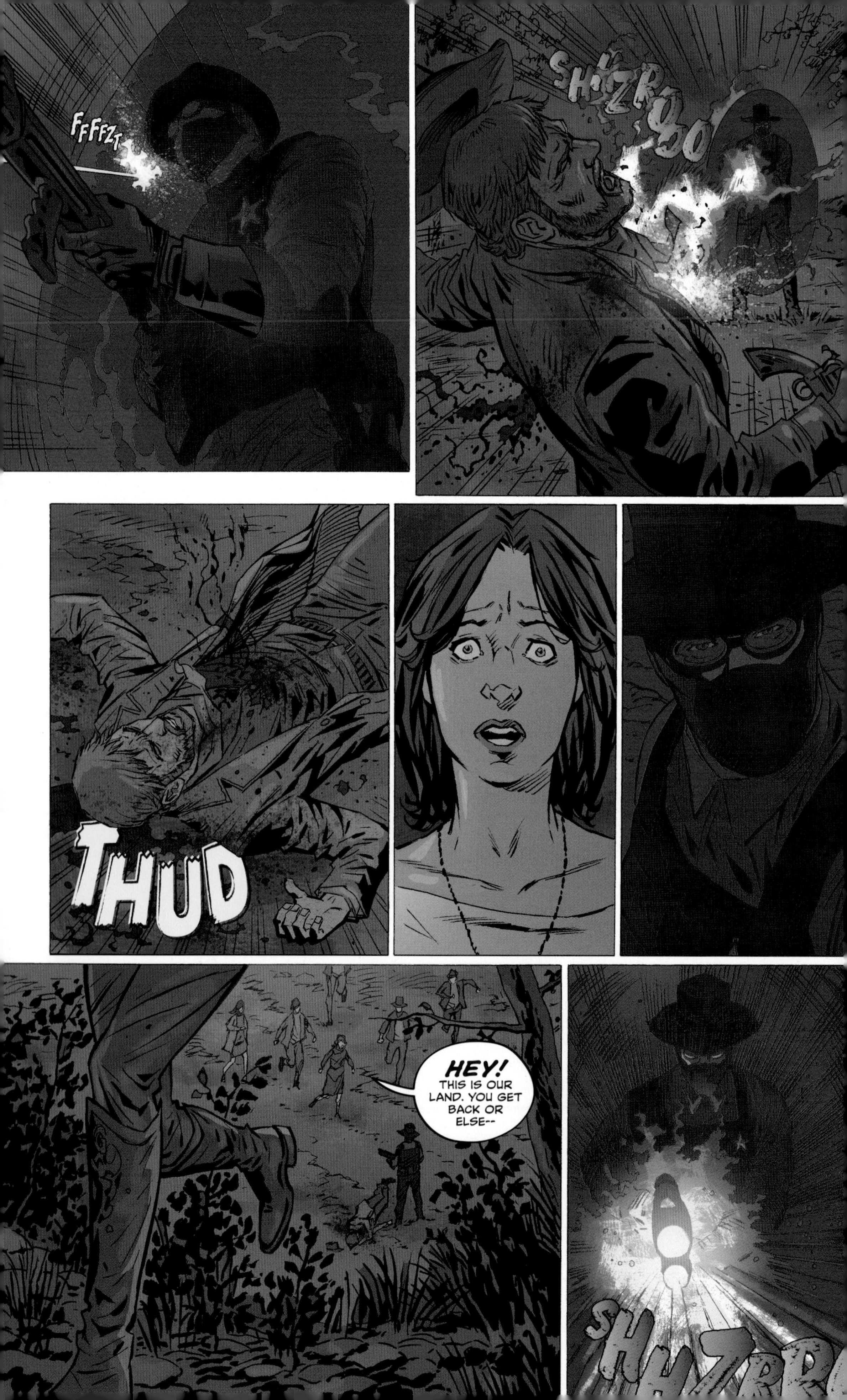
FFFFZT
SHZROOO
THUD
HEY! THIS IS OUR LAND. YOU GET BACK OR ELSE--
SHHZRR

FFZZT

VZZT

VZZZT

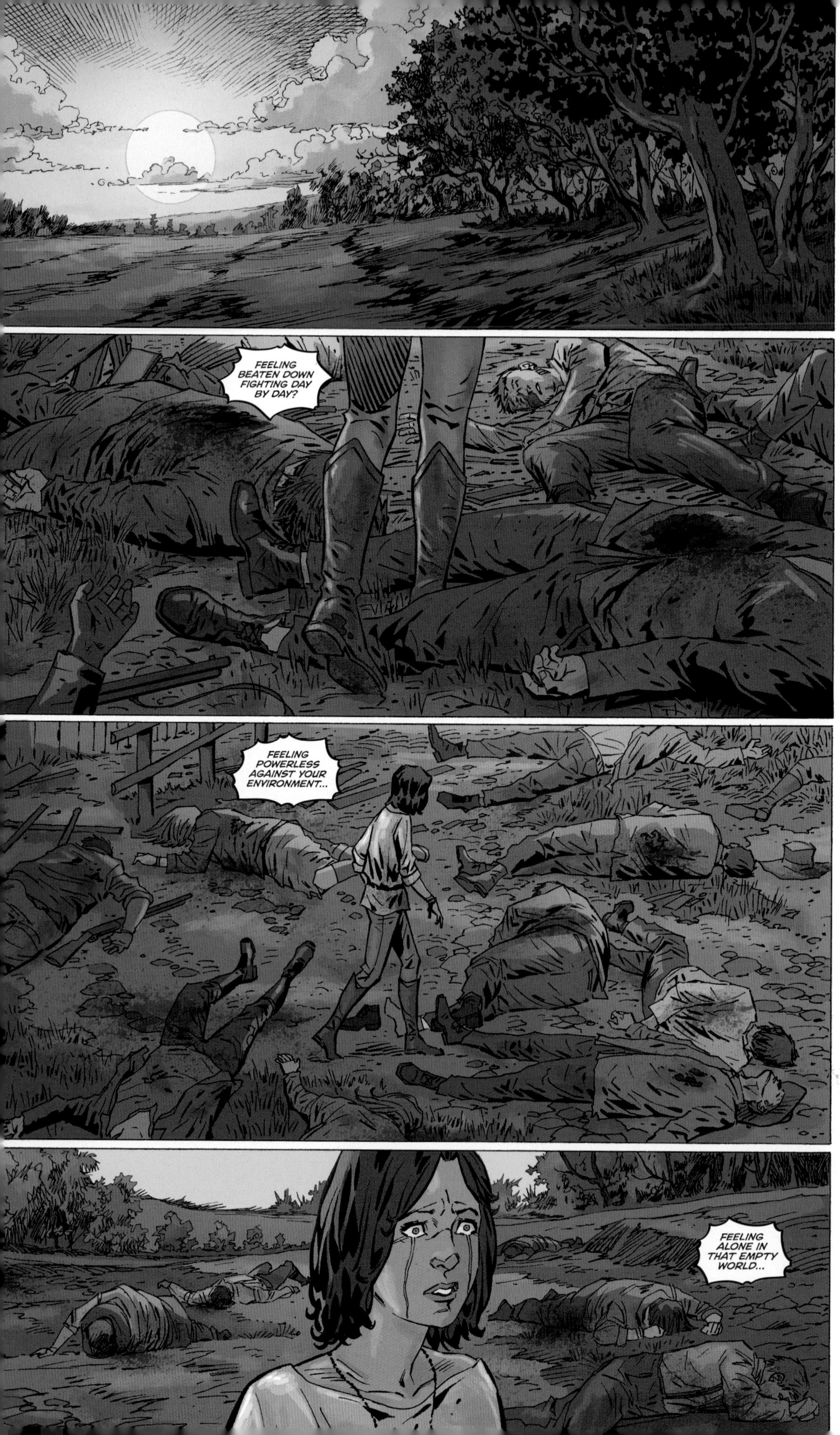
FEELING BEATEN DOWN FIGHTING DAY BY DAY?
FEELING POWERLESS AGAINST YOUR ENVIRONMENT...
FEELING ALONE IN THAT EMPTY WORLD...

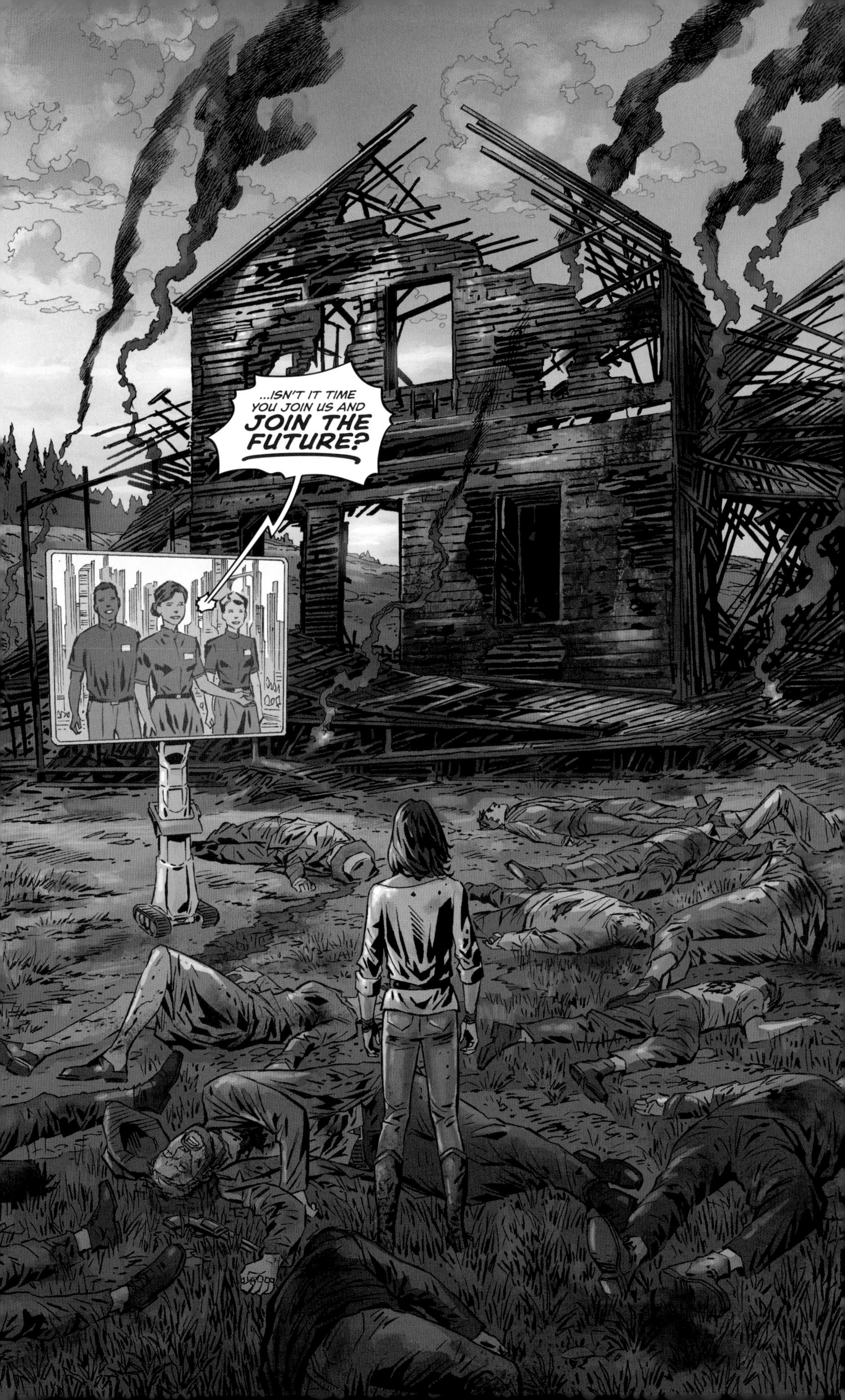
...ISN'T IT TIME YOU JOIN US AND JOIN THE FUTURE?

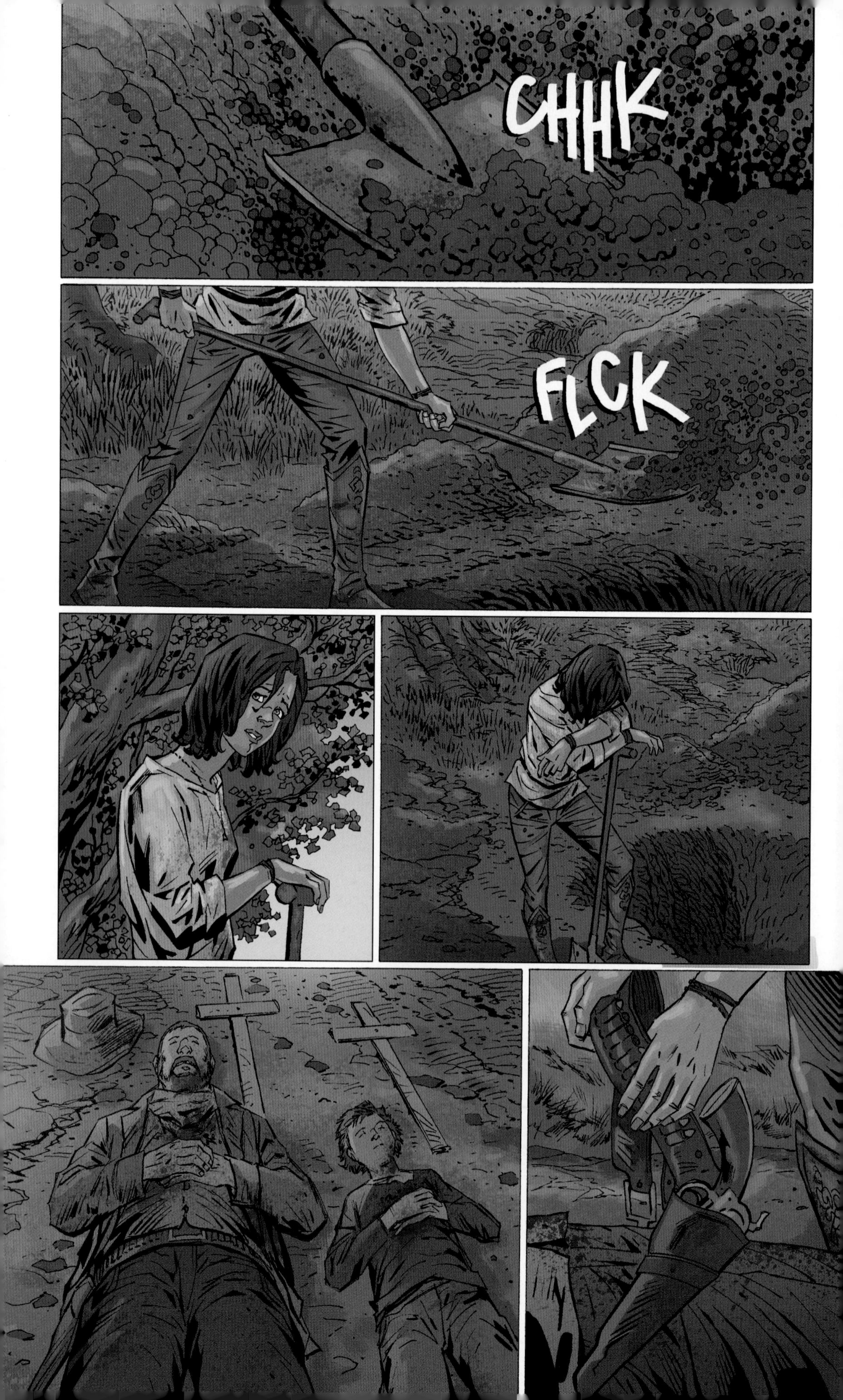
CHHK
FLCK

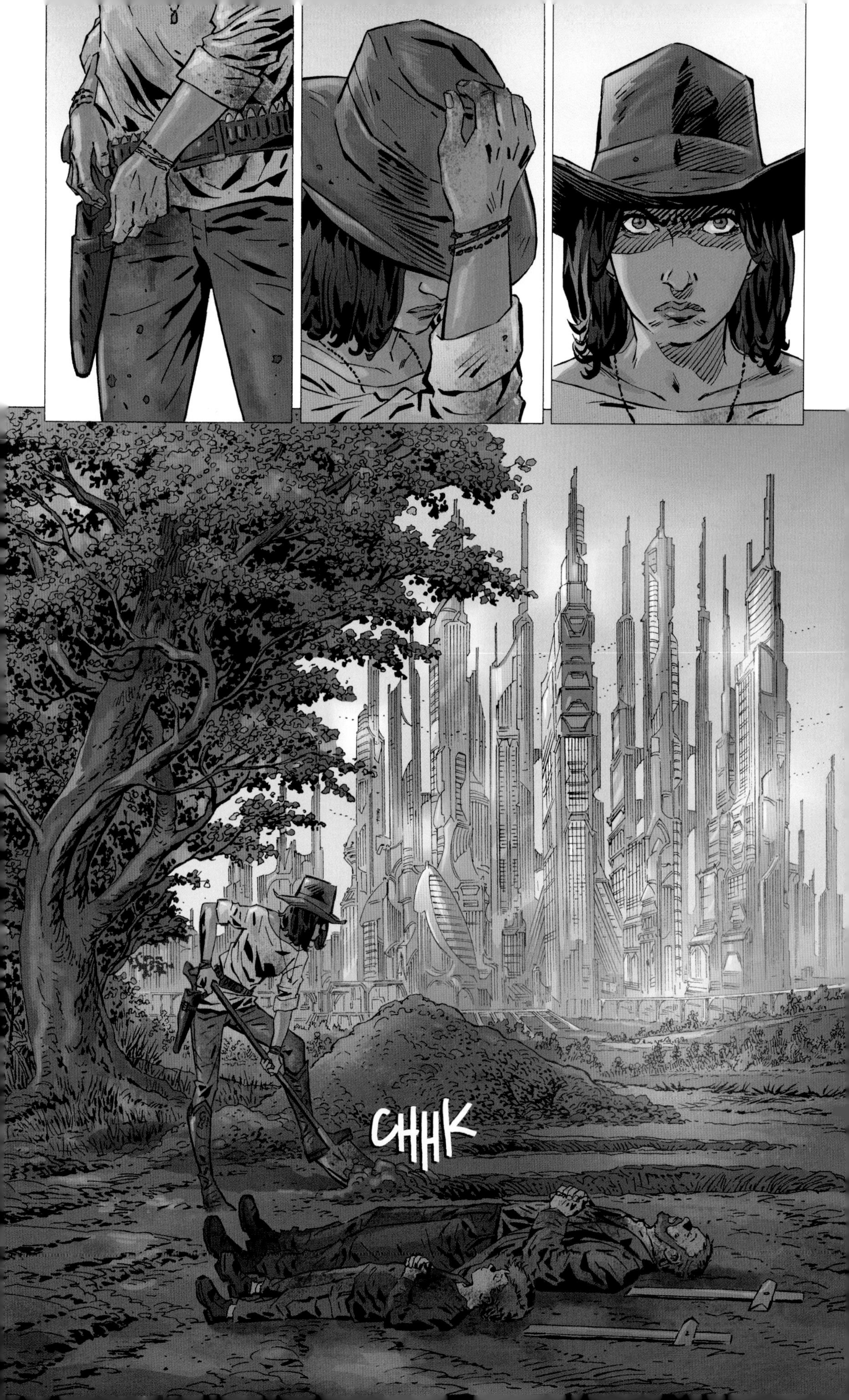
CHHK

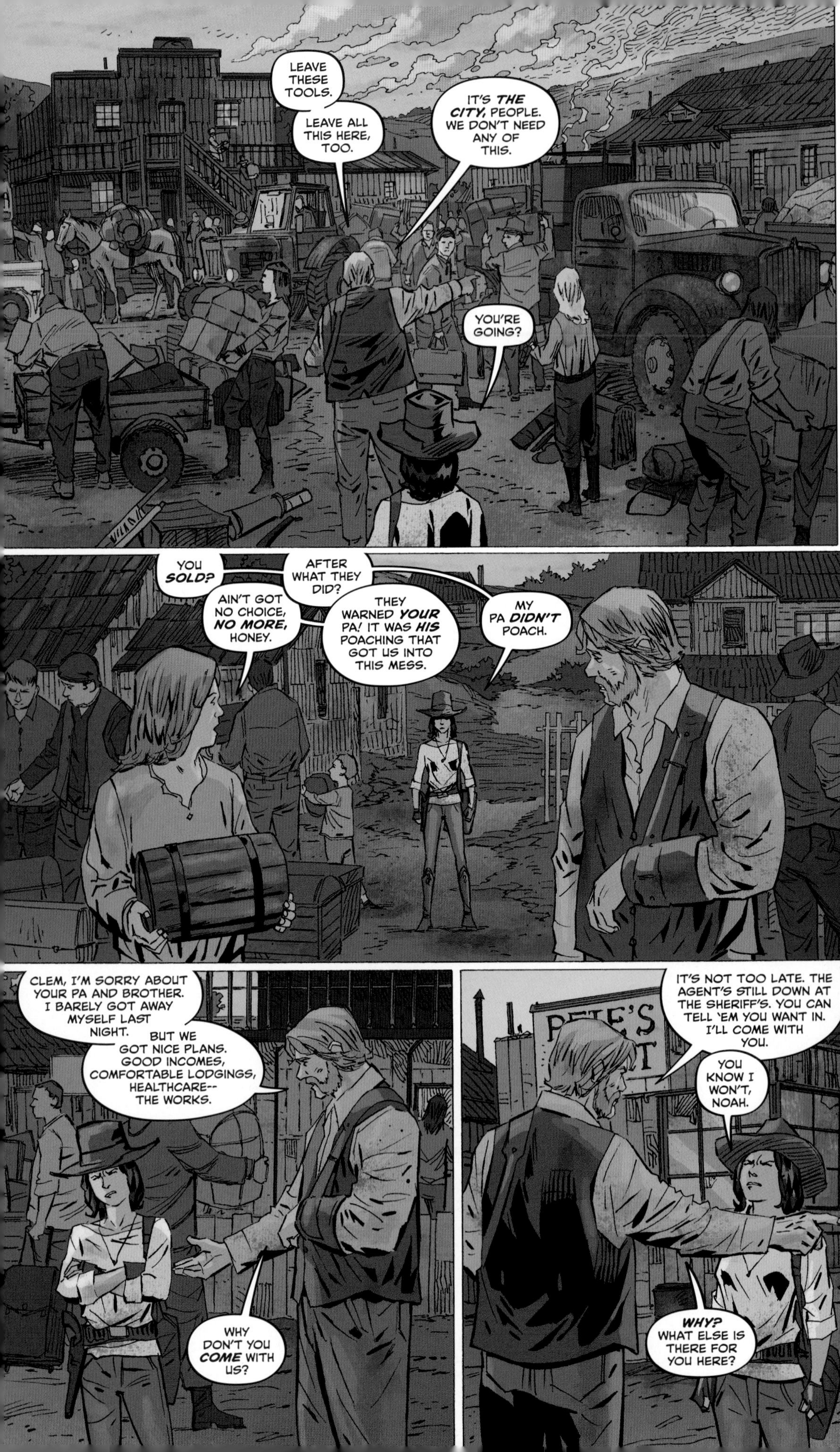
LEAVE THESE TOOLS.
LEAVE ALL THIS HERE, TOO.
IT'S THE CITY, PEOPLE. WE DON'T NEED ANY OF THIS.
YOU'RE GOING?
YOU SOLD?
AFTER WHAT THEY DID?
AIN'T GOT NO CHOICE, NO MORE, HONEY.
THEY WARNED YOUR PA! IT WAS HIS POACHING THAT GOT US INTO THIS MESS.
MY PA DIDN'T POACH.
CLEM, I'M SORRY ABOUT YOUR PA AND BROTHER. I BARELY GOT AWAY MYSELF LAST NIGHT.
BUT WE GOT NICE PLANS. GOOD INCOMES, COMFORTABLE LODGINGS, HEALTHCARE-- THE WORKS.
WHY DON'T YOU COME WITH US?
PETE'S
IT'S NOT TOO LATE. THE AGENT'S STILL DOWN AT THE SHERIFF'S. YOU CAN TELL 'EM YOU WANT IN. I'LL COME WITH YOU.
YOU KNOW I WON'T, NOAH.
WHY? WHAT ELSE IS THERE FOR YOU HERE?

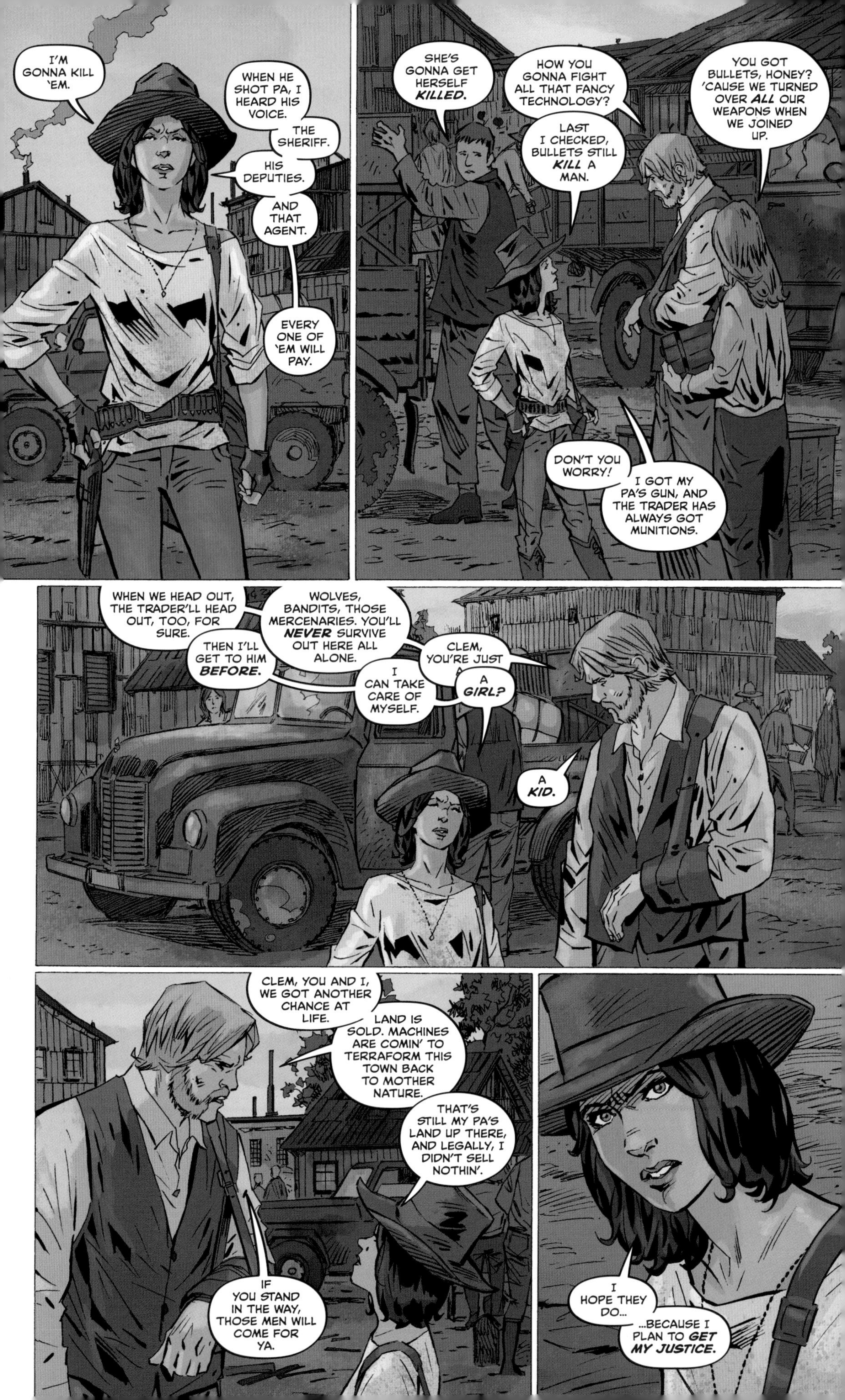

I'M GONNA KILL 'EM.
WHEN HE SHOT PA, I HEARD HIS VOICE.
THE SHERIFF.
HIS DEPUTIES.
AND THAT AGENT.
EVERY ONE OF 'EM WILL PAY.
SHE'S GONNA GET HERSELF KILLED.
HOW YOU GONNA FIGHT ALL THAT FANCY TECHNOLOGY?
LAST I CHECKED, BULLETS STILL KILL A MAN.
YOU GOT BULLETS, HONEY? 'CAUSE WE TURNED OVER ALL OUR WEAPONS WHEN WE JOINED UP.
DON'T YOU WORRY!
I GOT MY PA'S GUN, AND THE TRADER HAS ALWAYS GOT MUNITIONS.
WHEN WE HEAD OUT, THE TRADER'LL HEAD OUT, TOO, FOR SURE.
THEN I'LL GET TO HIM BEFORE.
WOLVES, BANDITS, THOSE MERCENARIES. YOU'LL NEVER SURVIVE OUT HERE ALL ALONE.
I CAN TAKE CARE OF MYSELF.
CLEM, YOU'RE JUST A
A GIRL?
A KID.
CLEM, YOU AND I, WE GOT ANOTHER CHANCE AT LIFE.
LAND IS SOLD. MACHINES ARE COMIN' TO TERRAFORM THIS TOWN BACK TO MOTHER NATURE.
THAT'S STILL MY PA'S LAND UP THERE, AND LEGALLY, I DIDN'T SELL NOTHIN'.
IF YOU STAND IN THE WAY, THOSE MEN WILL COME FOR YA.
I HOPE THEY DO...
...BECAUSE I PLAN TO GET MY JUSTICE.

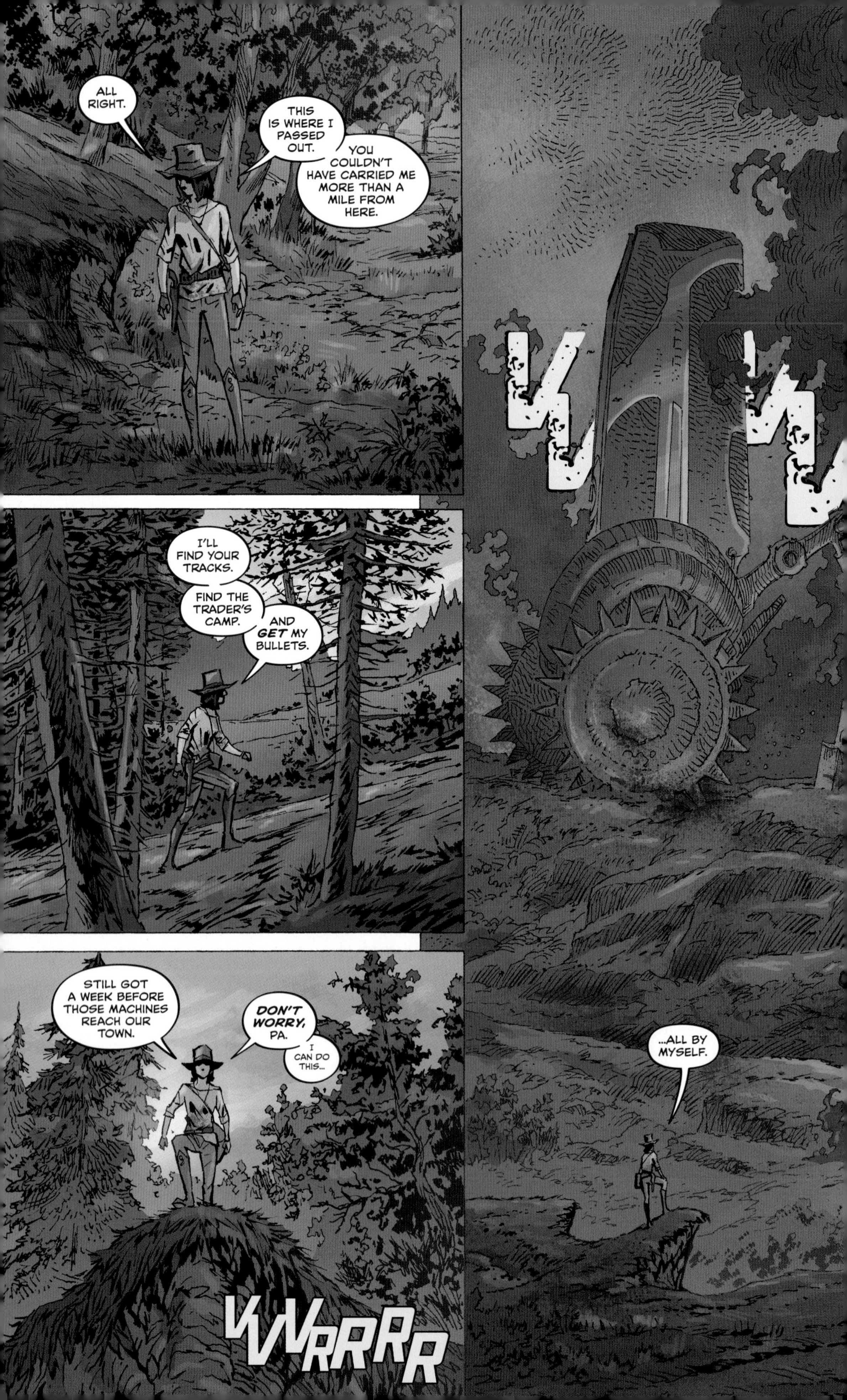
ALL RIGHT.
THIS IS WHERE I PASSED OUT.
YOU COULDN'T HAVE CARRIED ME MORE THAN A MILE FROM HERE.
I'LL FIND YOUR TRACKS.
FIND THE TRADER'S CAMP.
AND *GET* MY BULLETS.
STILL GOT A WEEK BEFORE THOSE MACHINES REACH OUR TOWN.
DON'T WORRY, PA.
I CAN DO THIS...
VVVRRRRR
...ALL BY MYSELF.

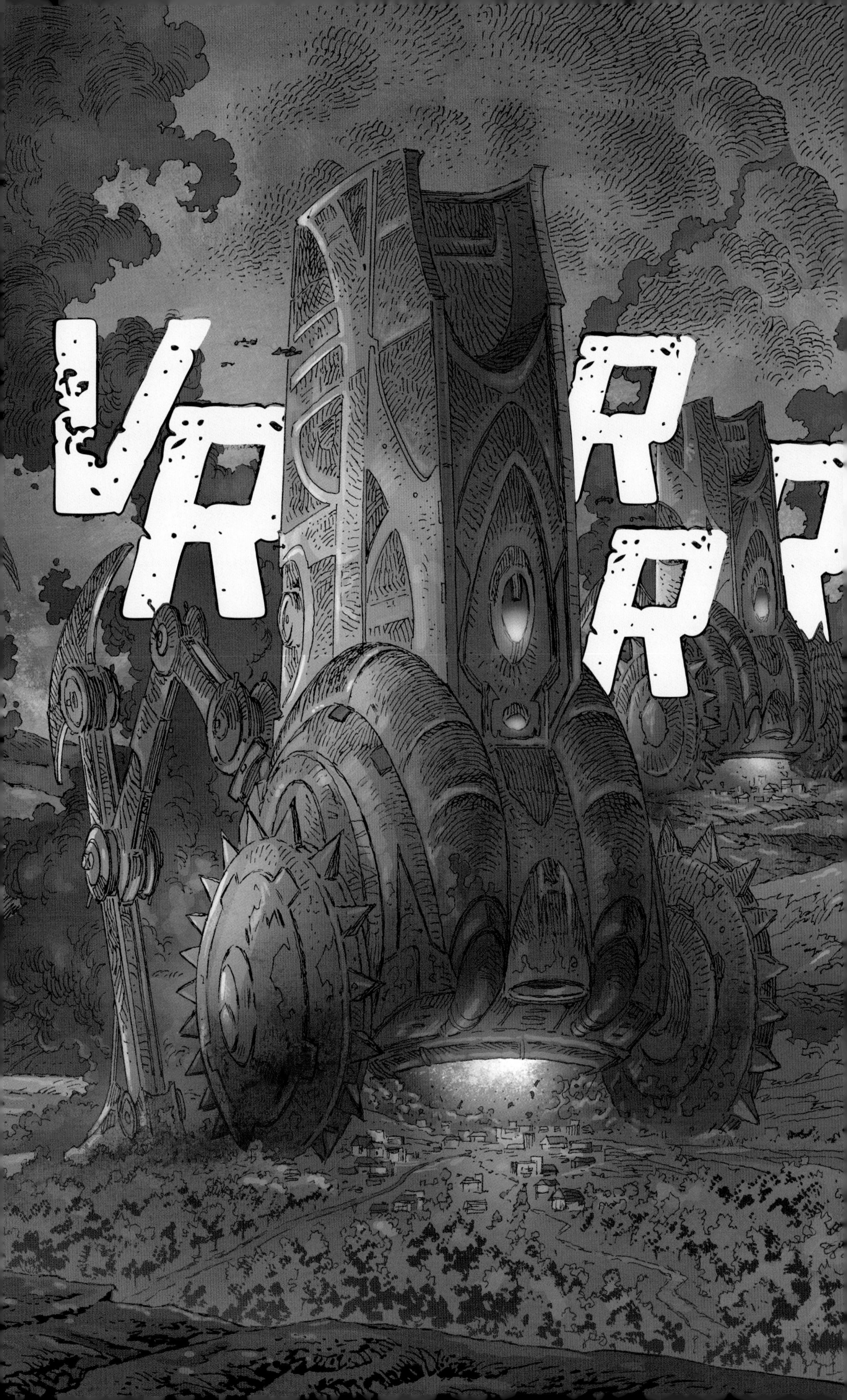
VRRRR

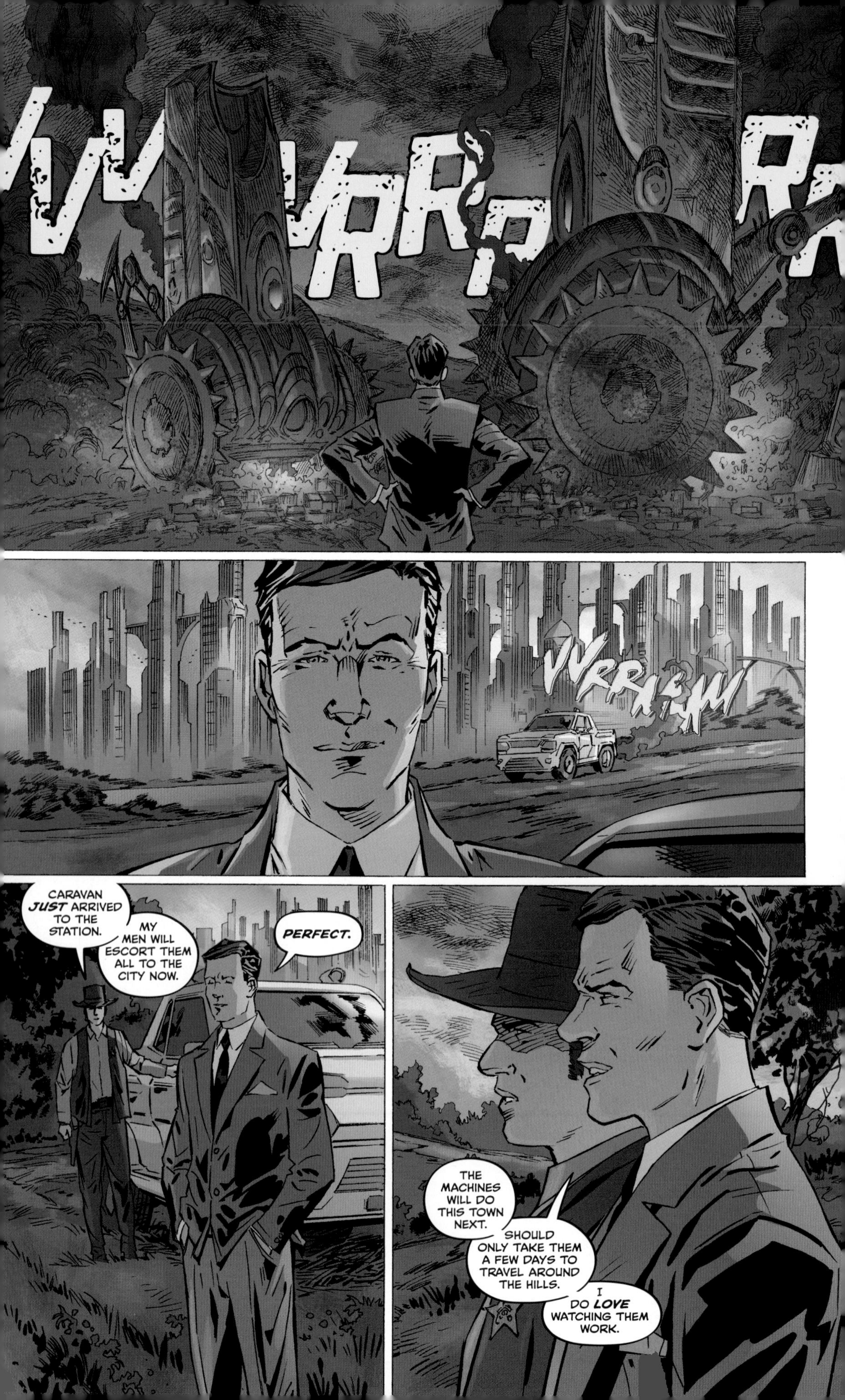
VVVRRRRRA
VVRRRMMM
CARAVAN JUST ARRIVED TO THE STATION.
MY MEN WILL ESCORT THEM ALL TO THE CITY NOW.
PERFECT.
THE MACHINES WILL DO THIS TOWN NEXT.
SHOULD ONLY TAKE THEM A FEW DAYS TO TRAVEL AROUND THE HILLS.
I DO LOVE WATCHING THEM WORK.

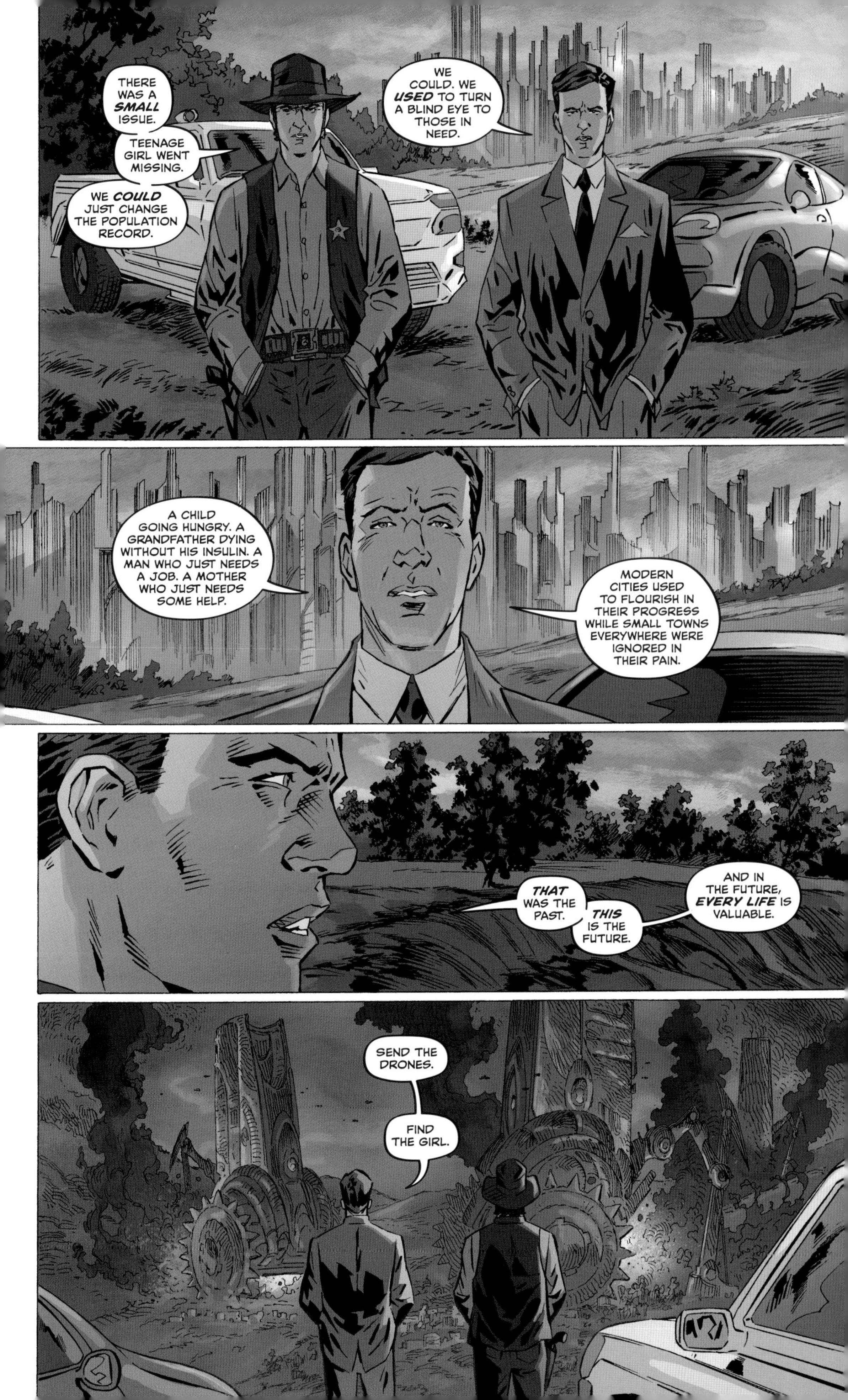
THERE WAS A SMALL ISSUE.
TEENAGE GIRL WENT MISSING.
WE COULD JUST CHANGE THE POPULATION RECORD.
WE COULD. WE USED TO TURN A BLIND EYE TO THOSE IN NEED.
A CHILD GOING HUNGRY. A GRANDFATHER DYING WITHOUT HIS INSULIN. A MAN WHO JUST NEEDS A JOB. A MOTHER WHO JUST NEEDS SOME HELP.
MODERN CITIES USED TO FLOURISH IN THEIR PROGRESS WHILE SMALL TOWNS EVERYWHERE WERE IGNORED IN THEIR PAIN.
THAT WAS THE PAST.
THIS IS THE FUTURE.
AND IN THE FUTURE, EVERY LIFE IS VALUABLE.
SEND THE DRONES.
FIND THE GIRL.

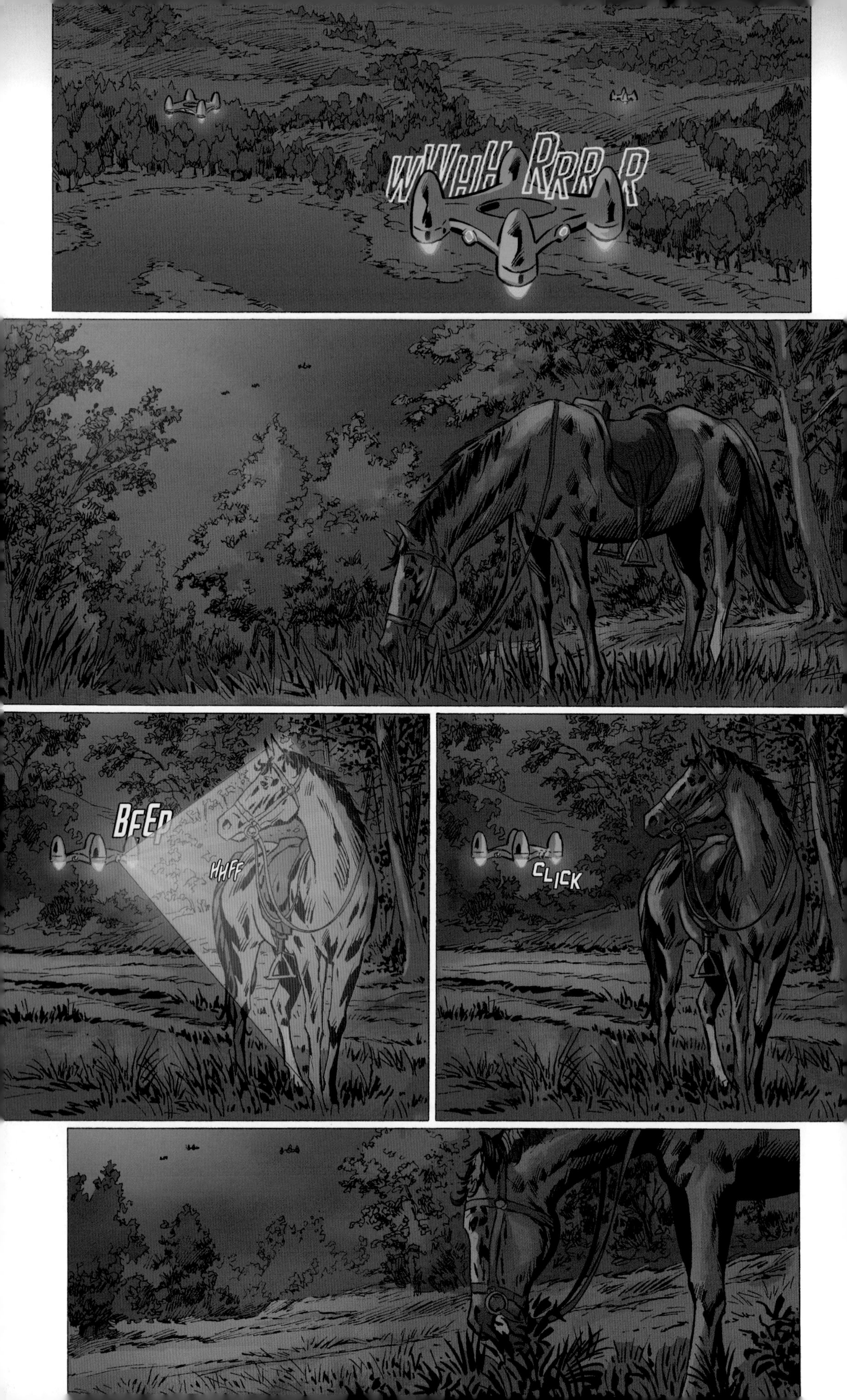
WHHH RRRR
BEEP
HHFF
CLICK

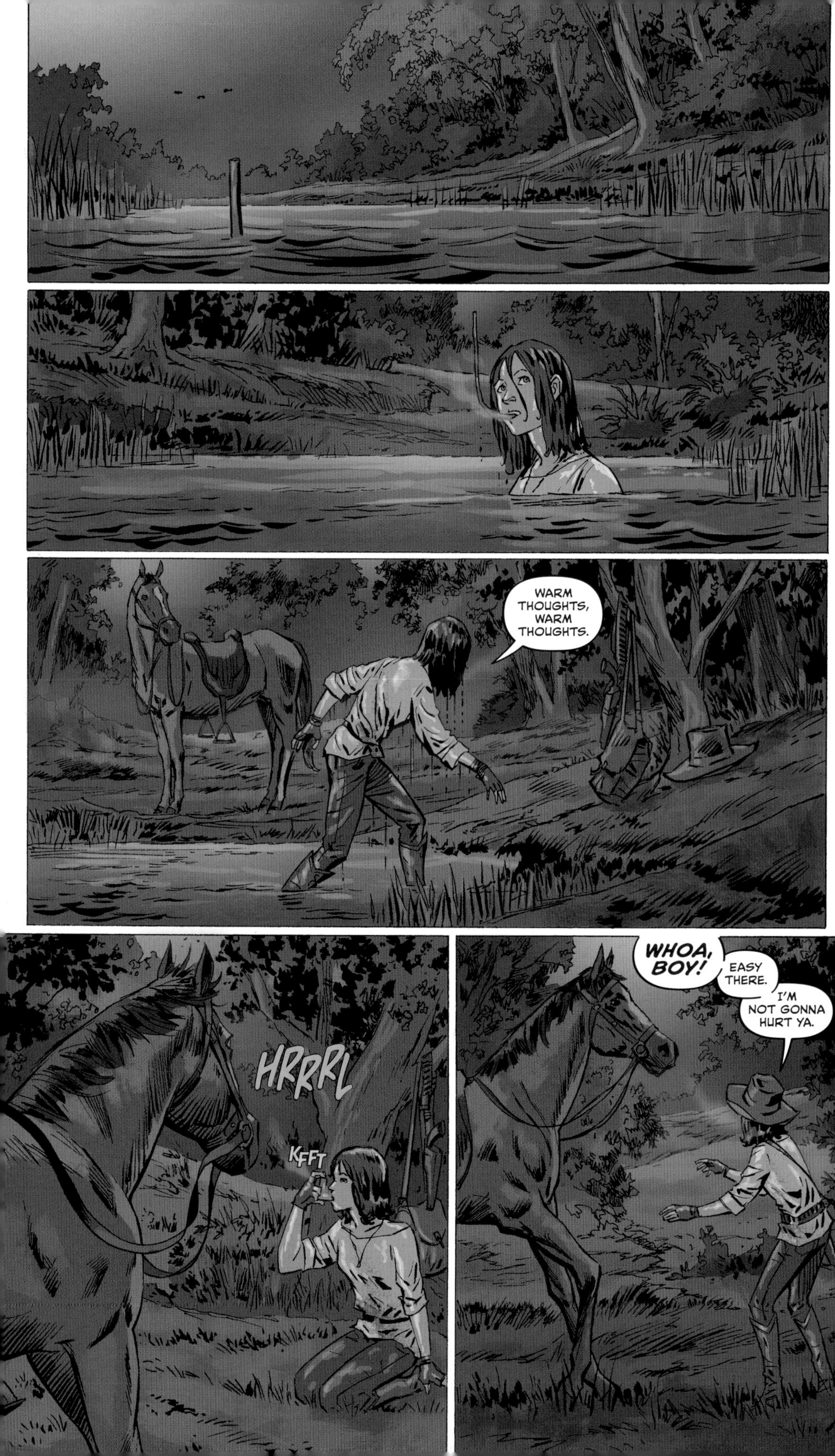
WARM THOUGHTS, WARM THOUGHTS.
HRRRL
KFFT
WHOA, BOY!
EASY THERE.
I'M NOT GONNA HURT YA.

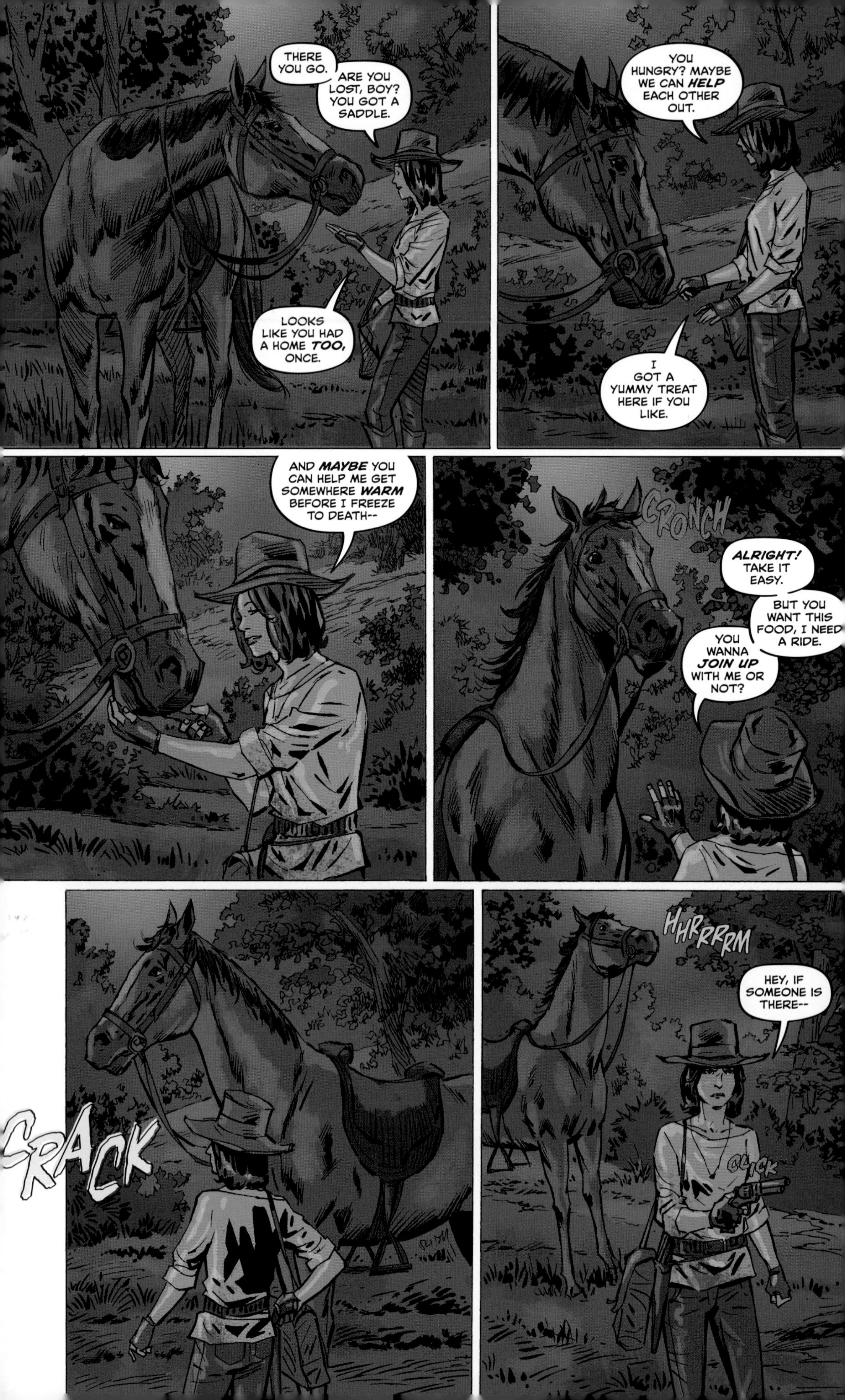

THERE YOU GO.
ARE YOU LOST, BOY? YOU GOT A SADDLE.
LOOKS LIKE YOU HAD A HOME TOO, ONCE.
YOU HUNGRY? MAYBE WE CAN HELP EACH OTHER OUT.
I GOT A YUMMY TREAT HERE IF YOU LIKE.
AND MAYBE YOU CAN HELP ME GET SOMEWHERE WARM BEFORE I FREEZE TO DEATH--
CRONCH
ALRIGHT! TAKE IT EASY.
BUT YOU WANT THIS FOOD, I NEED A RIDE.
YOU WANNA JOIN UP WITH ME OR NOT?
CRACK
HHRRRRM
HEY, IF SOMEONE IS THERE--
CLICK

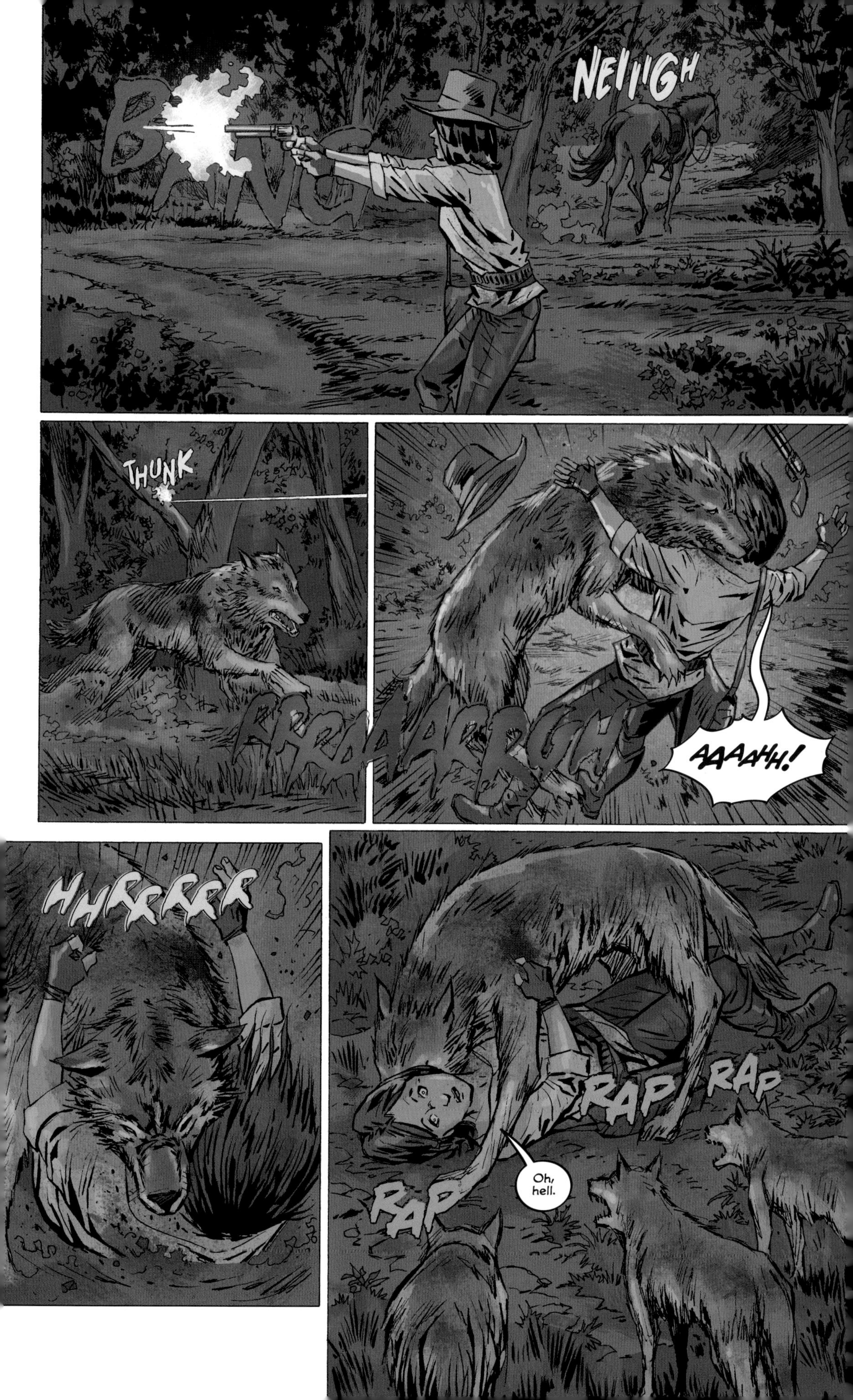
BLAM
NEIIIGH
THUNK
RRRAARRGH
AAAAHH!
HHRRRRR
RAP RAP
RAP
Oh, hell.

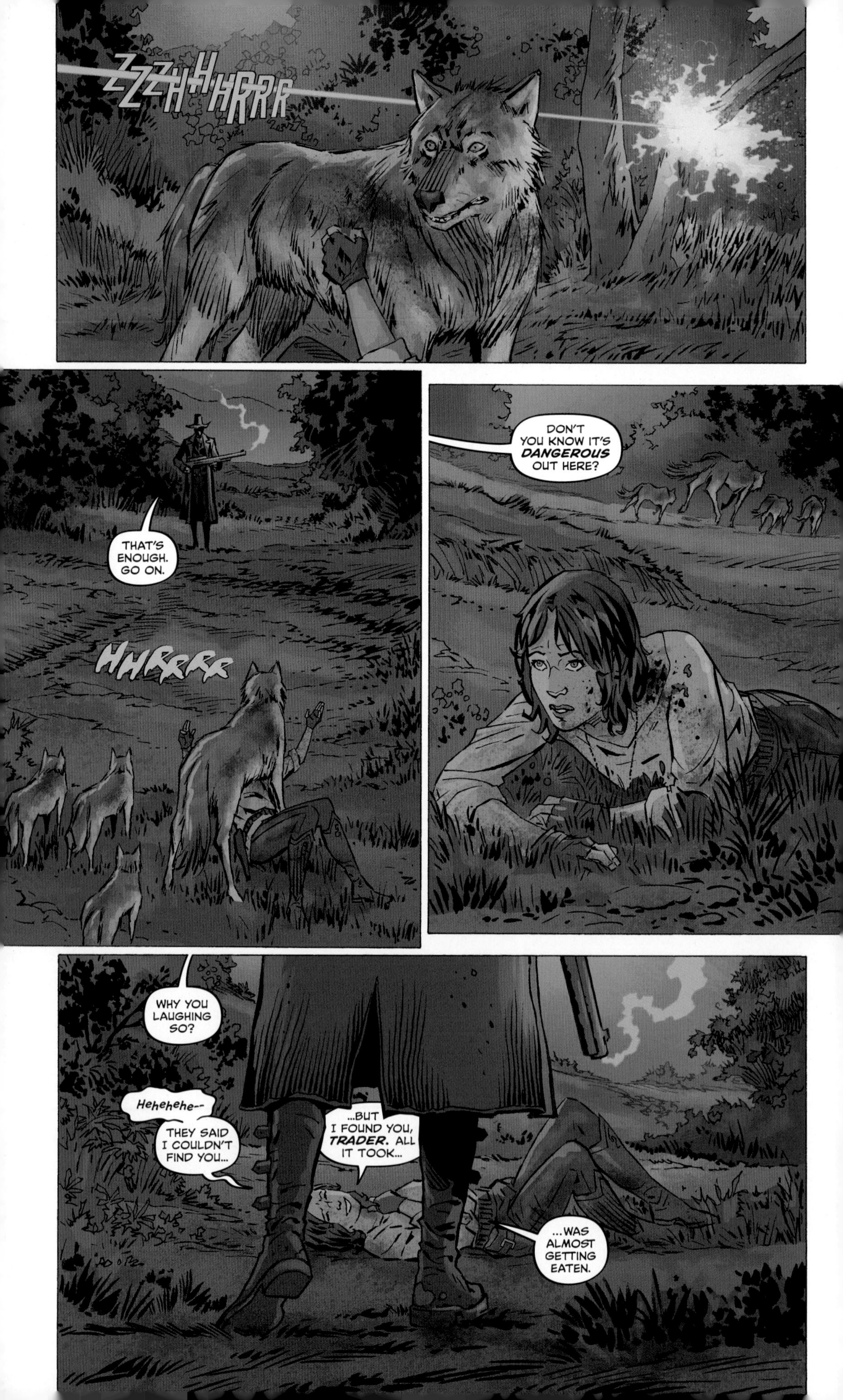
ZZZHHHRRRR
THAT'S ENOUGH. GO ON.
HHRRRR
DON'T YOU KNOW IT'S DANGEROUS OUT HERE?
WHY YOU LAUGHING SO?
Hehehehe--
THEY SAID I COULDN'T FIND YOU...
...BUT I FOUND YOU, TRADER. ALL IT TOOK...
...WAS ALMOST GETTING EATEN.

3

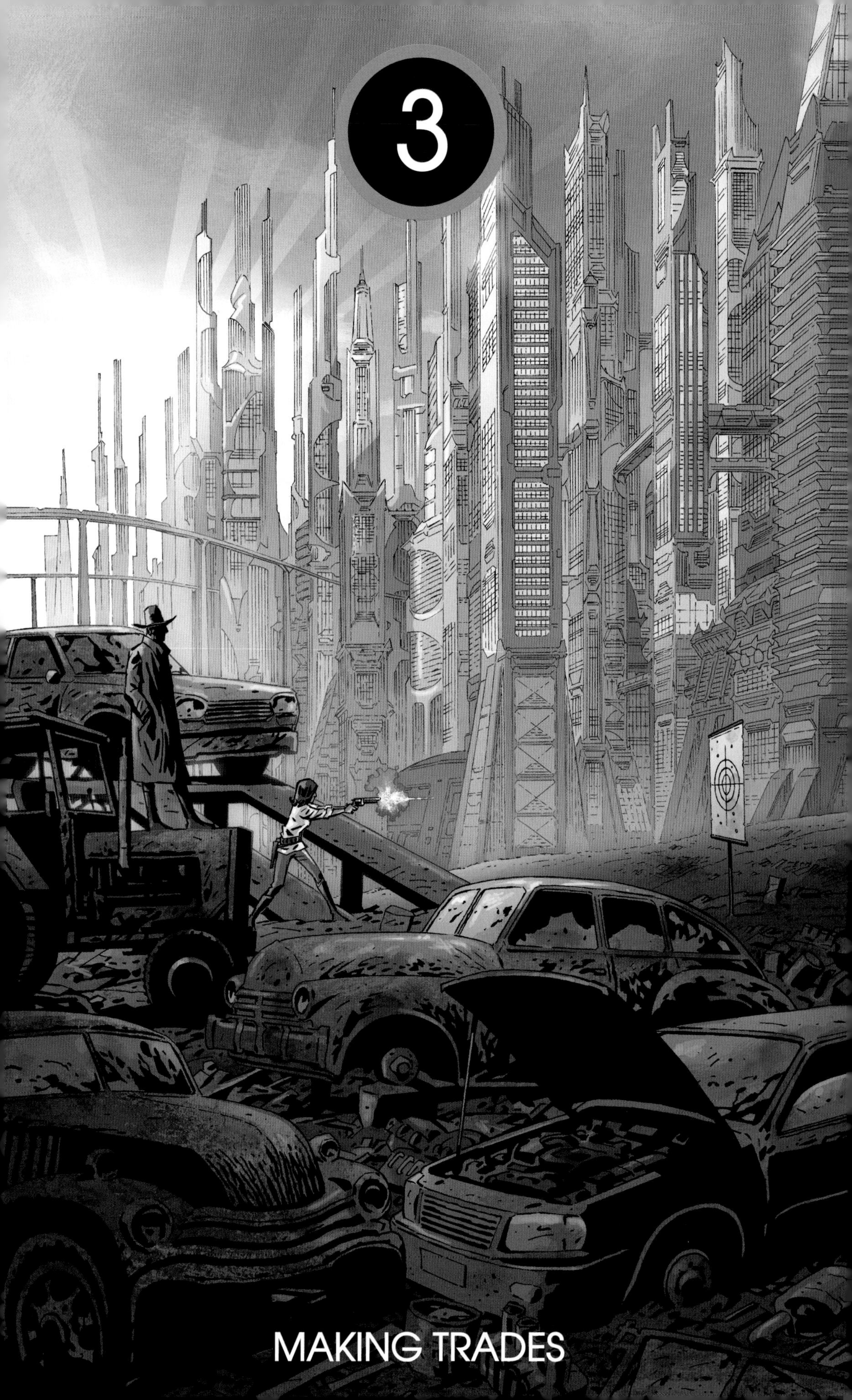

MAKING TRADES

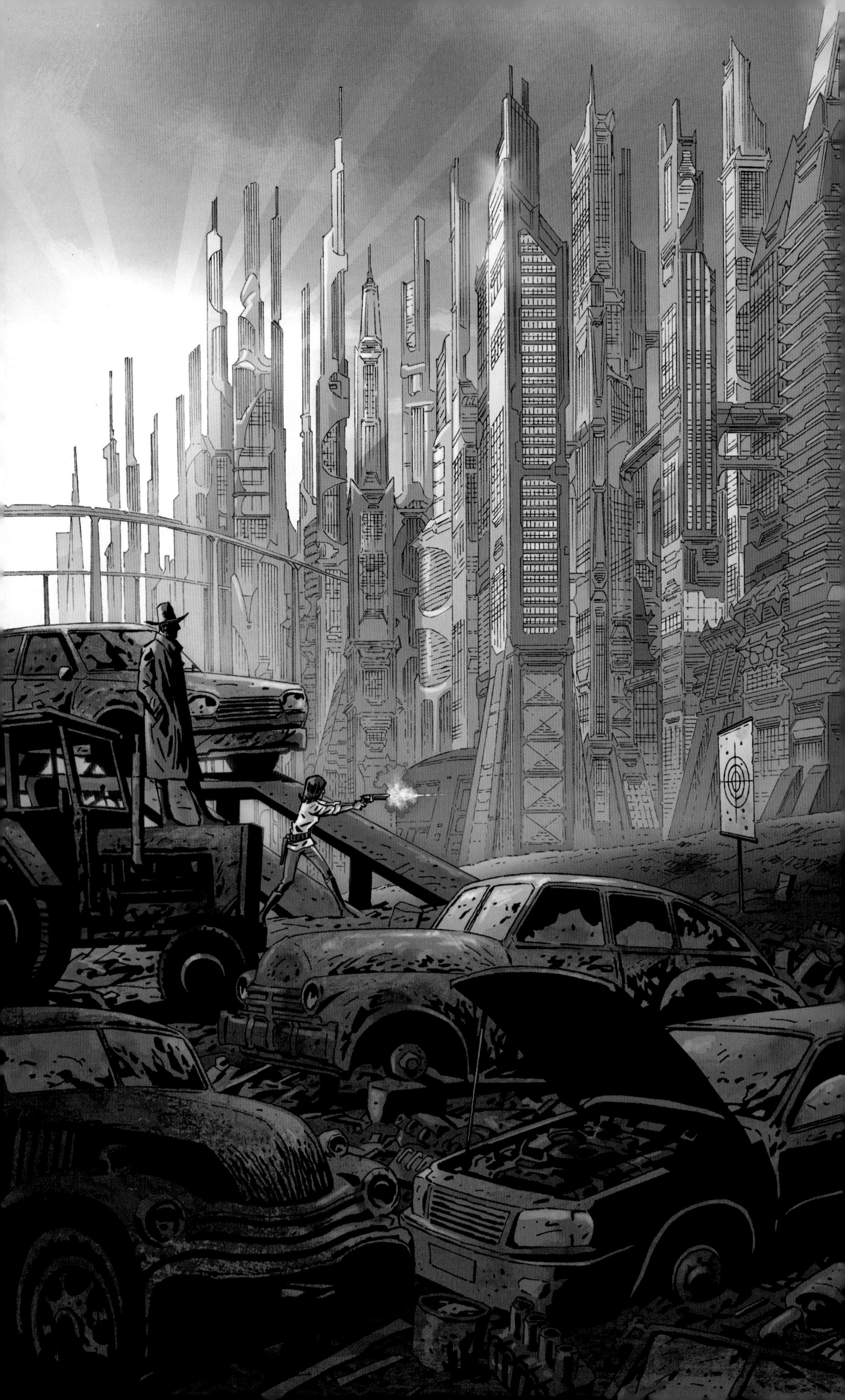

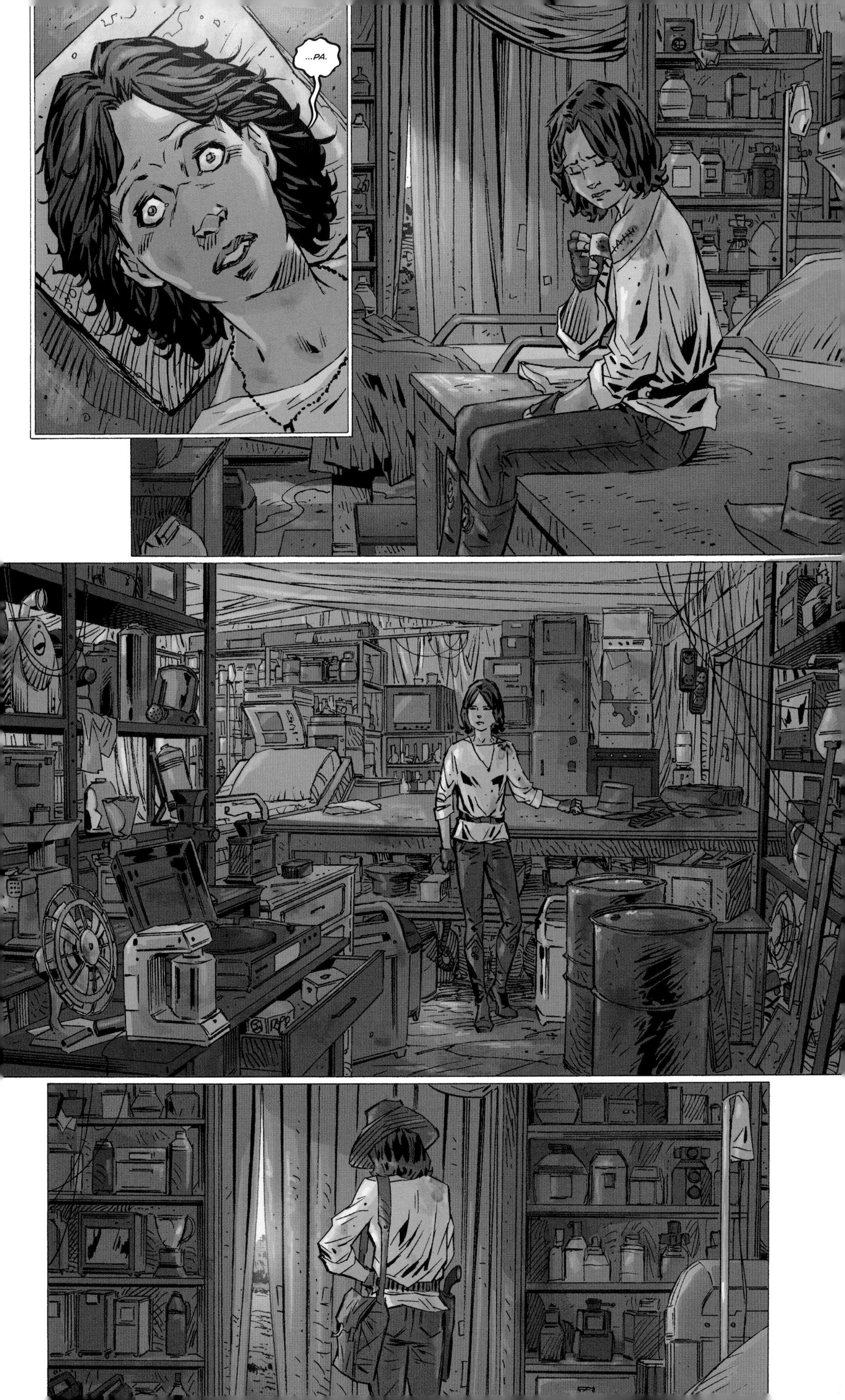
...PA.

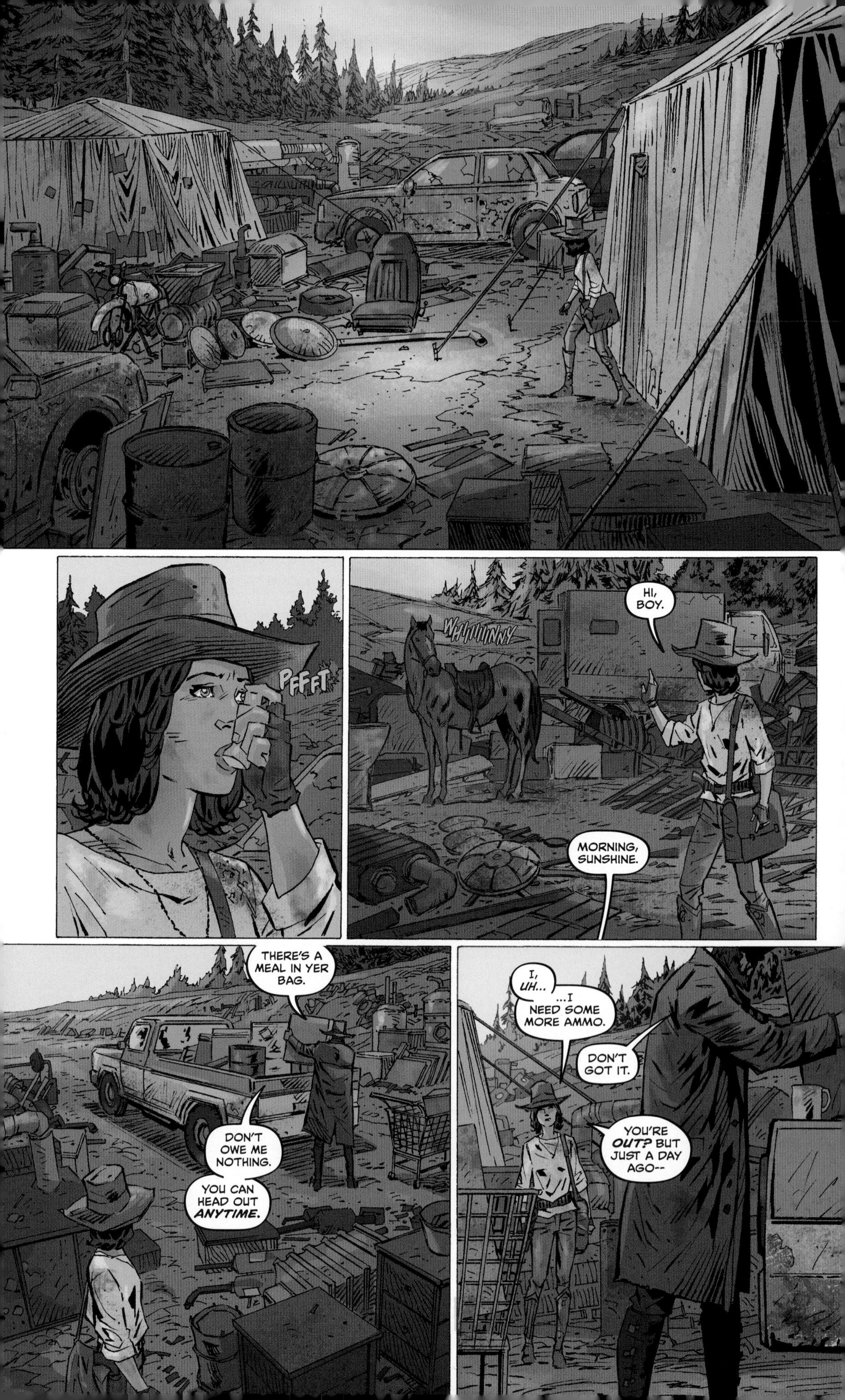
PFFFT
WHIIIIINNY
HI, BOY.
MORNING, SUNSHINE.
THERE'S A MEAL IN YER BAG.
DON'T OWE ME NOTHING.
YOU CAN HEAD OUT ANYTIME.
I, UH...
...I NEED SOME MORE AMMO.
DON'T GOT IT.
YOU'RE OUT? BUT JUST A DAY AGO--

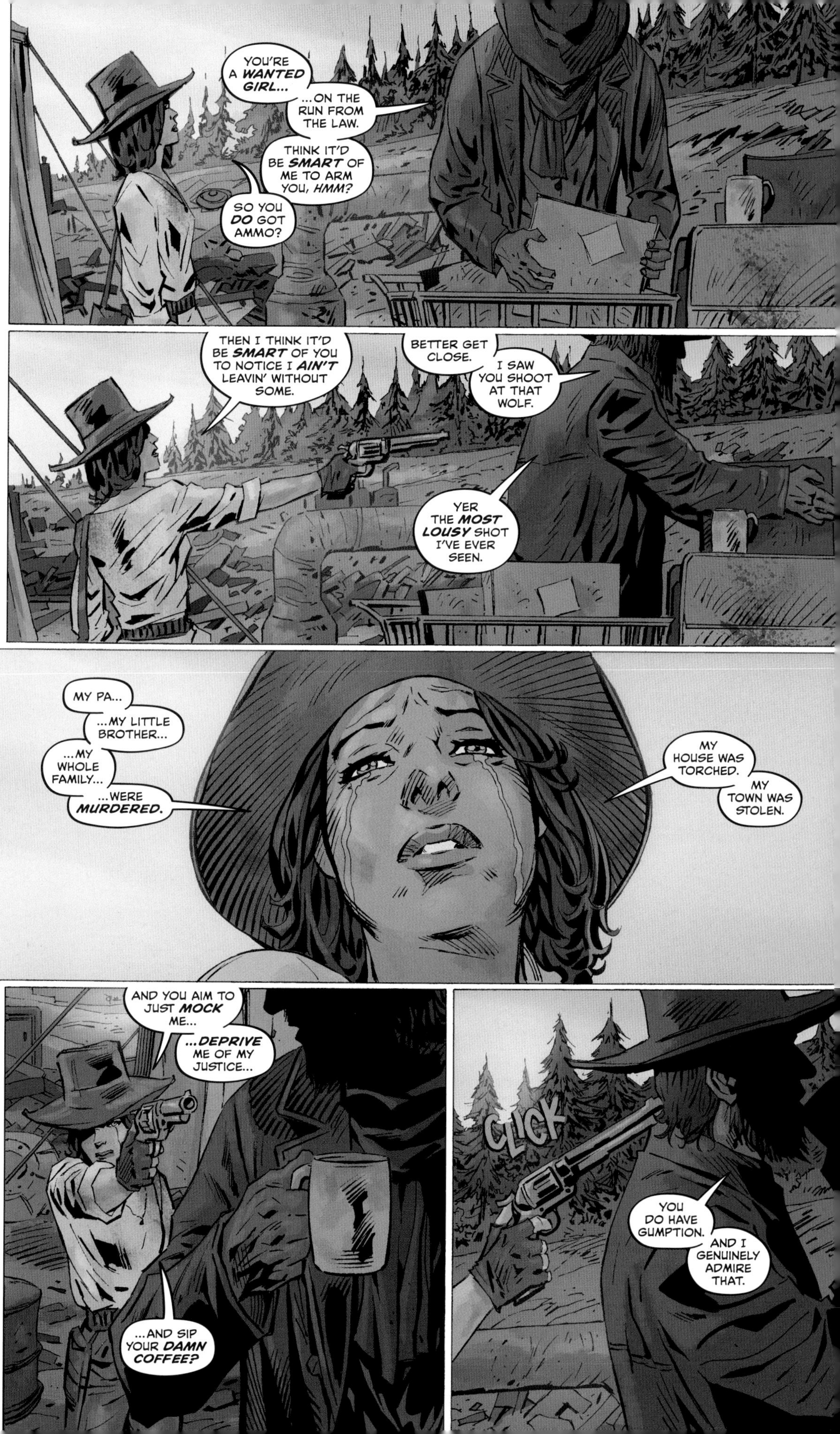
YOU'RE A WANTED GIRL...
...ON THE RUN FROM THE LAW.
THINK IT'D BE SMART OF ME TO ARM YOU, HMM?
SO YOU DO GOT AMMO?
THEN I THINK IT'D BE SMART OF YOU TO NOTICE I AIN'T LEAVIN' WITHOUT SOME.
BETTER GET CLOSE.
I SAW YOU SHOOT AT THAT WOLF.
YER THE MOST LOUSY SHOT I'VE EVER SEEN.
MY PA...
...MY LITTLE BROTHER...
...MY WHOLE FAMILY...
...WERE MURDERED.
MY HOUSE WAS TORCHED.
MY TOWN WAS STOLEN.
AND YOU AIM TO JUST MOCK ME...
...DEPRIVE ME OF MY JUSTICE...
...AND SIP YOUR DAMN COFFEE?
CLICK
YOU DO HAVE GUMPTION.
AND I GENUINELY ADMIRE THAT.

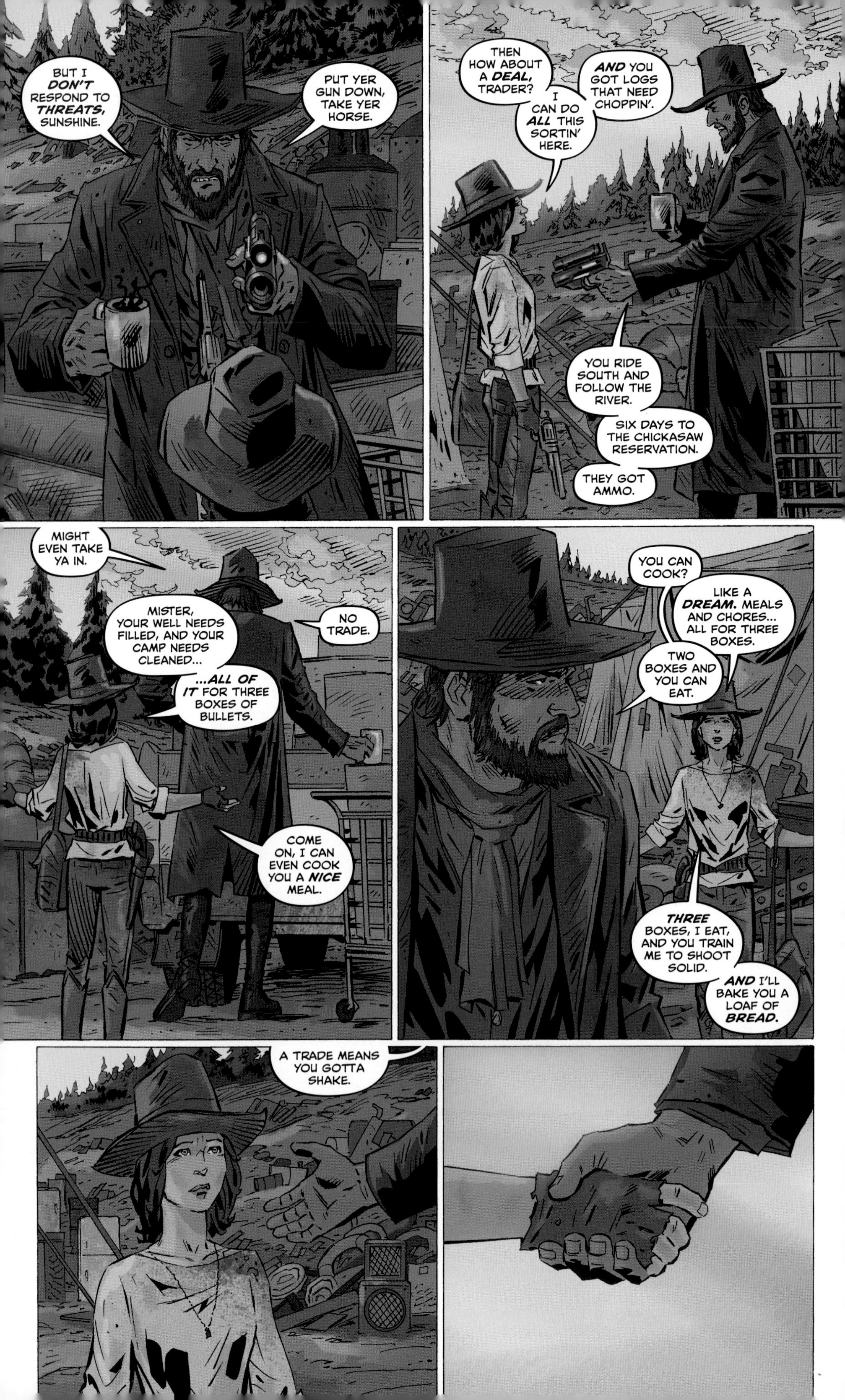
BUT I DON'T RESPOND TO THREATS, SUNSHINE.
PUT YER GUN DOWN, TAKE YER HORSE.
THEN HOW ABOUT A DEAL, TRADER?
I CAN DO ALL THIS SORTIN' HERE.
AND YOU GOT LOGS THAT NEED CHOPPIN'.
YOU RIDE SOUTH AND FOLLOW THE RIVER.
SIX DAYS TO THE CHICKASAW RESERVATION.
THEY GOT AMMO.
MIGHT EVEN TAKE YA IN.
MISTER, YOUR WELL NEEDS FILLED, AND YOUR CAMP NEEDS CLEANED...
...ALL OF IT FOR THREE BOXES OF BULLETS.
NO TRADE.
COME ON, I CAN EVEN COOK YOU A NICE MEAL.
YOU CAN COOK?
LIKE A DREAM. MEALS AND CHORES... ALL FOR THREE BOXES.
TWO BOXES AND YOU CAN EAT.
THREE BOXES, I EAT, AND YOU TRAIN ME TO SHOOT SOLID.
AND I'LL BAKE YOU A LOAF OF BREAD.
A TRADE MEANS YOU GOTTA SHAKE.

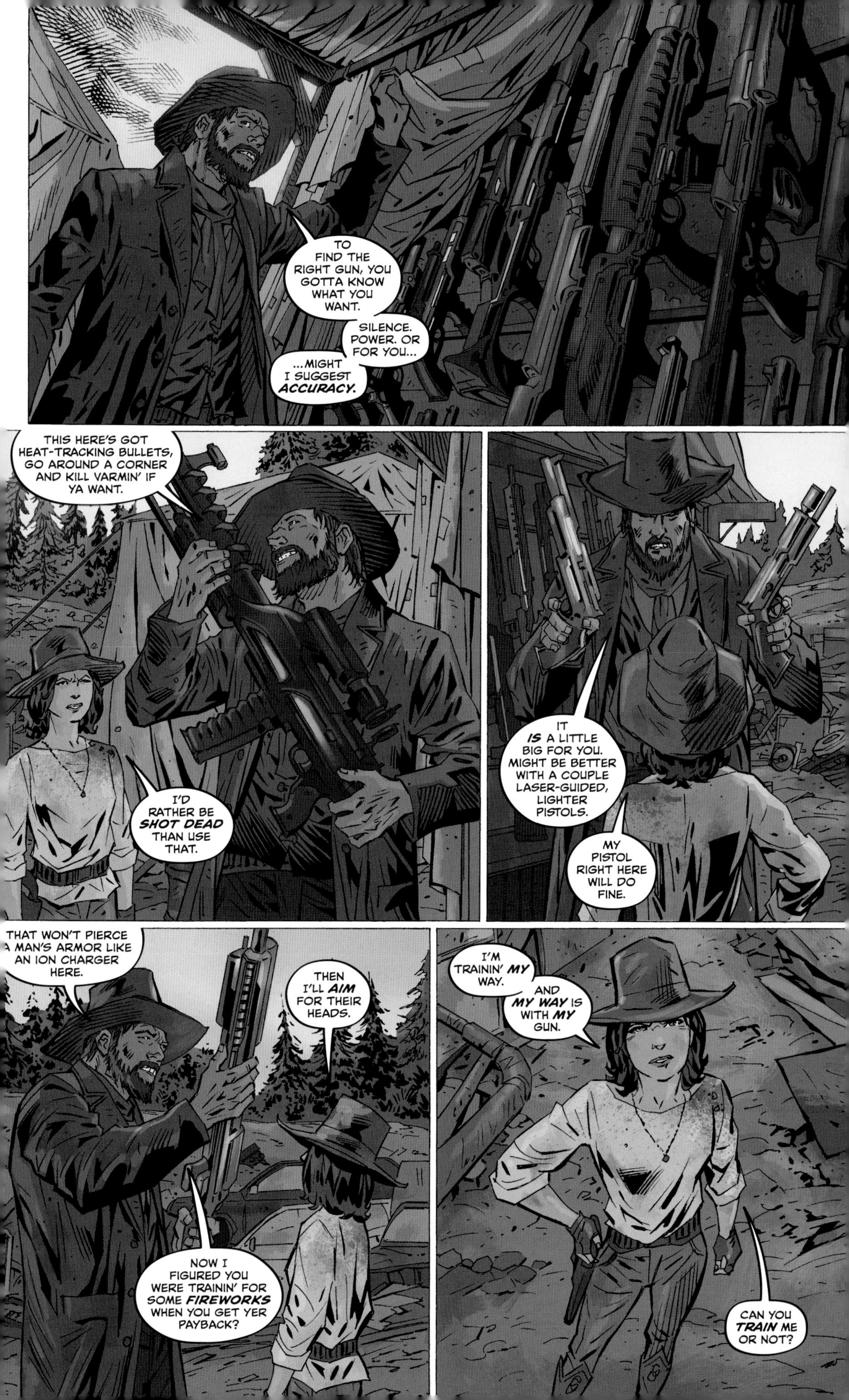
TO FIND THE RIGHT GUN, YOU GOTTA KNOW WHAT YOU WANT.
SILENCE. POWER. OR FOR YOU...
...MIGHT I SUGGEST ***ACCURACY.***
THIS HERE'S GOT HEAT-TRACKING BULLETS, GO AROUND A CORNER AND KILL VARMIN' IF YA WANT.
I'D RATHER BE ***SHOT DEAD*** THAN USE THAT.
IT ***IS*** A LITTLE BIG FOR YOU. MIGHT BE BETTER WITH A COUPLE LASER-GUIDED, LIGHTER PISTOLS.
MY PISTOL RIGHT HERE WILL DO FINE.
THAT WON'T PIERCE A MAN'S ARMOR LIKE AN ION CHARGER HERE.
THEN I'LL ***AIM*** FOR THEIR HEADS.
NOW I FIGURED YOU WERE TRAININ' FOR SOME ***FIREWORKS*** WHEN YOU GET YER PAYBACK?
I'M TRAININ' ***MY*** WAY.
AND ***MY WAY*** IS WITH ***MY*** GUN.
CAN YOU ***TRAIN*** ME OR NOT?

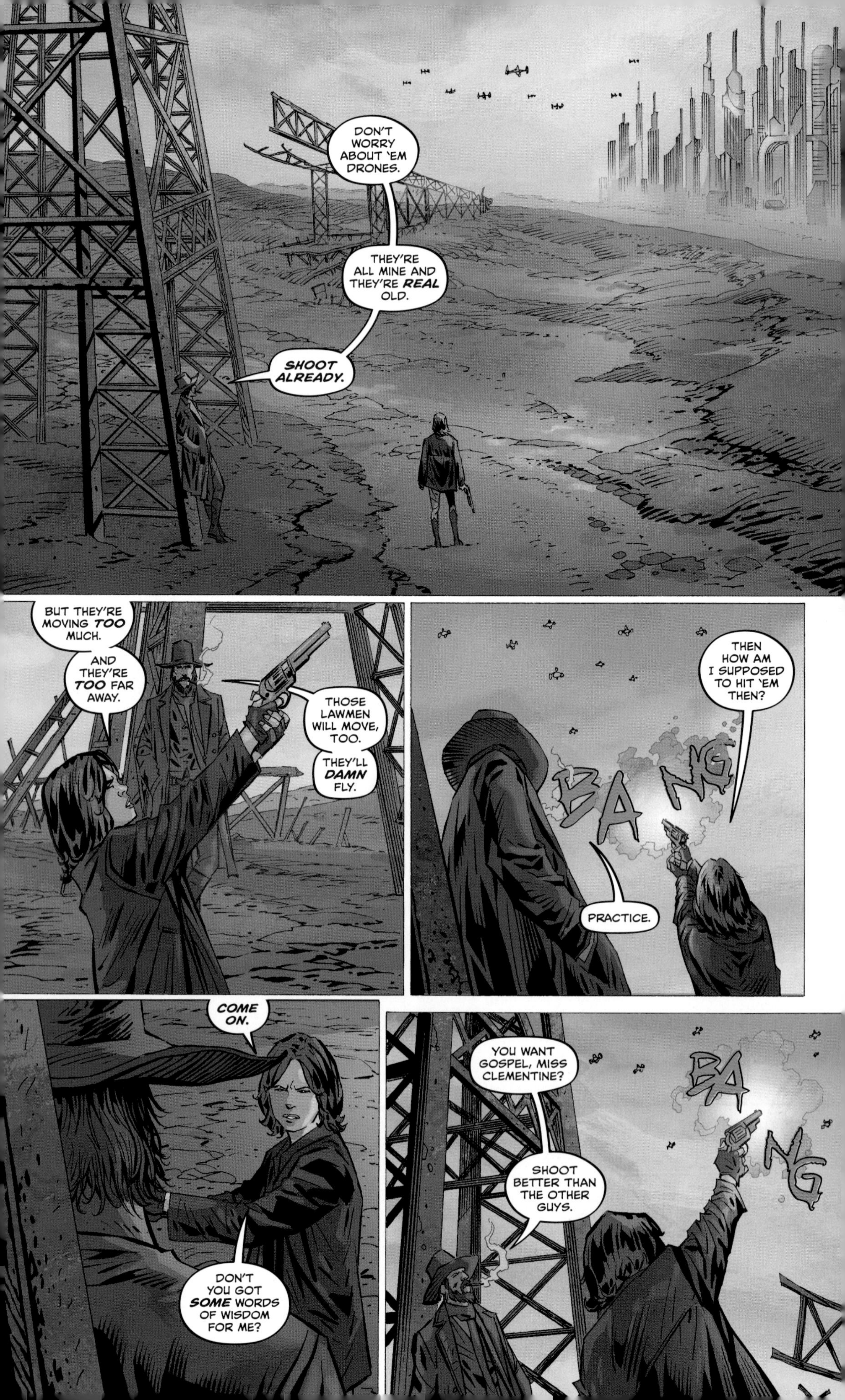

DON'T WORRY ABOUT 'EM DRONES.
THEY'RE ALL MINE AND THEY'RE REAL OLD.
SHOOT ALREADY.
BUT THEY'RE MOVING TOO MUCH.
AND THEY'RE TOO FAR AWAY.
THOSE LAWMEN WILL MOVE, TOO.
THEY'LL DAMN FLY.
BANG
THEN HOW AM I SUPPOSED TO HIT 'EM THEN?
PRACTICE.
COME ON.
DON'T YOU GOT SOME WORDS OF WISDOM FOR ME?
YOU WANT GOSPEL, MISS CLEMENTINE?
SHOOT BETTER THAN THE OTHER GUYS.
BANG

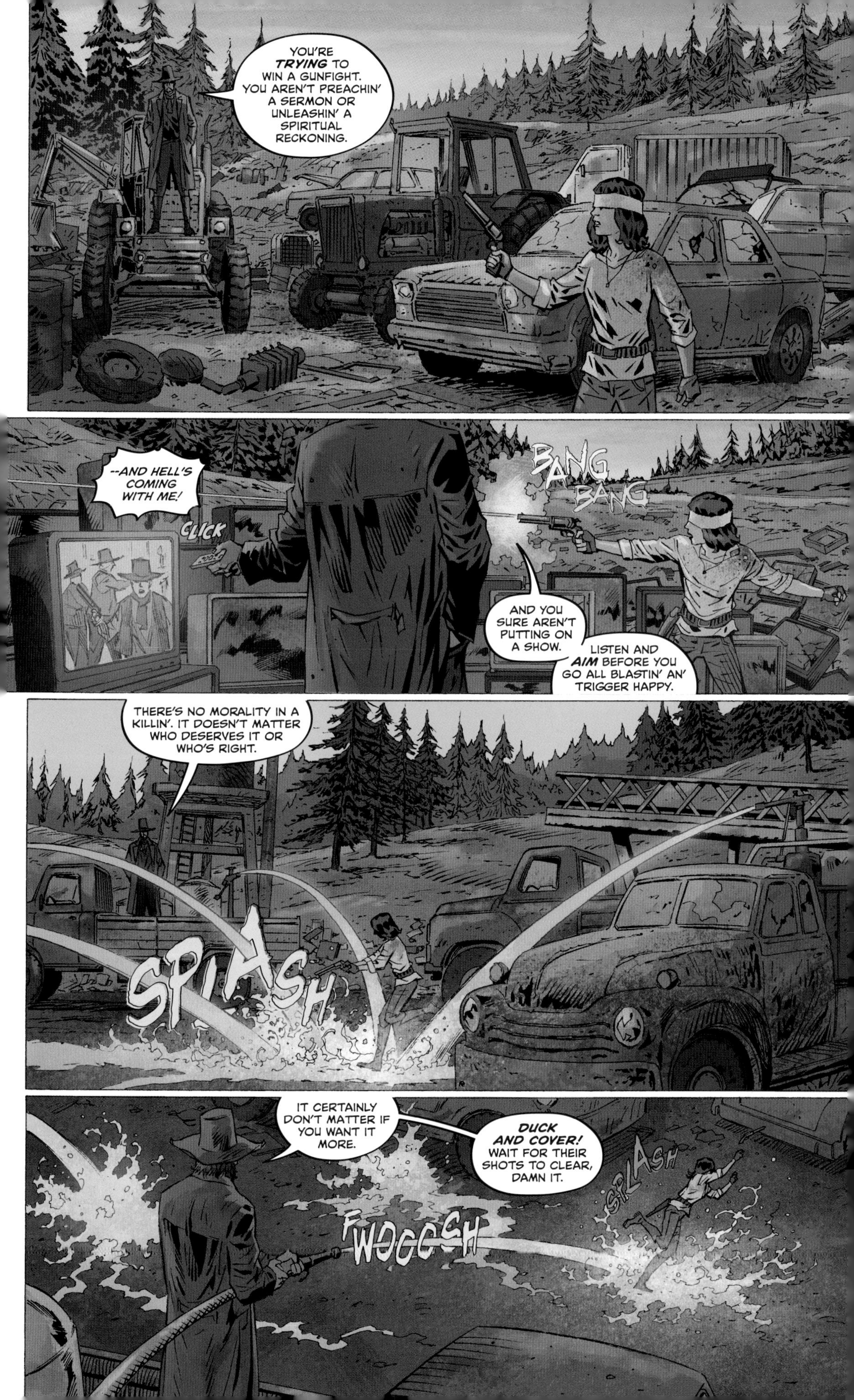
YOU'RE TRYING TO WIN A GUNFIGHT. YOU AREN'T PREACHIN' A SERMON OR UNLEASHIN' A SPIRITUAL RECKONING.
--AND HELL'S COMING WITH ME!
CLICK
BANG BANG
AND YOU SURE AREN'T PUTTING ON A SHOW.
LISTEN AND AIM BEFORE YOU GO ALL BLASTIN' AN' TRIGGER HAPPY.
THERE'S NO MORALITY IN A KILLIN'. IT DOESN'T MATTER WHO DESERVES IT OR WHO'S RIGHT.
SPLASH
IT CERTAINLY DON'T MATTER IF YOU WANT IT MORE.
DUCK AND COVER! WAIT FOR THEIR SHOTS TO CLEAR, DAMN IT.
SPLASH
FWOOOSH

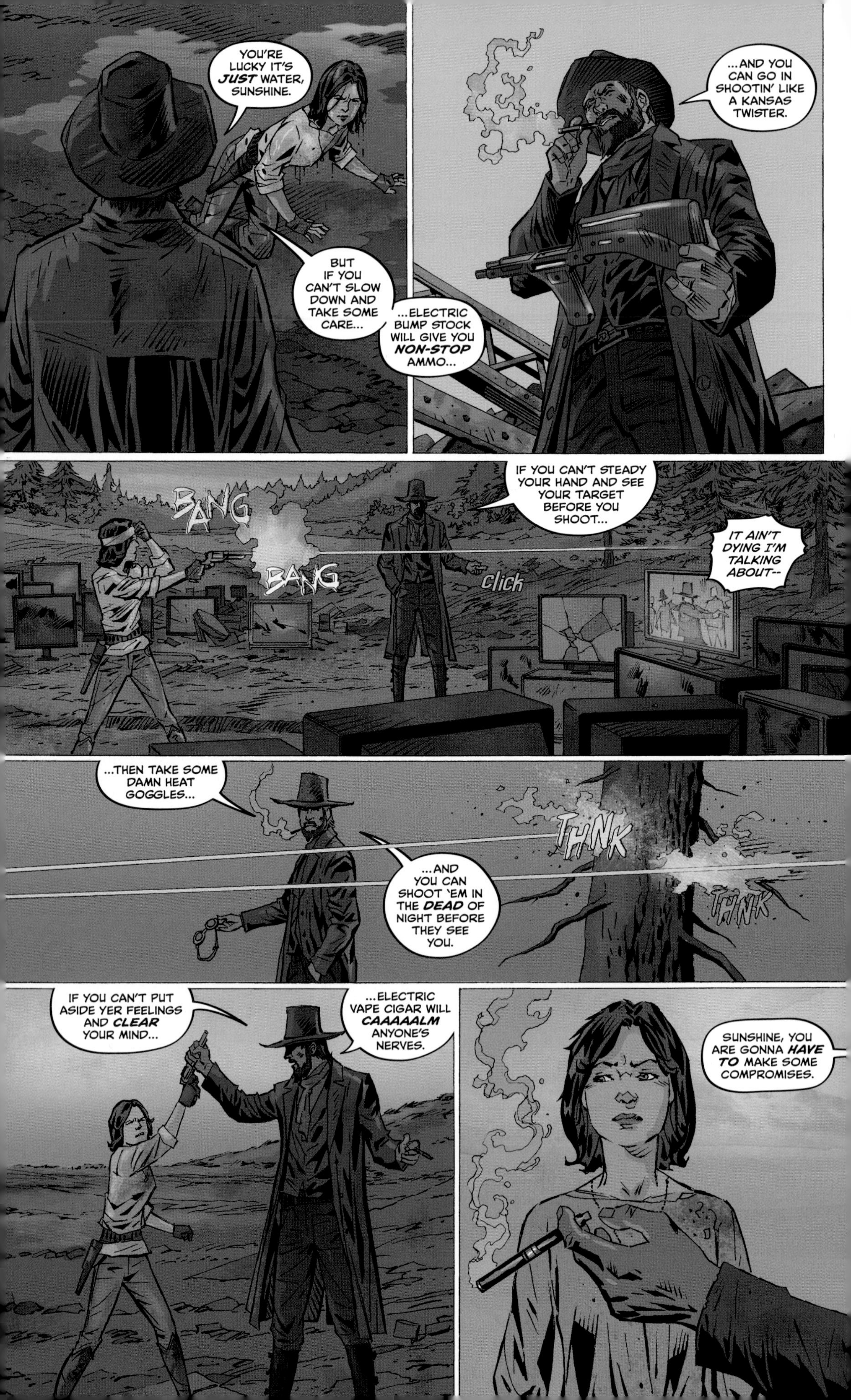

YOU'RE LUCKY IT'S *JUST* WATER, SUNSHINE.
BUT IF YOU CAN'T SLOW DOWN AND TAKE SOME CARE...
...ELECTRIC BUMP STOCK WILL GIVE YOU *NON-STOP* AMMO...
...AND YOU CAN GO IN SHOOTIN' LIKE A KANSAS TWISTER.
BANG
BANG
IF YOU CAN'T STEADY YOUR HAND AND SEE YOUR TARGET BEFORE YOU SHOOT...
click
IT AIN'T DYING I'M TALKING ABOUT--
...THEN TAKE SOME DAMN HEAT GOGGLES...
THNK
...AND YOU CAN SHOOT 'EM IN THE *DEAD* OF NIGHT BEFORE THEY SEE YOU.
THNK
IF YOU CAN'T PUT ASIDE YER FEELINGS AND *CLEAR* YOUR MIND...
...ELECTRIC VAPE CIGAR WILL *CAAAAALM* ANYONE'S NERVES.
SUNSHINE, YOU ARE GONNA *HAVE TO* MAKE SOME COMPROMISES.

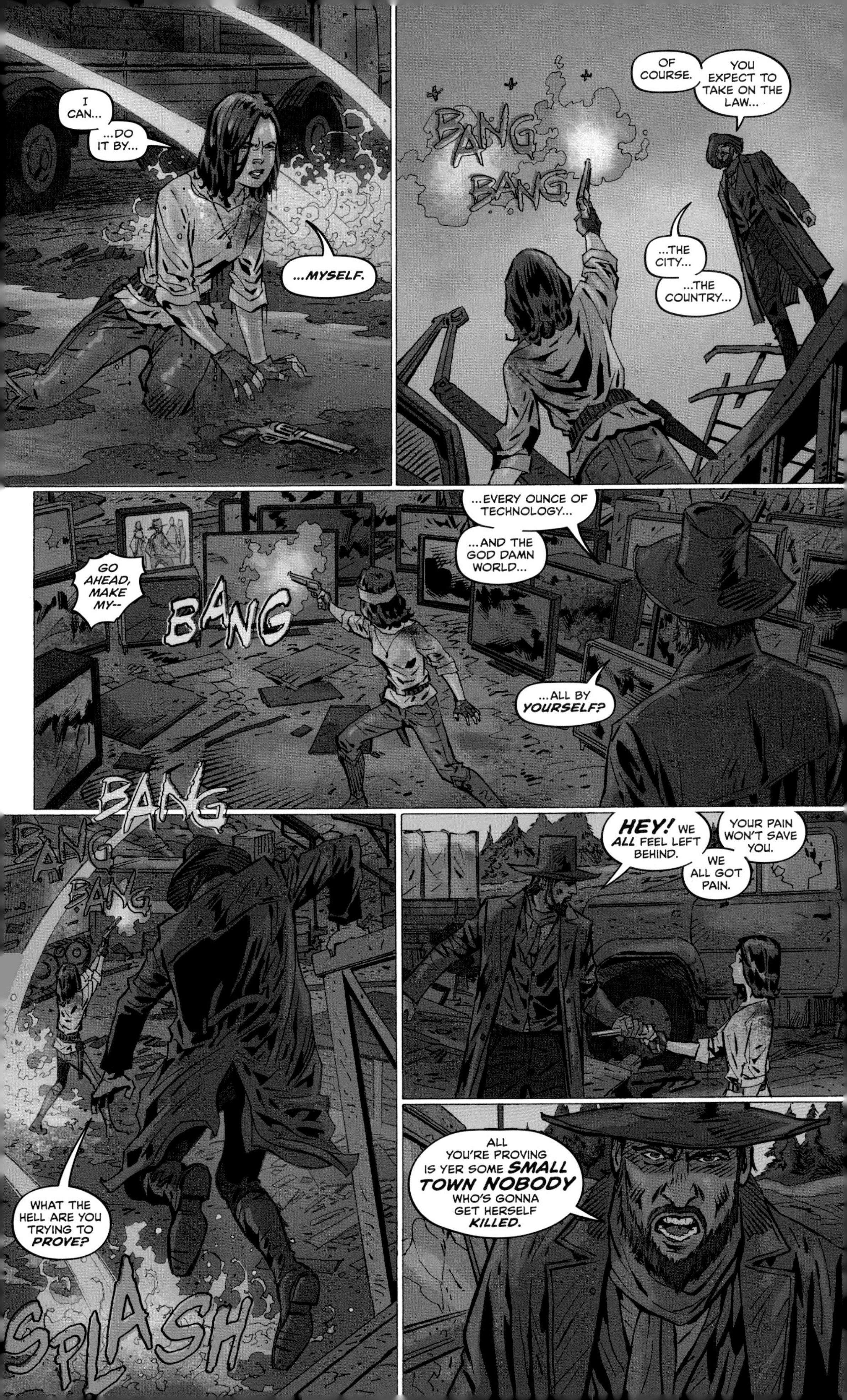
I CAN...
...DO IT BY...
...MYSELF.
BANG
BANG
OF COURSE.
YOU EXPECT TO TAKE ON THE LAW...
...THE CITY...
...THE COUNTRY...
GO AHEAD, MAKE MY--
BANG
...EVERY OUNCE OF TECHNOLOGY...
...AND THE GOD DAMN WORLD...
...ALL BY YOURSELF?
BANG
BANG
BANG
WHAT THE HELL ARE YOU TRYING TO PROVE?
SPLASH
HEY! WE ALL FEEL LEFT BEHIND.
YOUR PAIN WON'T SAVE YOU.
WE ALL GOT PAIN.
ALL YOU'RE PROVING IS YER SOME SMALL TOWN NOBODY WHO'S GONNA GET HERSELF KILLED.

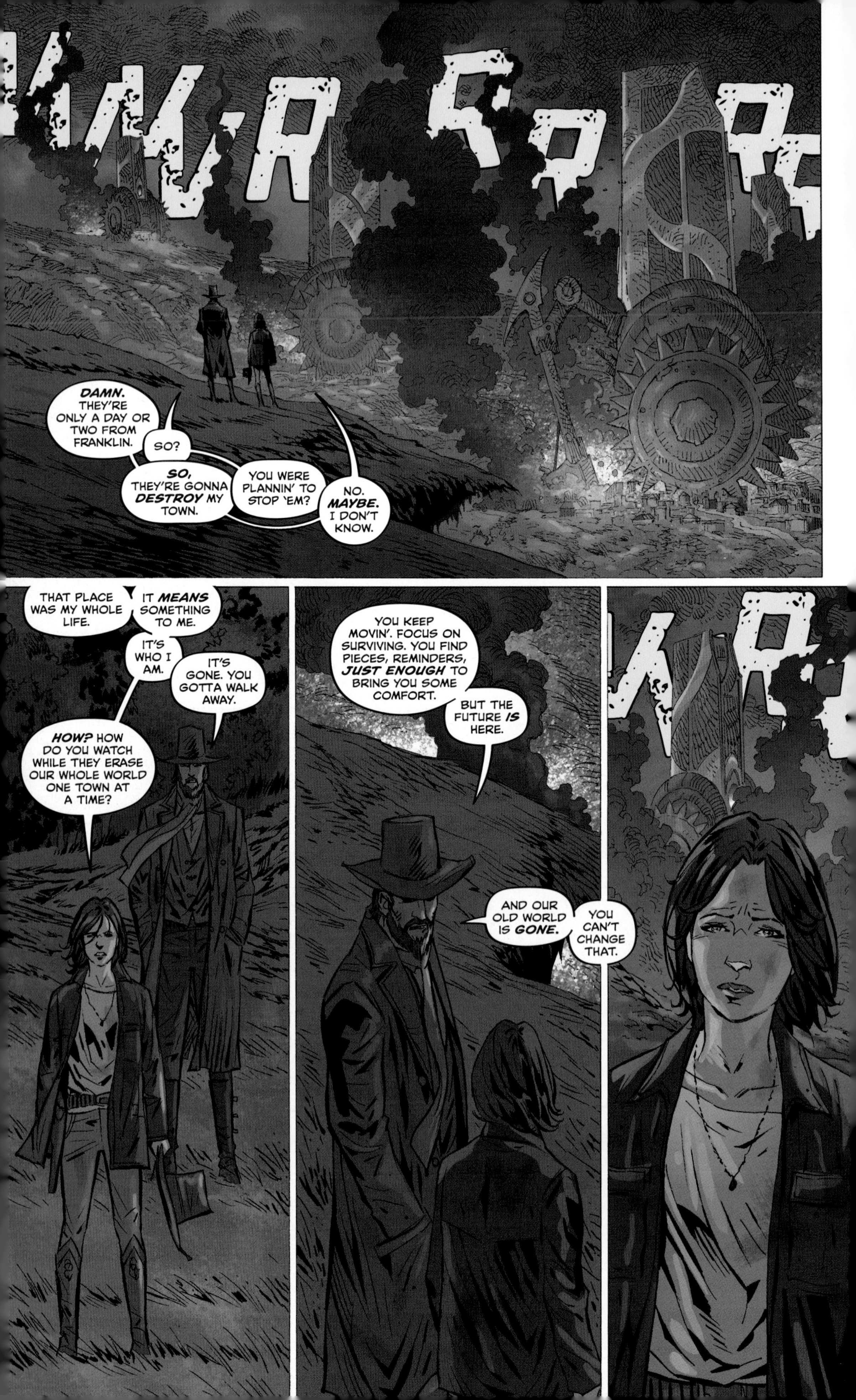
DAMN. THEY'RE ONLY A DAY OR TWO FROM FRANKLIN.
SO?
SO, THEY'RE GONNA DESTROY MY TOWN.
YOU WERE PLANNIN' TO STOP 'EM?
NO. MAYBE. I DON'T KNOW.
THAT PLACE WAS MY WHOLE LIFE.
IT MEANS SOMETHING TO ME.
IT'S WHO I AM.
IT'S GONE. YOU GOTTA WALK AWAY.
HOW? HOW DO YOU WATCH WHILE THEY ERASE OUR WHOLE WORLD ONE TOWN AT A TIME?
YOU KEEP MOVIN'. FOCUS ON SURVIVING. YOU FIND PIECES, REMINDERS, JUST ENOUGH TO BRING YOU SOME COMFORT.
BUT THE FUTURE IS HERE.
AND OUR OLD WORLD IS GONE.
YOU CAN'T CHANGE THAT.

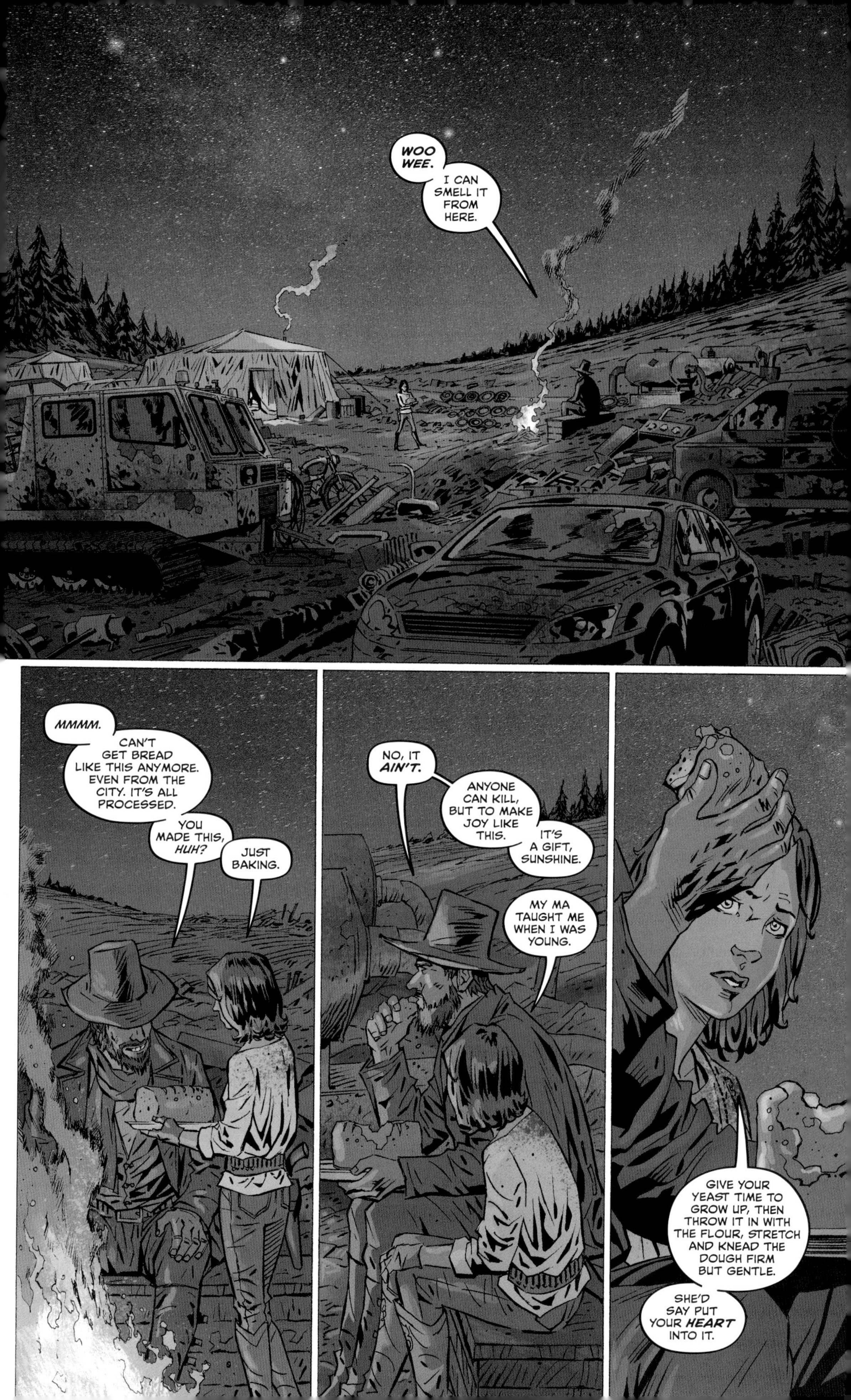

WOO WEE.
I CAN SMELL IT FROM HERE.
MMMM.
CAN'T GET BREAD LIKE THIS ANYMORE. EVEN FROM THE CITY. IT'S ALL PROCESSED.
YOU MADE THIS, HUH?
JUST BAKING.
NO, IT AIN'T.
ANYONE CAN KILL, BUT TO MAKE JOY LIKE THIS.
IT'S A GIFT, SUNSHINE.
MY MA TAUGHT ME WHEN I WAS YOUNG.
GIVE YOUR YEAST TIME TO GROW UP, THEN THROW IT IN WITH THE FLOUR, STRETCH AND KNEAD THE DOUGH FIRM BUT GENTLE.
SHE'D SAY PUT YOUR HEART INTO IT.

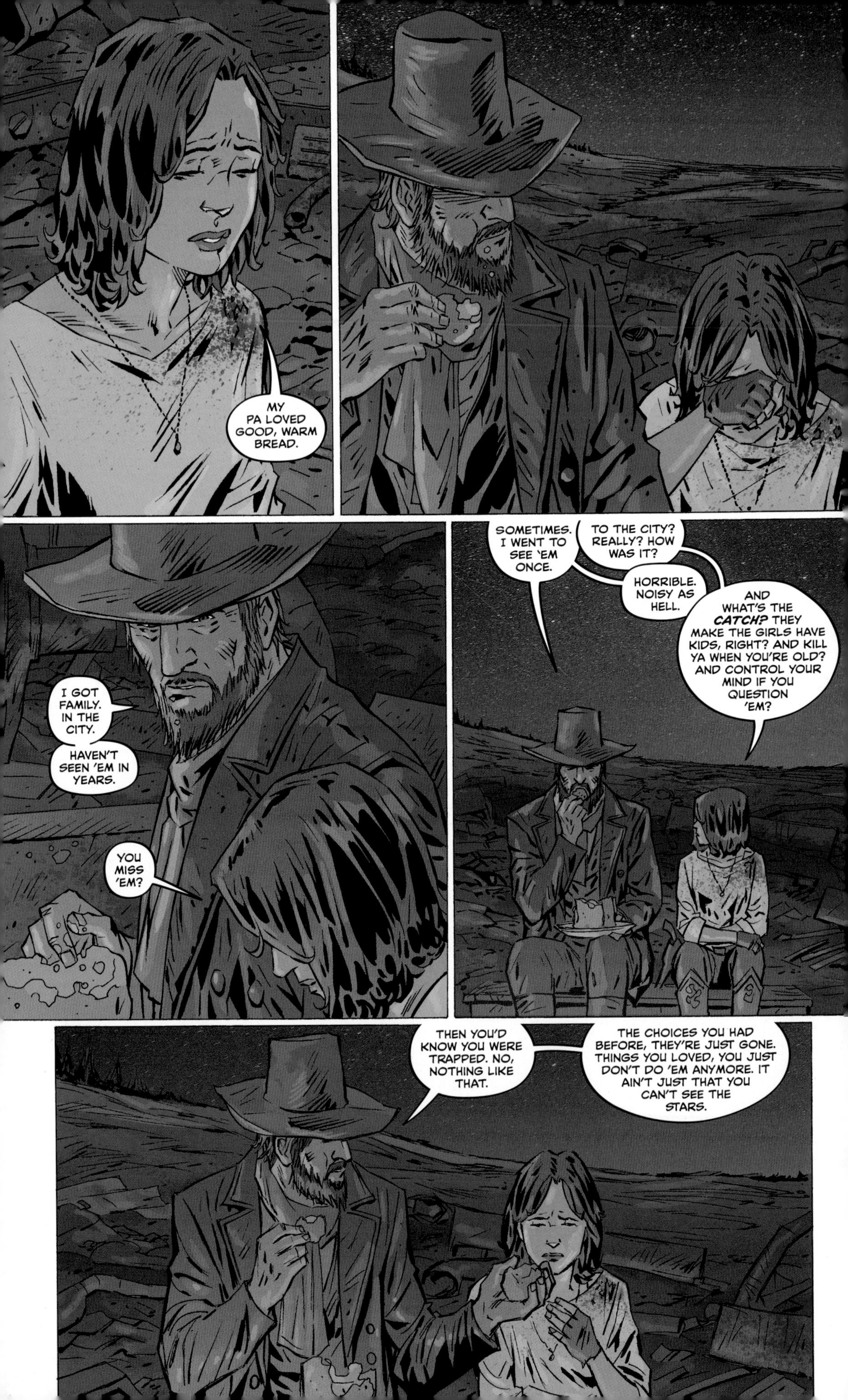
MY PA LOVED GOOD, WARM BREAD.
I GOT FAMILY. IN THE CITY.
HAVEN'T SEEN 'EM IN YEARS.
YOU MISS 'EM?
SOMETIMES. I WENT TO SEE 'EM ONCE.
TO THE CITY? REALLY? HOW WAS IT?
HORRIBLE. NOISY AS HELL.
AND WHAT'S THE *CATCH?* THEY MAKE THE GIRLS HAVE KIDS, RIGHT? AND KILL YA WHEN YOU'RE OLD? AND CONTROL YOUR MIND IF YOU QUESTION 'EM?
THEN YOU'D KNOW YOU WERE TRAPPED. NO, NOTHING LIKE THAT.
THE CHOICES YOU HAD BEFORE, THEY'RE JUST GONE. THINGS YOU LOVED, YOU JUST DON'T DO 'EM ANYMORE. IT AIN'T JUST THAT YOU CAN'T SEE THE STARS.

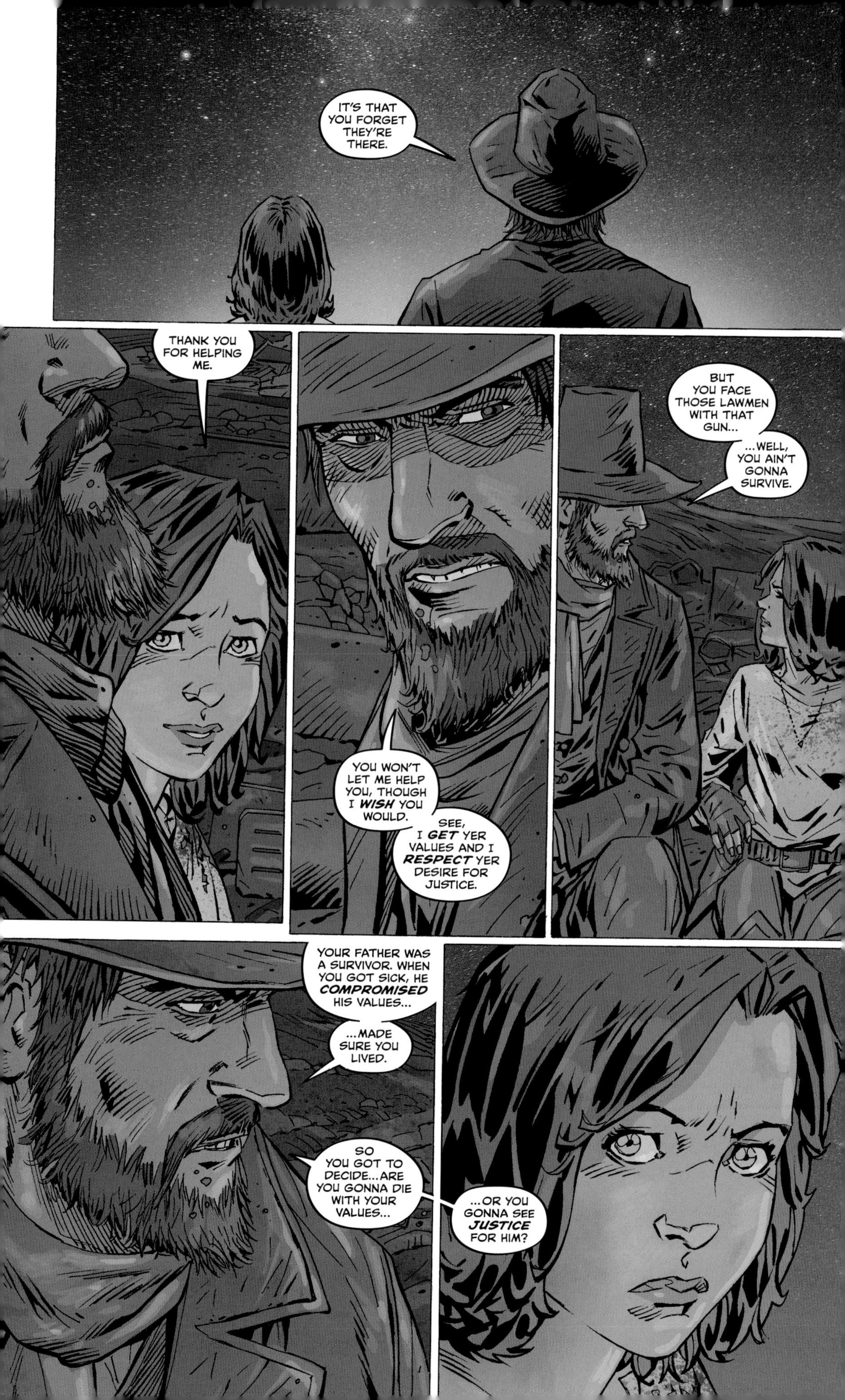
IT'S THAT YOU FORGET THEY'RE THERE.
THANK YOU FOR HELPING ME.
YOU WON'T LET ME HELP YOU, THOUGH I WISH YOU WOULD.
SEE, I GET YER VALUES AND I RESPECT YER DESIRE FOR JUSTICE.
BUT YOU FACE THOSE LAWMEN WITH THAT GUN...
...WELL, YOU AIN'T GONNA SURVIVE.
YOUR FATHER WAS A SURVIVOR. WHEN YOU GOT SICK, HE COMPROMISED HIS VALUES...
...MADE SURE YOU LIVED.
SO YOU GOT TO DECIDE...ARE YOU GONNA DIE WITH YOUR VALUES...
...OR YOU GONNA SEE JUSTICE FOR HIM?

LISTEN CLOSELY. YOU CHARGE THE LASER WITH THE FIRST GRIP TRIGGER. LOCK THE CHARGE IN WITH THE SECOND HANDLE.

AND *FIRE!*

ZZZCCHHHN!

BOOM

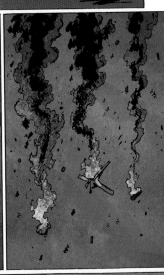

THAT FELT GOOD. *REAL* GOOD.

ONCE YOU FIRE, THAT LASER'S LIKE FLAME-THROWER.

EASY AS SLICIN' HAM.

THEY'LL NEVER SEE YOU COMIN', SUNSHINE.

THANK YOU, TRADER.

PLEASURE DOING BUSINESS WITH YOU.

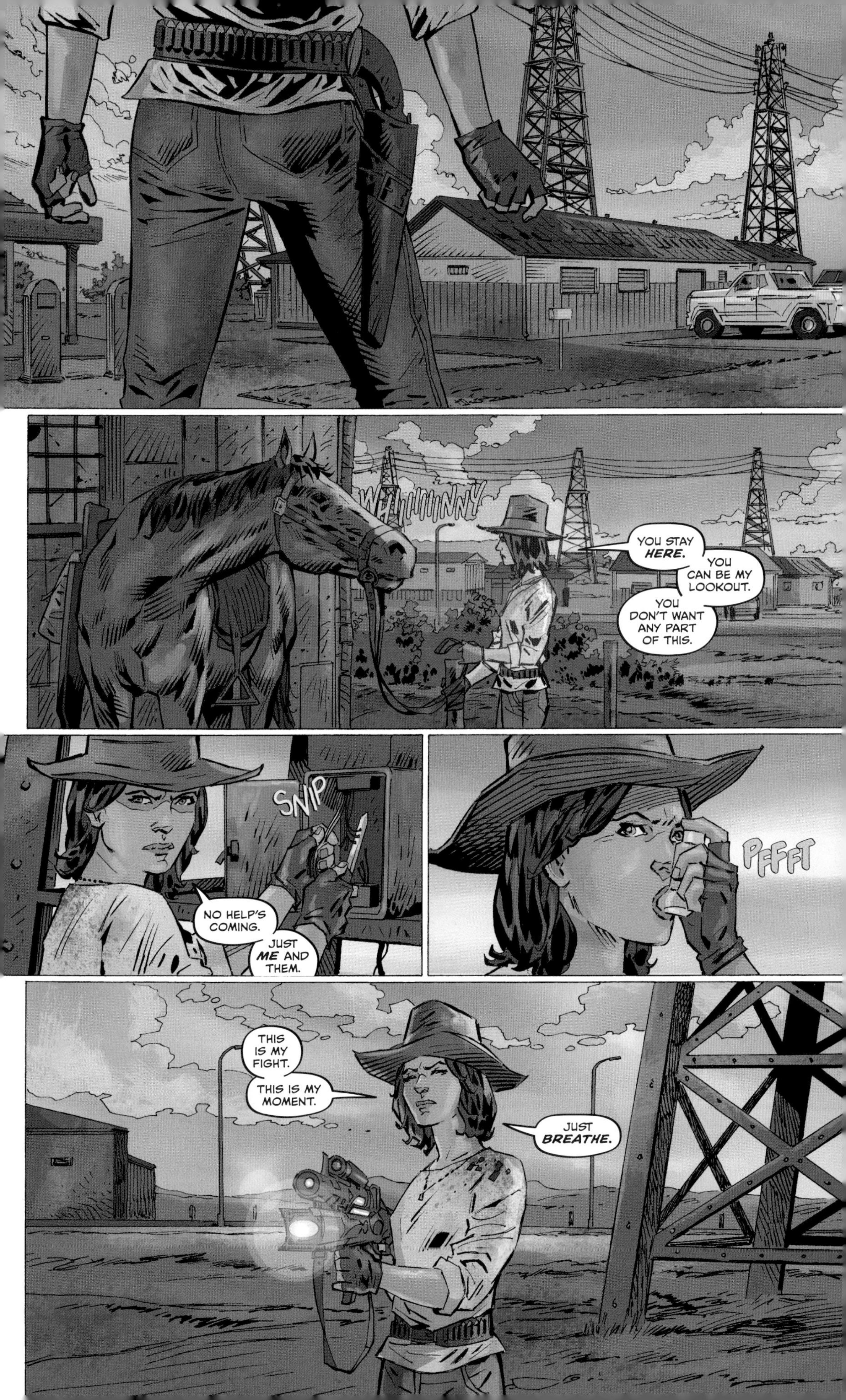
WHIIIIINNY
YOU STAY *HERE.*
YOU CAN BE MY LOOKOUT.
YOU DON'T WANT ANY PART OF THIS.
SNIP
NO HELP'S COMING.
JUST *ME* AND THEM.
PFFFT
THIS IS MY FIGHT.
THIS IS MY MOMENT.
JUST *BREATHE.*

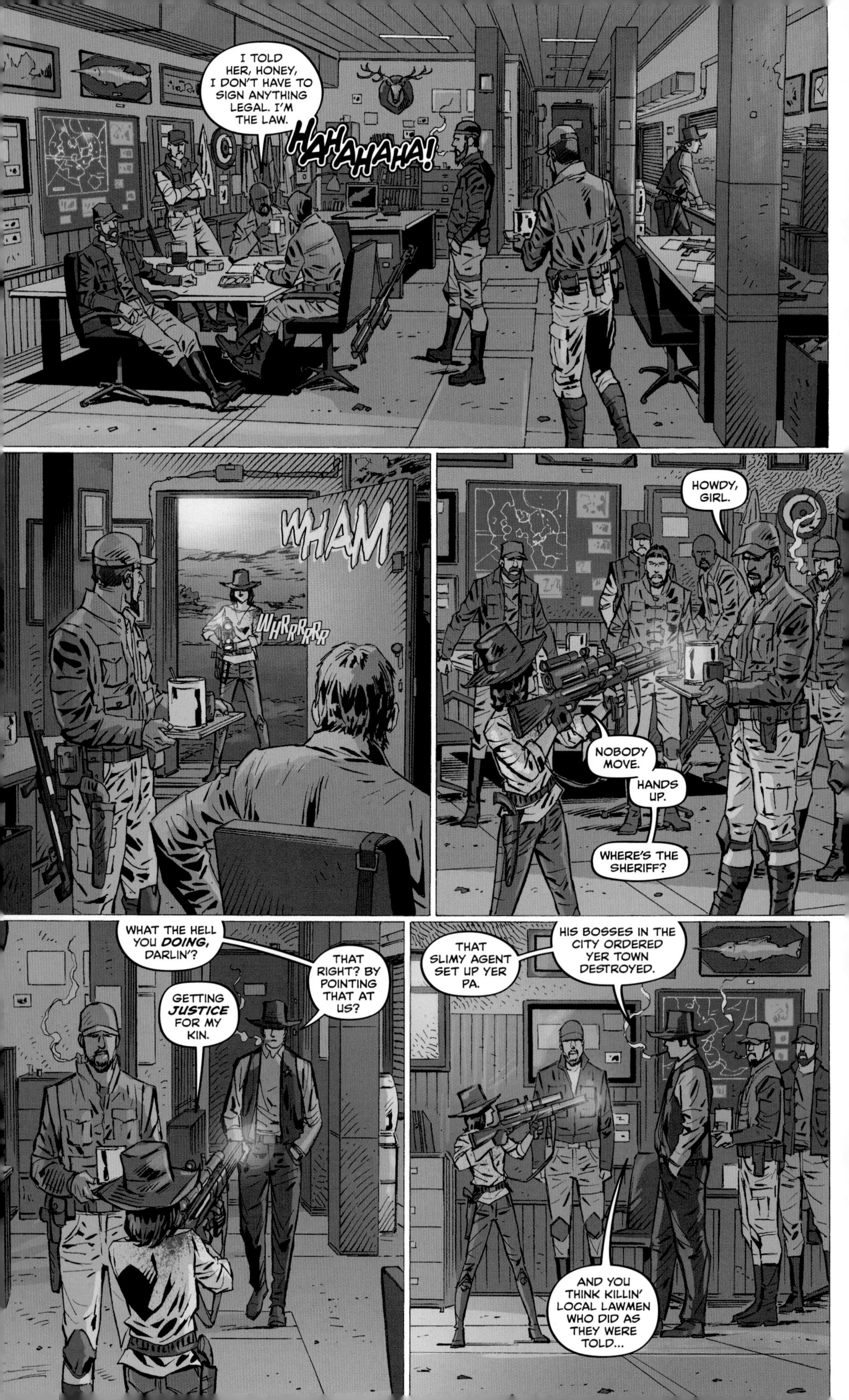
I TOLD HER, HONEY, I DON'T HAVE TO SIGN ANYTHING LEGAL. I'M THE LAW.
HAHAHAHAHA!
WHAM
WHRRRRRR
HOWDY, GIRL.
NOBODY MOVE.
HANDS UP.
WHERE'S THE SHERIFF?
WHAT THE HELL YOU **DOING,** DARLIN'?
GETTING ***JUSTICE*** FOR MY KIN.
THAT RIGHT? BY POINTING THAT AT US?
THAT SLIMY AGENT SET UP YER PA.
HIS BOSSES IN THE CITY ORDERED YER TOWN DESTROYED.
AND YOU THINK KILLIN' LOCAL LAWMEN WHO DID AS THEY WERE TOLD...

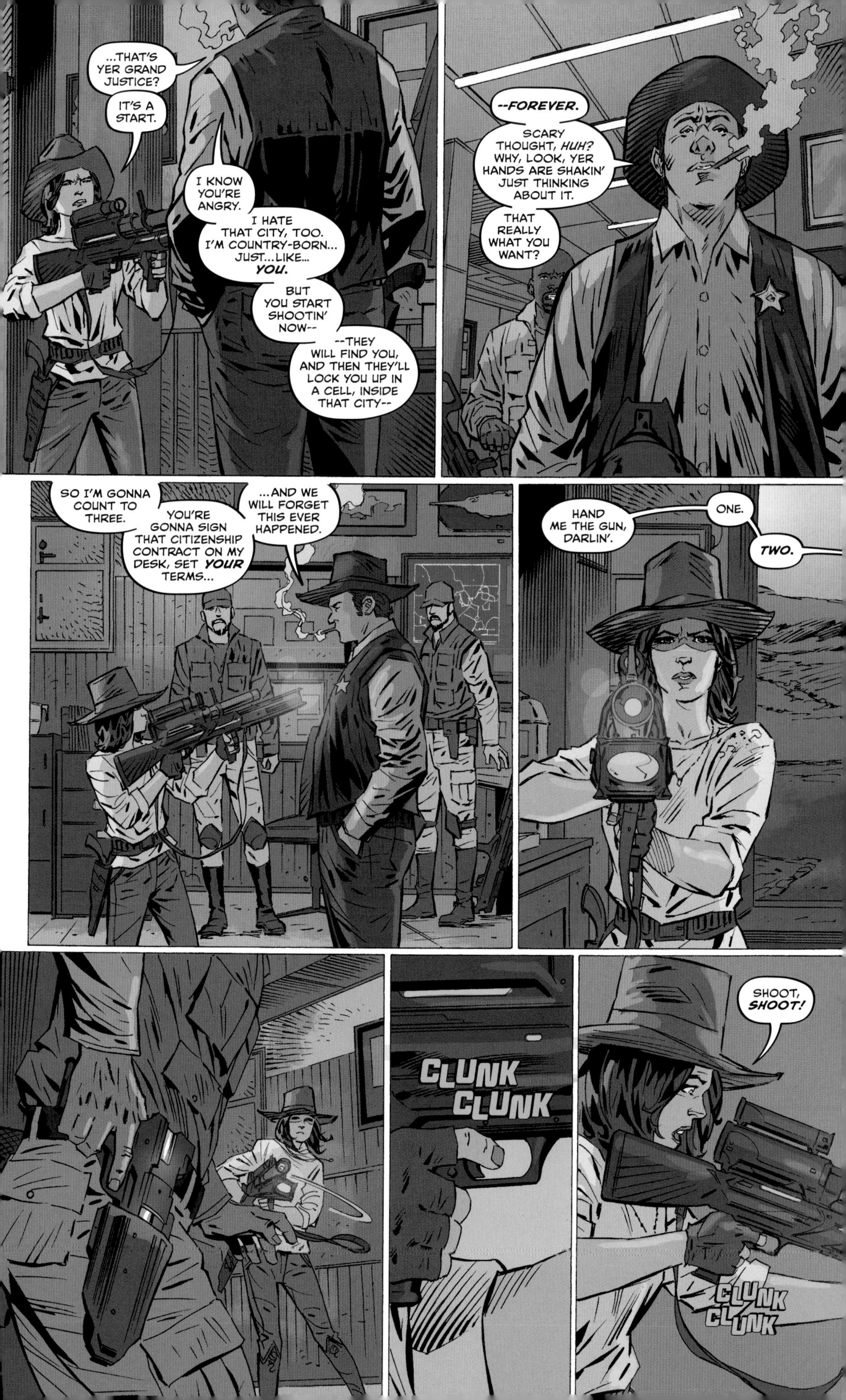
...THAT'S YER GRAND JUSTICE?
IT'S A START.
I KNOW YOU'RE ANGRY.
I HATE THAT CITY, TOO. I'M COUNTRY-BORN... JUST...LIKE... ***YOU.***
BUT YOU START SHOOTIN' NOW--
--THEY WILL FIND YOU, AND THEN THEY'LL LOCK YOU UP IN A CELL, INSIDE THAT CITY--
--FOREVER.
SCARY THOUGHT, ***HUH?*** WHY, LOOK, YER HANDS ARE SHAKIN' JUST THINKING ABOUT IT.
THAT REALLY WHAT YOU WANT?
SO I'M GONNA COUNT TO THREE.
YOU'RE GONNA SIGN THAT CITIZENSHIP CONTRACT ON MY DESK, SET ***YOUR*** TERMS...
...AND WE WILL FORGET THIS EVER HAPPENED.
HAND ME THE GUN, DARLIN'.
ONE.
TWO.
CLUNK CLUNK
SHOOT, ***SHOOT!***
CLUNK CLUNK

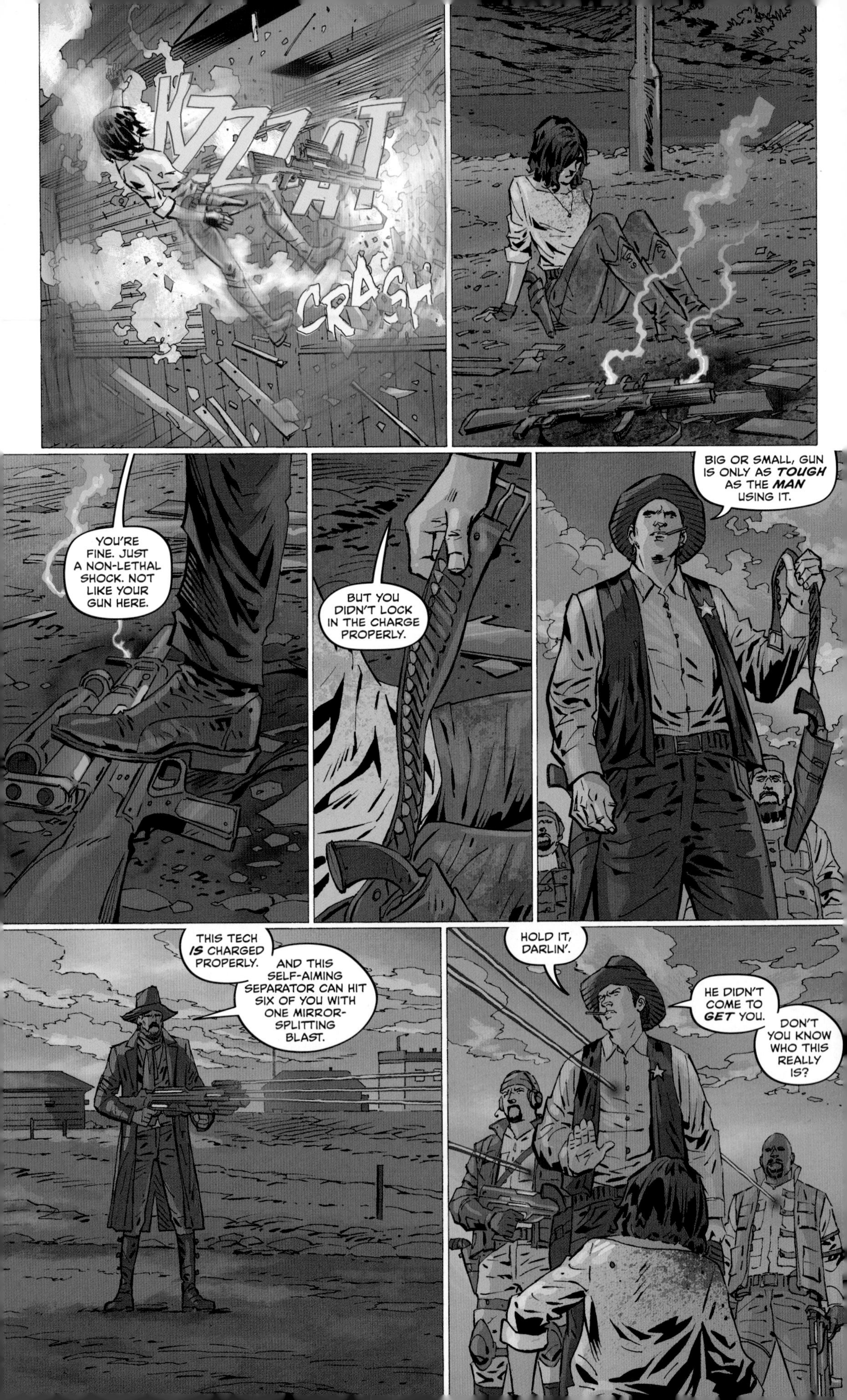
KZZZAT
CRASH
YOU'RE FINE. JUST A NON-LETHAL SHOCK. NOT LIKE YOUR GUN HERE.
BUT YOU DIDN'T LOCK IN THE CHARGE PROPERLY.
BIG OR SMALL, GUN IS ONLY AS *TOUGH* AS THE *MAN* USING IT.
THIS TECH *IS* CHARGED PROPERLY.
AND THIS SELF-AIMING SEPARATOR CAN HIT SIX OF YOU WITH ONE MIRROR-SPLITTING BLAST.
HOLD IT, DARLIN'.
HE DIDN'T COME TO *GET* YOU.
DON'T YOU KNOW WHO THIS REALLY IS?

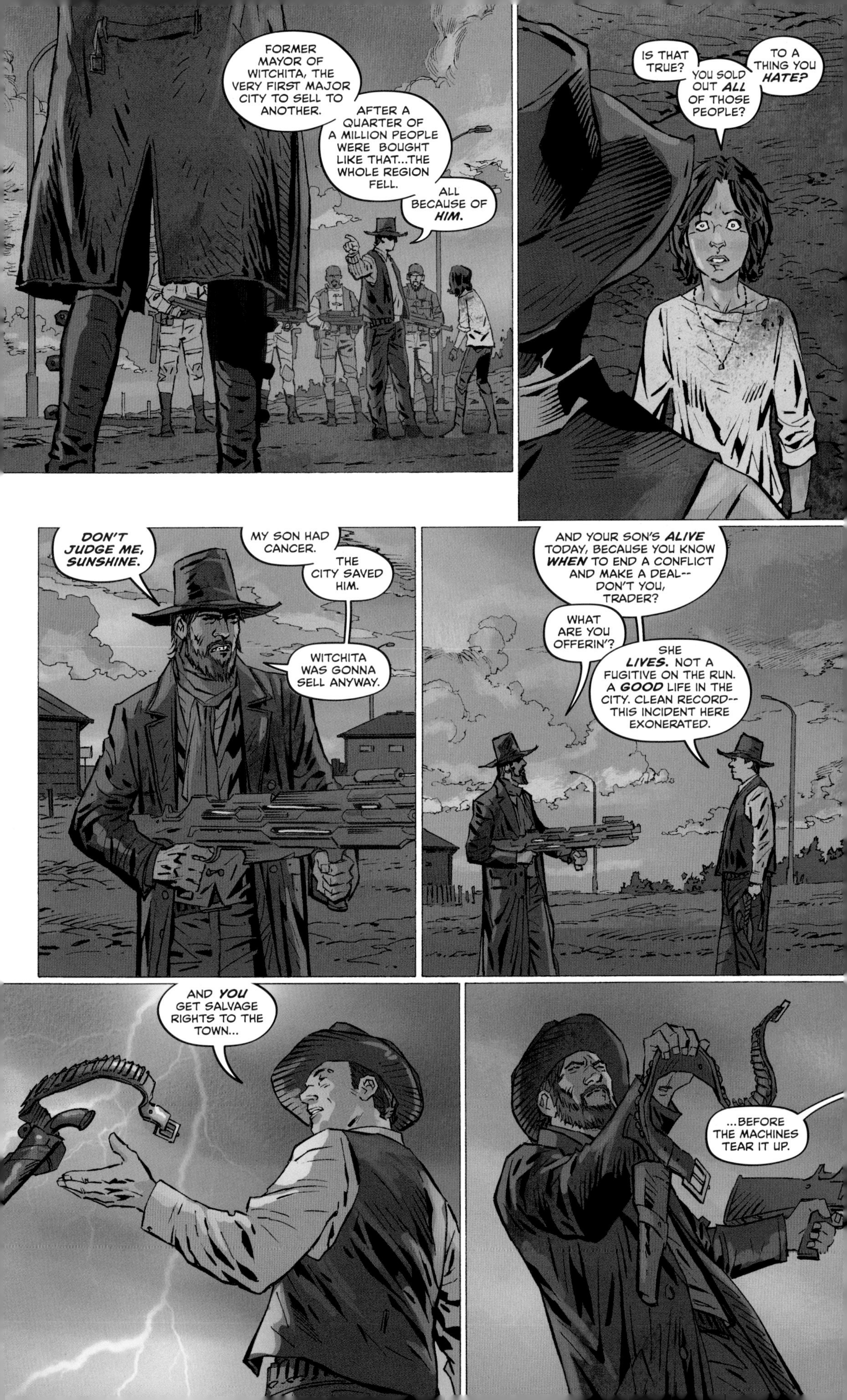
FORMER MAYOR OF WITCHITA, THE VERY FIRST MAJOR CITY TO SELL TO ANOTHER.
AFTER A QUARTER OF A MILLION PEOPLE WERE BOUGHT LIKE THAT...THE WHOLE REGION FELL.
ALL BECAUSE OF *HIM.*
IS THAT TRUE?
YOU SOLD OUT *ALL* OF THOSE PEOPLE?
TO A THING YOU *HATE?*
DON'T JUDGE ME, SUNSHINE.
MY SON HAD CANCER.
THE CITY SAVED HIM.
WITCHITA WAS GONNA SELL ANYWAY.
AND YOUR SON'S *ALIVE* TODAY, BECAUSE YOU KNOW *WHEN* TO END A CONFLICT AND MAKE A DEAL-- DON'T YOU, TRADER?
WHAT ARE YOU OFFERIN'?
SHE *LIVES.* NOT A FUGITIVE ON THE RUN. A *GOOD* LIFE IN THE CITY. CLEAN RECORD-- THIS INCIDENT HERE EXONERATED.
AND *YOU* GET SALVAGE RIGHTS TO THE TOWN...
...BEFORE THE MACHINES TEAR IT UP.

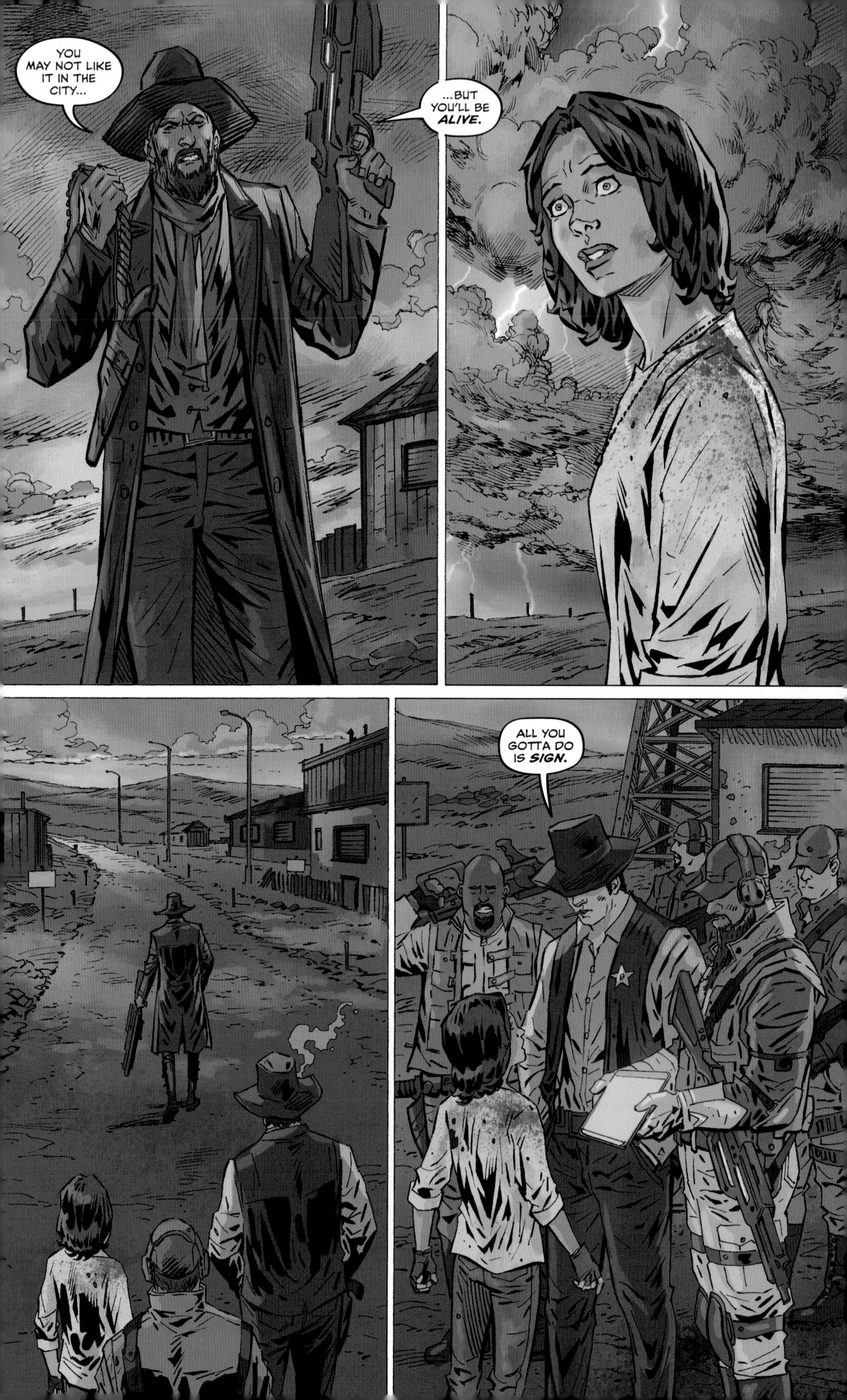
YOU MAY NOT LIKE IT IN THE CITY...
...BUT YOU'LL BE *ALIVE*.
ALL YOU GOTTA DO IS *SIGN*.

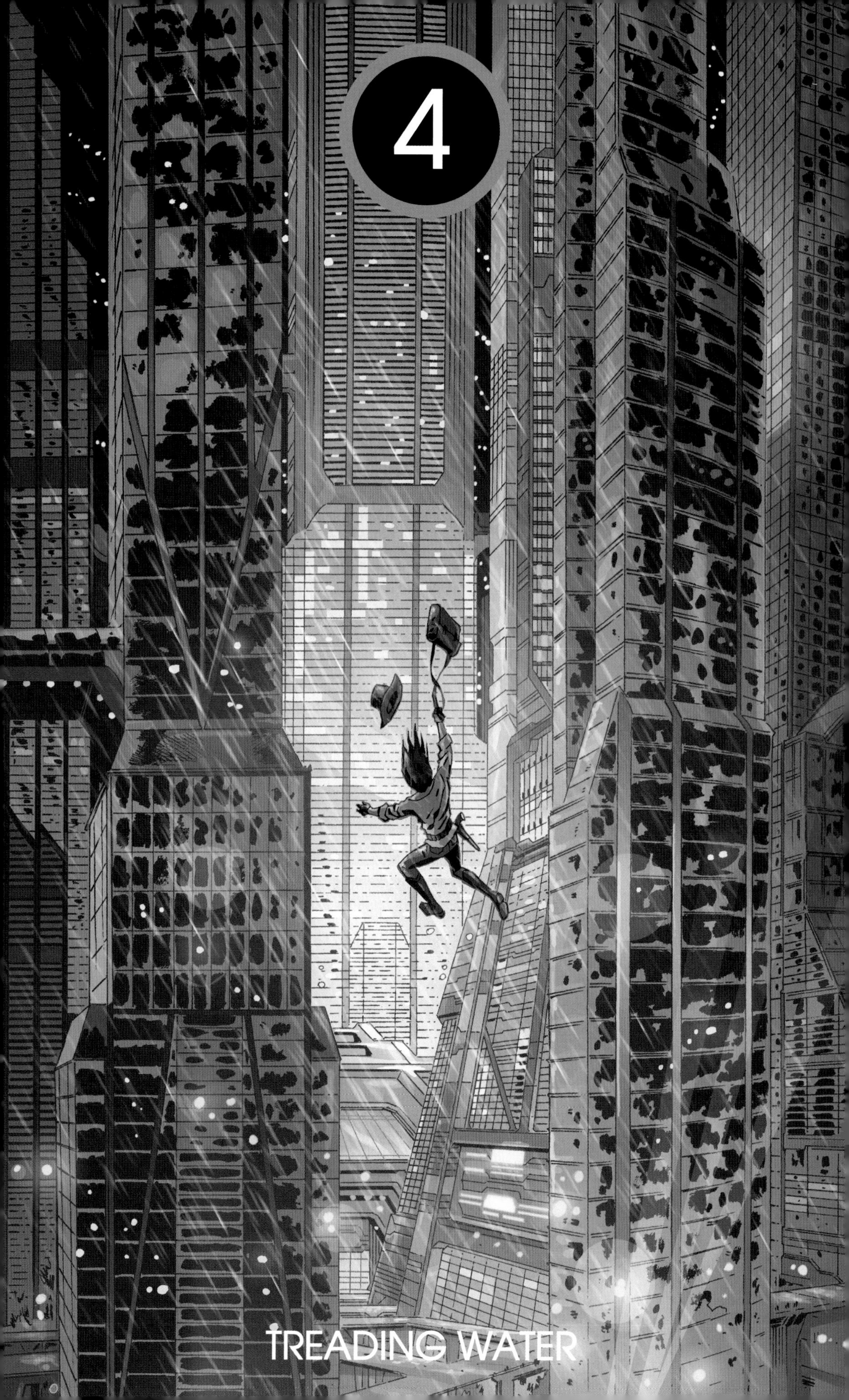
4
TREADING WATER

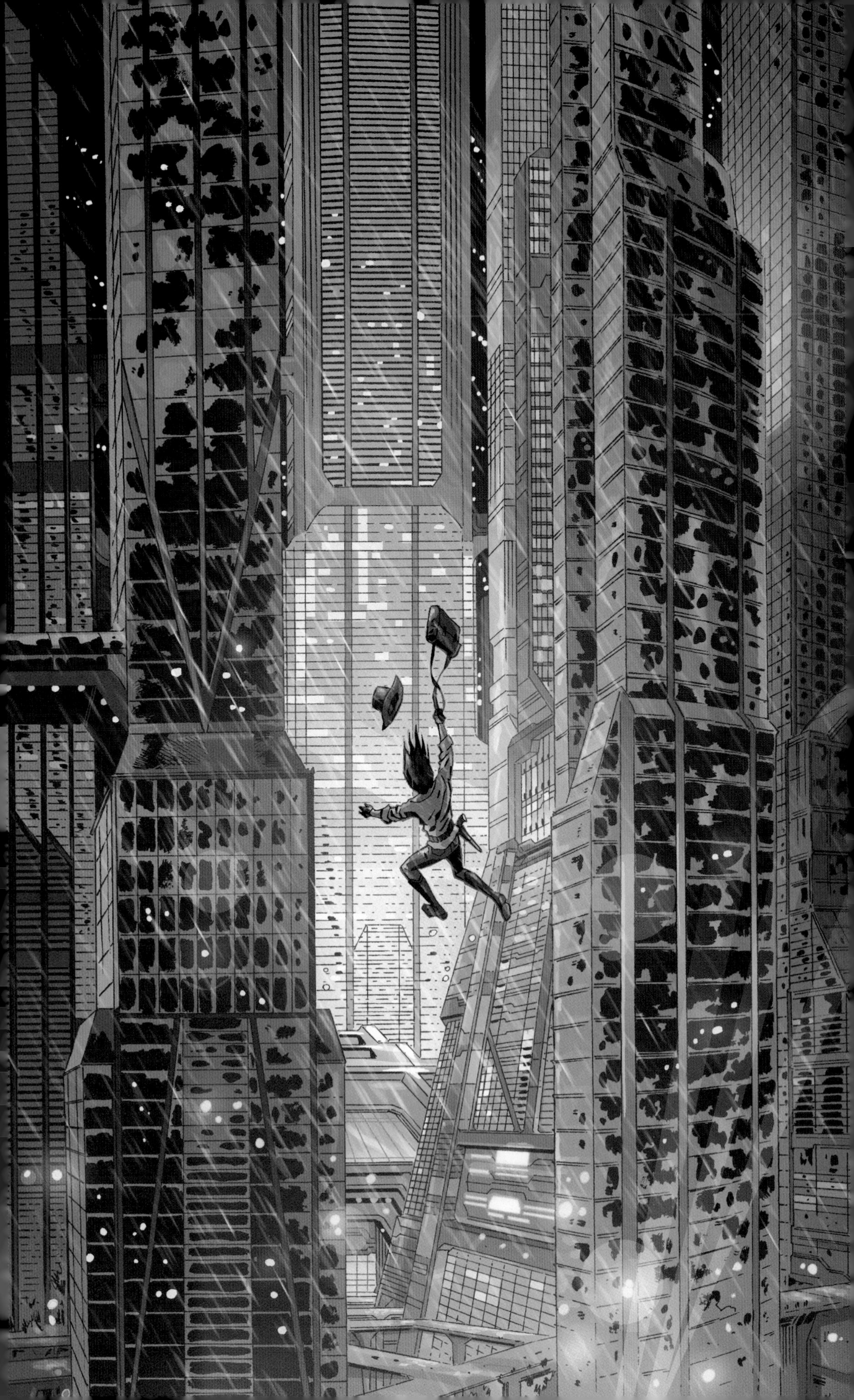

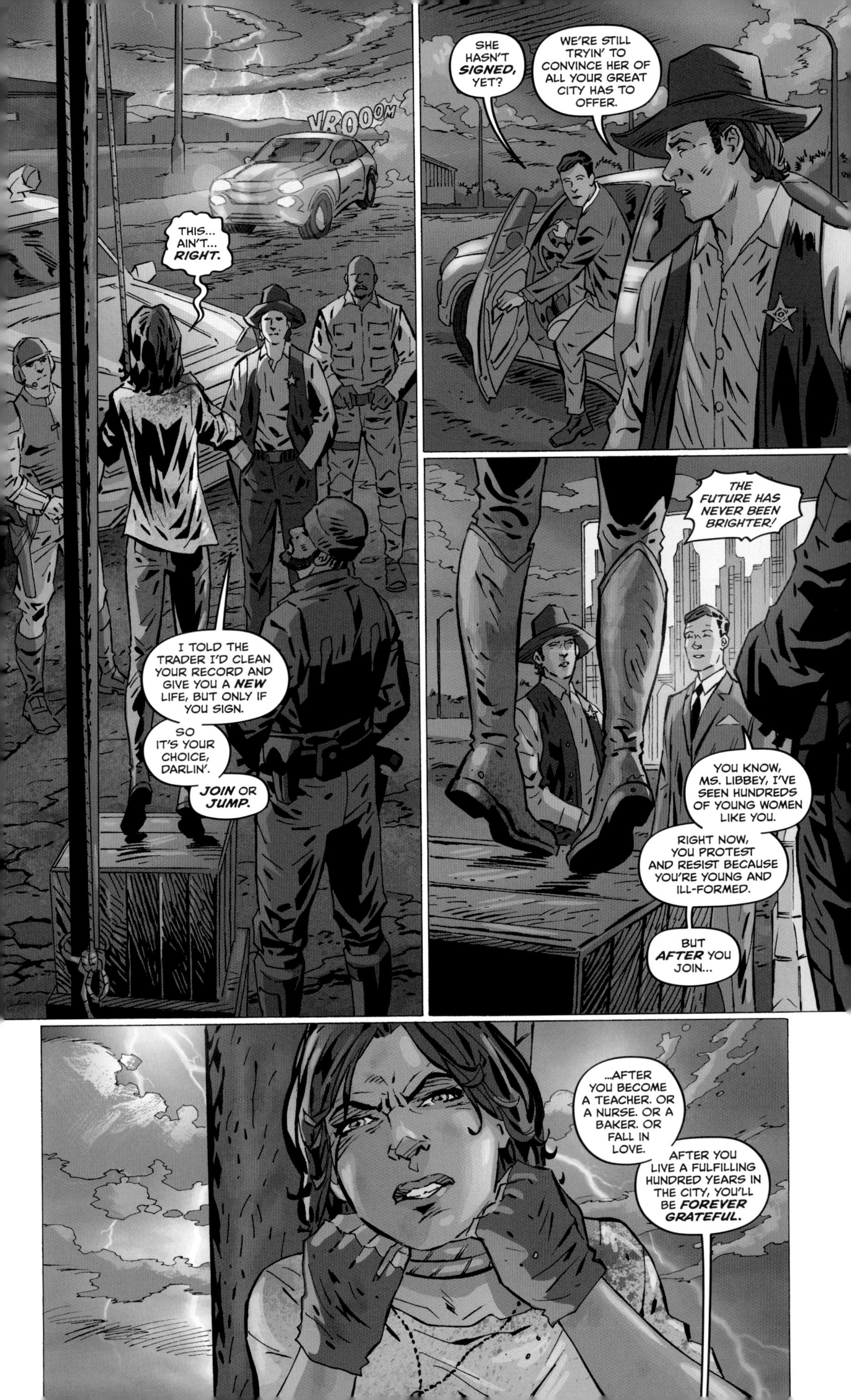
VROOOM
THIS... AIN'T... RIGHT.
SHE HASN'T SIGNED, YET?
WE'RE STILL TRYIN' TO CONVINCE HER OF ALL YOUR GREAT CITY HAS TO OFFER.
I TOLD THE TRADER I'D CLEAN YOUR RECORD AND GIVE YOU A NEW LIFE, BUT ONLY IF YOU SIGN.
SO IT'S YOUR CHOICE, DARLIN'.
JOIN OR JUMP.
THE FUTURE HAS NEVER BEEN BRIGHTER!
YOU KNOW, MS. LIBBEY, I'VE SEEN HUNDREDS OF YOUNG WOMEN LIKE YOU.
RIGHT NOW, YOU PROTEST AND RESIST BECAUSE YOU'RE YOUNG AND ILL-FORMED.
BUT AFTER YOU JOIN...
...AFTER YOU BECOME A TEACHER. OR A NURSE. OR A BAKER. OR FALL IN LOVE.
AFTER YOU LIVE A FULFILLING HUNDRED YEARS IN THE CITY, YOU'LL BE FOREVER GRATEFUL.

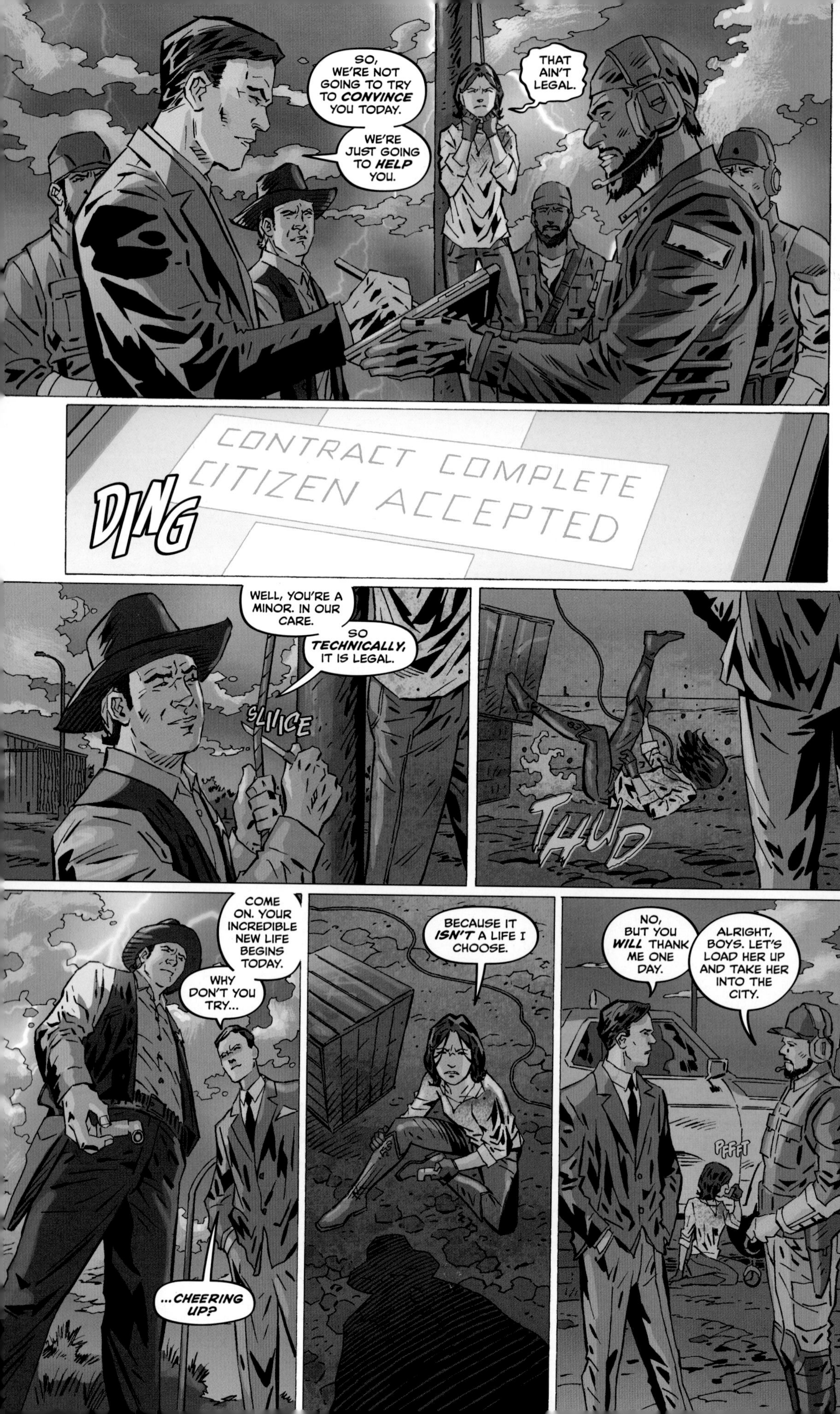
SO, WE'RE NOT GOING TO TRY TO CONVINCE YOU TODAY.
WE'RE JUST GOING TO HELP YOU.
THAT AIN'T LEGAL.
CONTRACT COMPLETE
CITIZEN ACCEPTED
DING
WELL, YOU'RE A MINOR. IN OUR CARE.
SO TECHNICALLY, IT IS LEGAL.
SLIIICE
THUD
COME ON. YOUR INCREDIBLE NEW LIFE BEGINS TODAY.
WHY DON'T YOU TRY...
...CHEERING UP?
BECAUSE IT ISN'T A LIFE I CHOOSE.
NO, BUT YOU WILL THANK ME ONE DAY.
ALRIGHT, BOYS. LET'S LOAD HER UP AND TAKE HER INTO THE CITY.
PFFFT

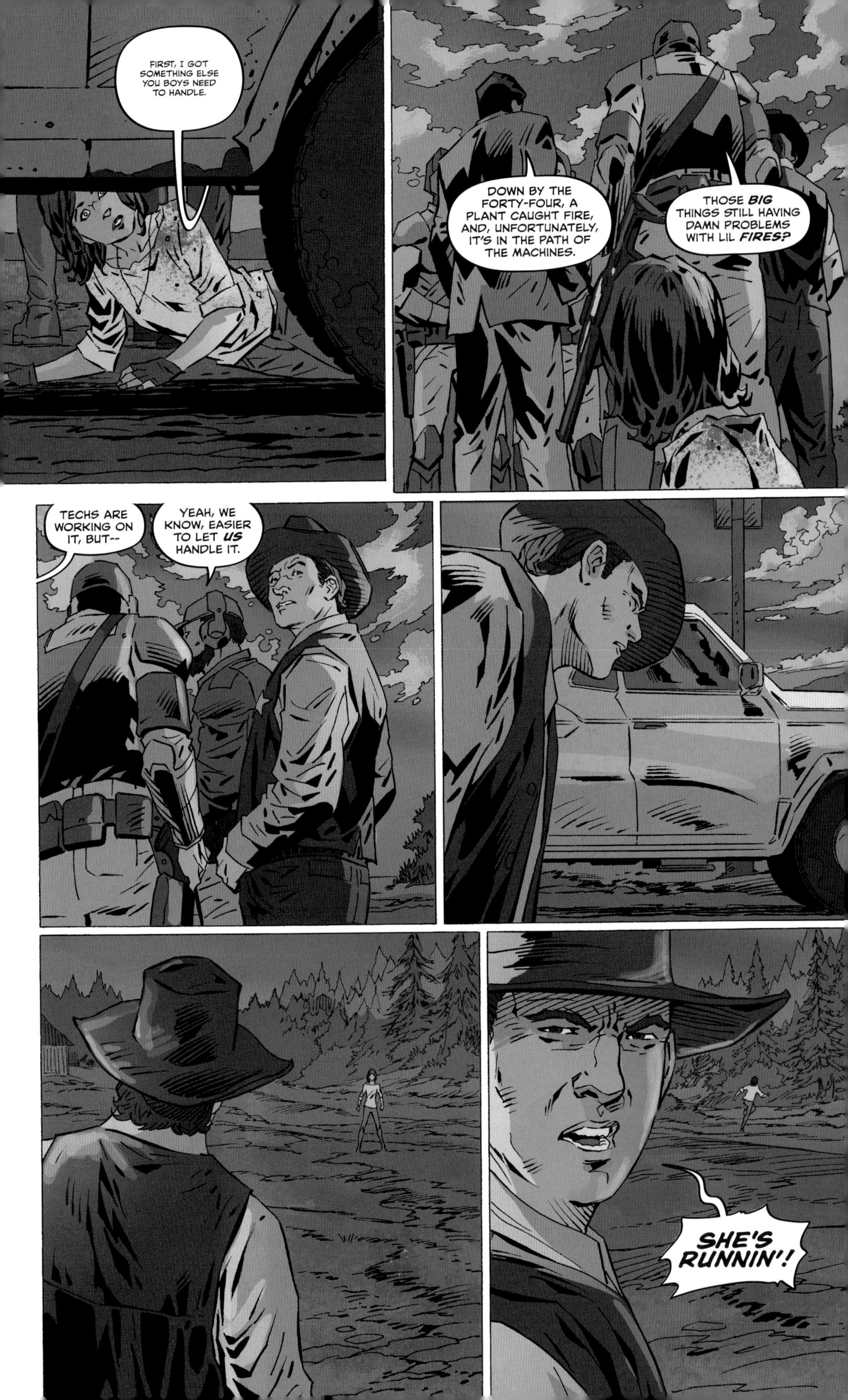
FIRST, I GOT SOMETHING ELSE YOU BOYS NEED TO HANDLE.
DOWN BY THE FORTY-FOUR, A PLANT CAUGHT FIRE, AND, UNFORTUNATELY, IT'S IN THE PATH OF THE MACHINES.
THOSE BIG THINGS STILL HAVING DAMN PROBLEMS WITH LIL FIRES?
TECHS ARE WORKING ON IT, BUT--
YEAH, WE KNOW, EASIER TO LET US HANDLE IT.
SHE'S RUNNIN'!

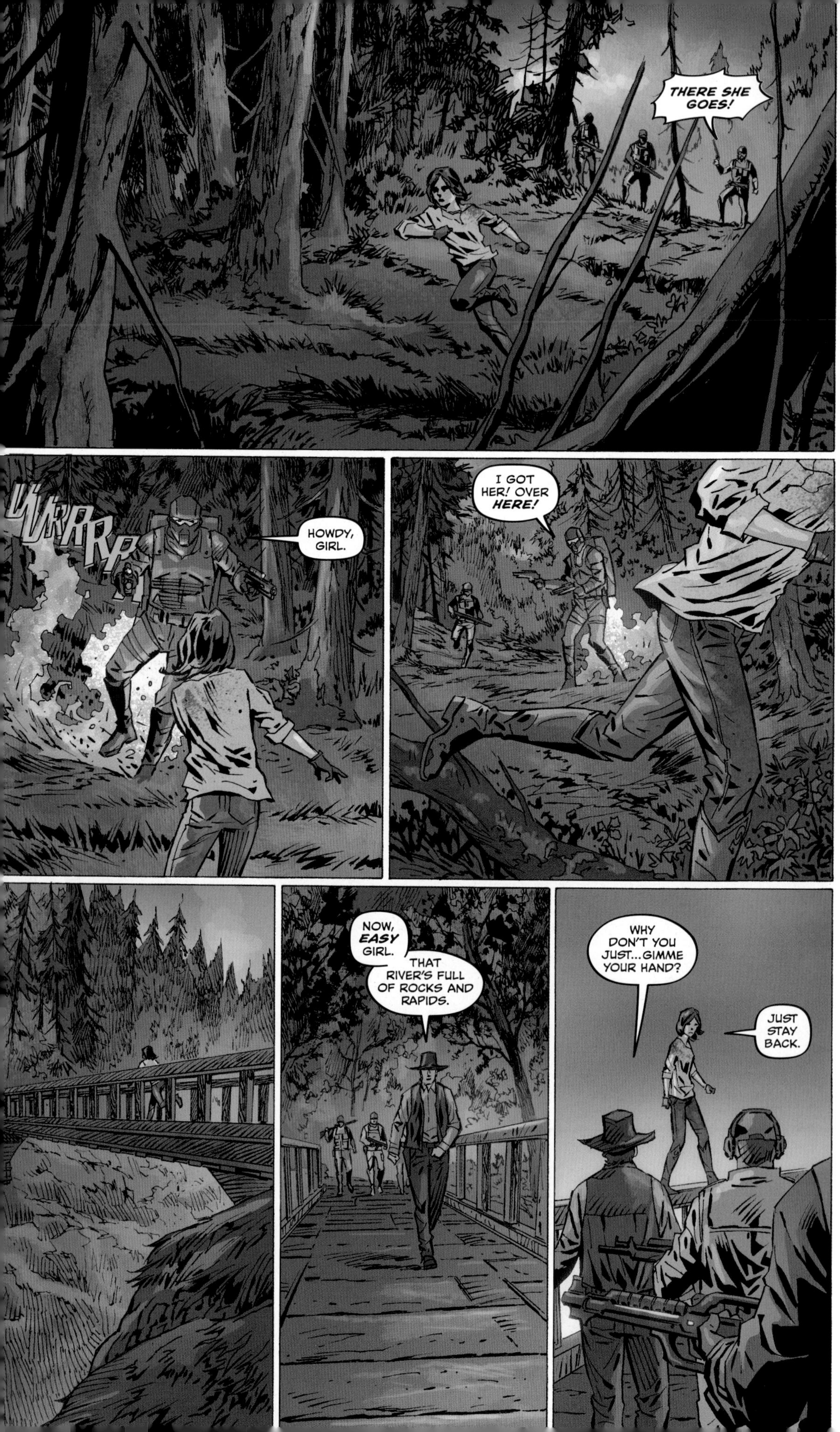
THERE SHE GOES!
VVVRRRRP
HOWDY, GIRL.
I GOT HER! OVER HERE!
NOW, EASY GIRL.
THAT RIVER'S FULL OF ROCKS AND RAPIDS.
WHY DON'T YOU JUST...GIMME YOUR HAND?
JUST STAY BACK.

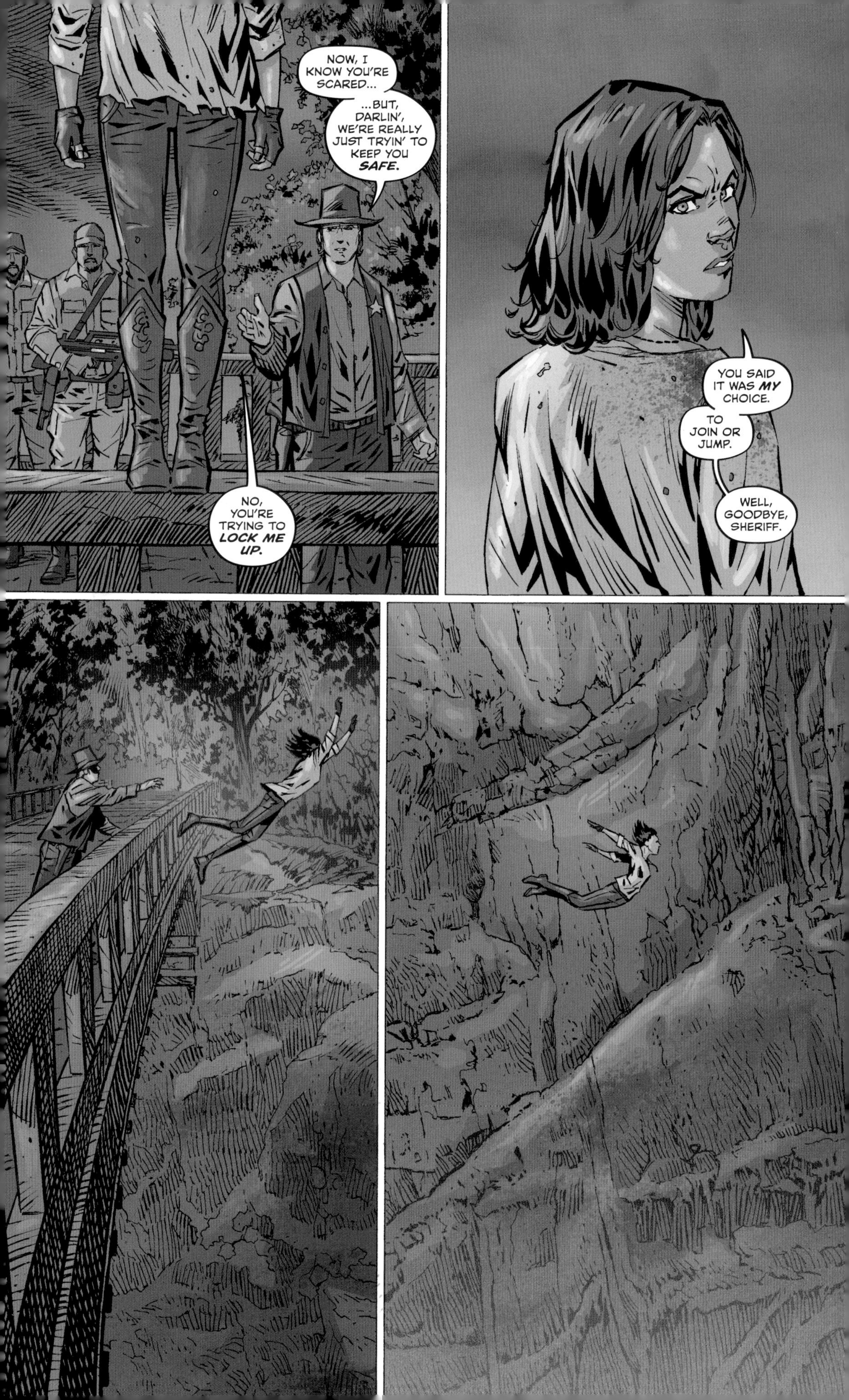
NOW, I KNOW YOU'RE SCARED...
...BUT, DARLIN', WE'RE REALLY JUST TRYIN' TO KEEP YOU SAFE.
NO, YOU'RE TRYING TO LOCK ME UP.
YOU SAID IT WAS MY CHOICE.
TO JOIN OR JUMP.
WELL, GOODBYE, SHERIFF.

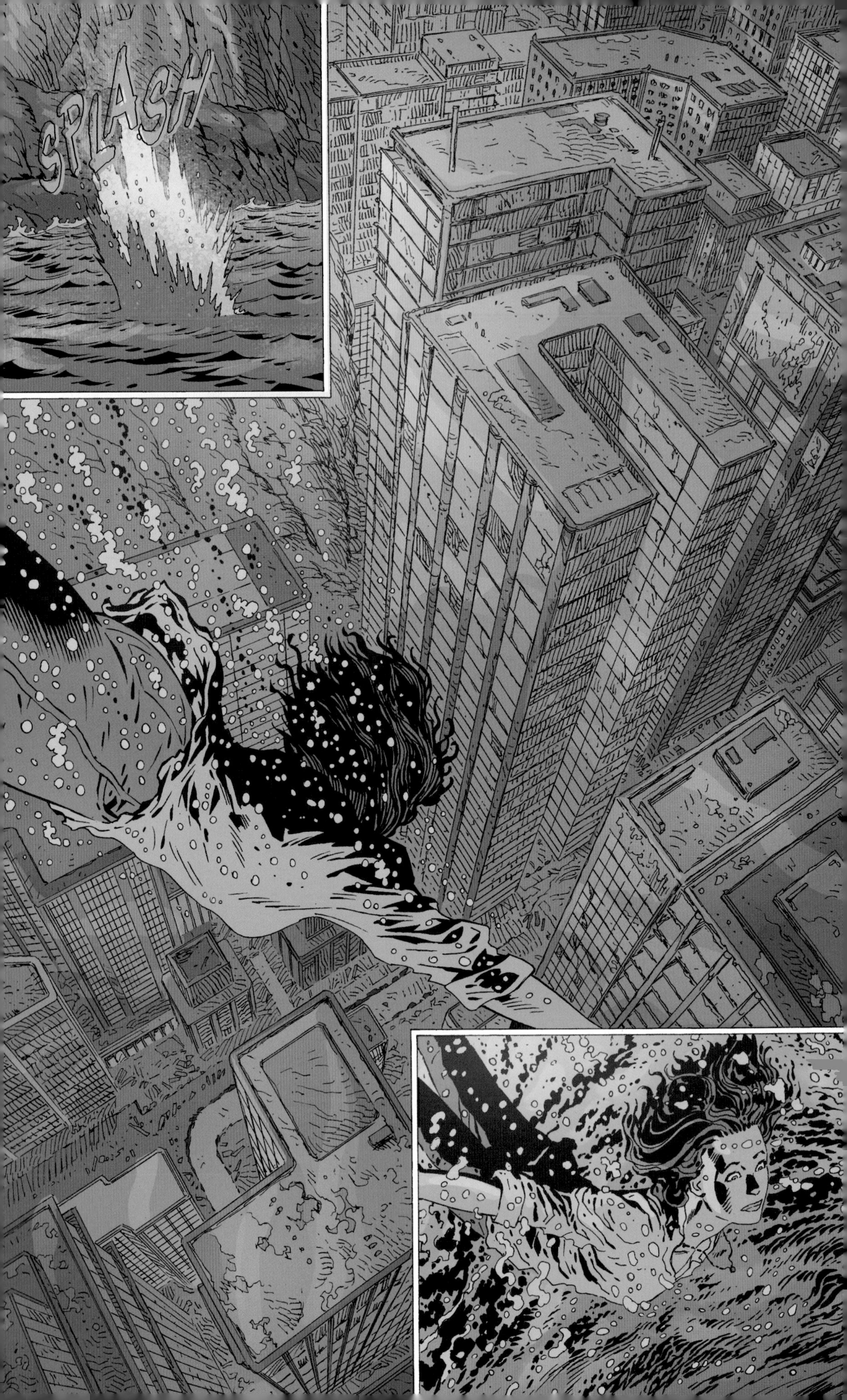
SPLASH

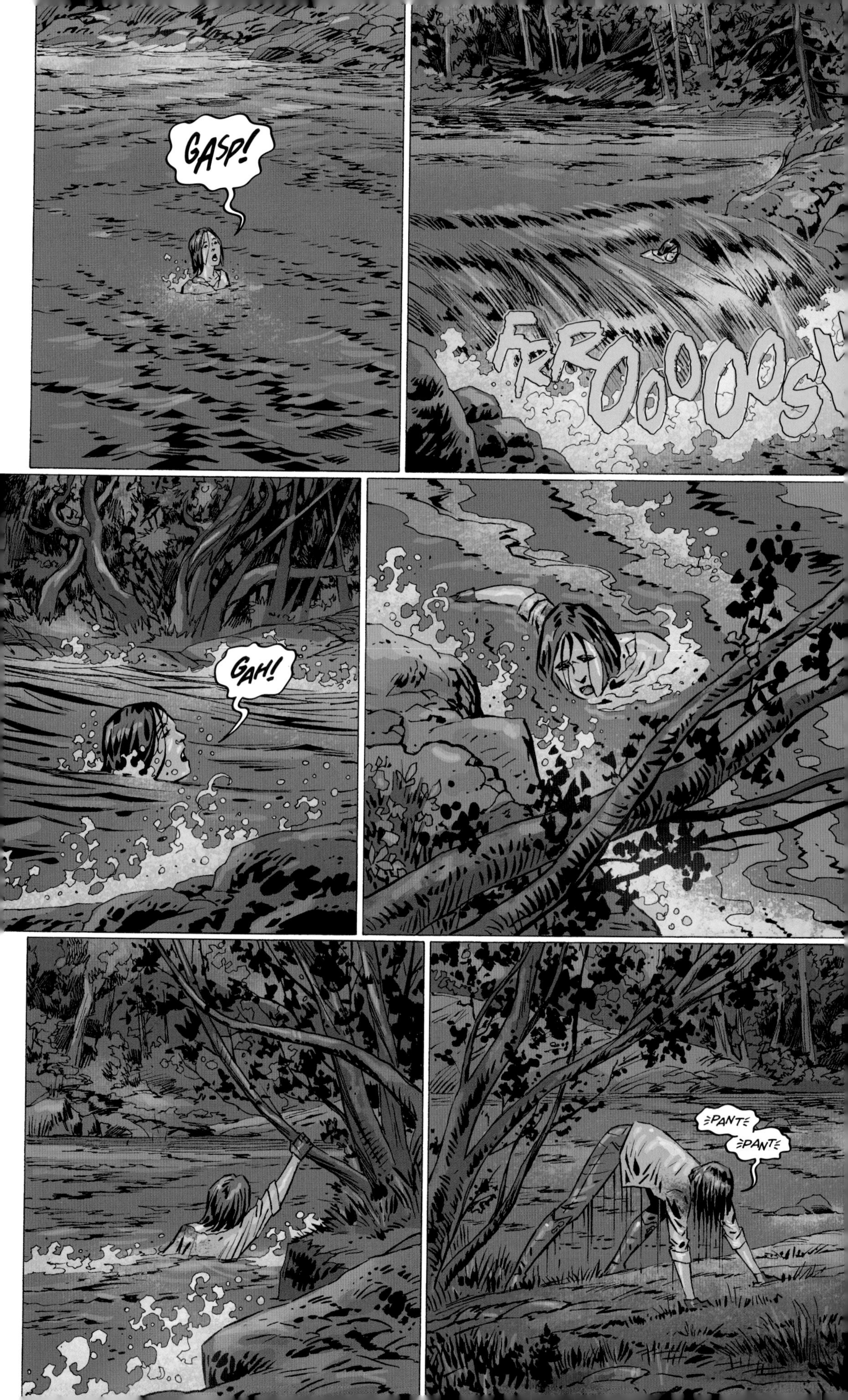
GASP!
FRROOOOSH
GAH!
PANT
PANT

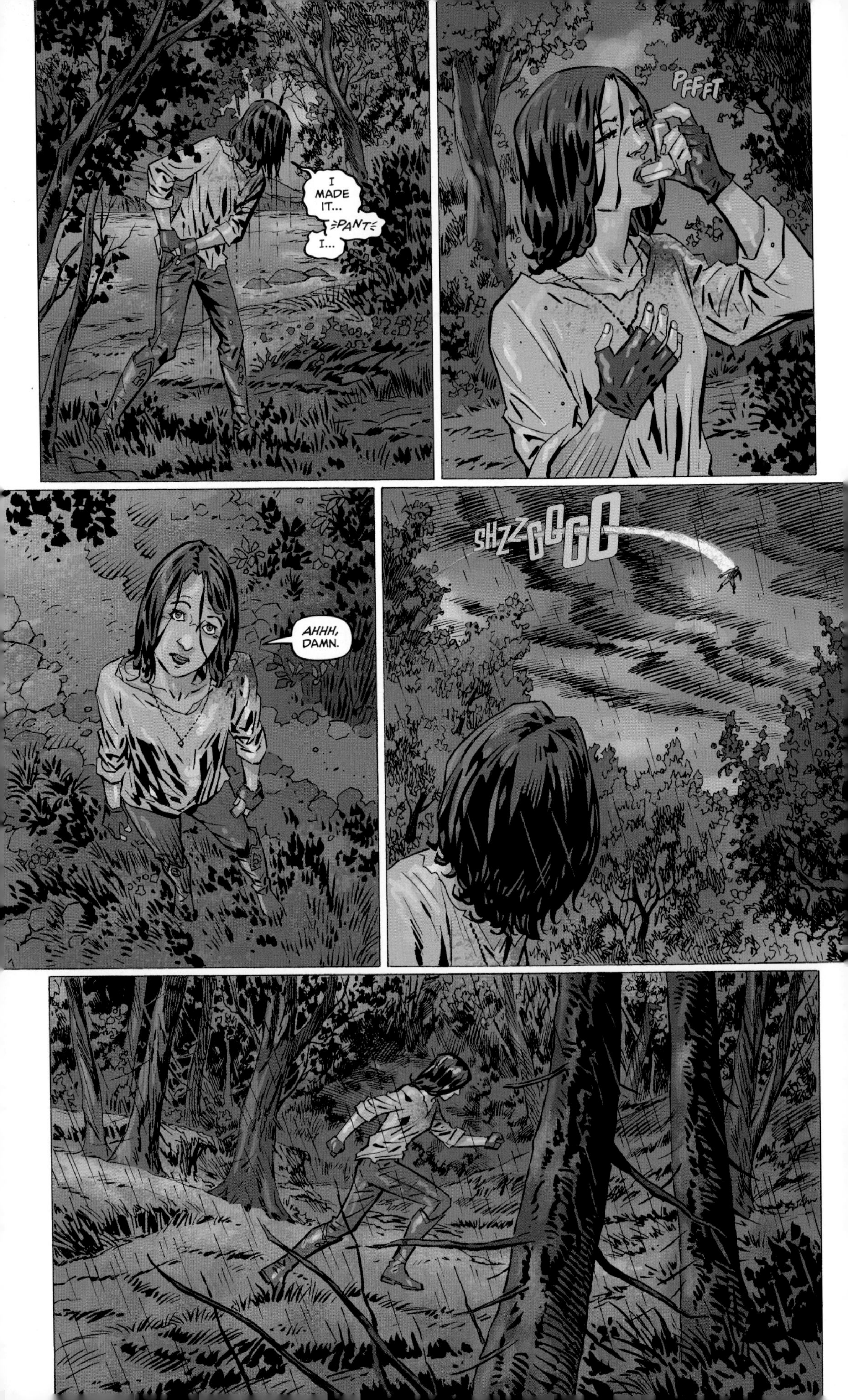
I MADE IT...
PANT
I...
PFFFT
AHHH, DAMN.
SHZZGOGO

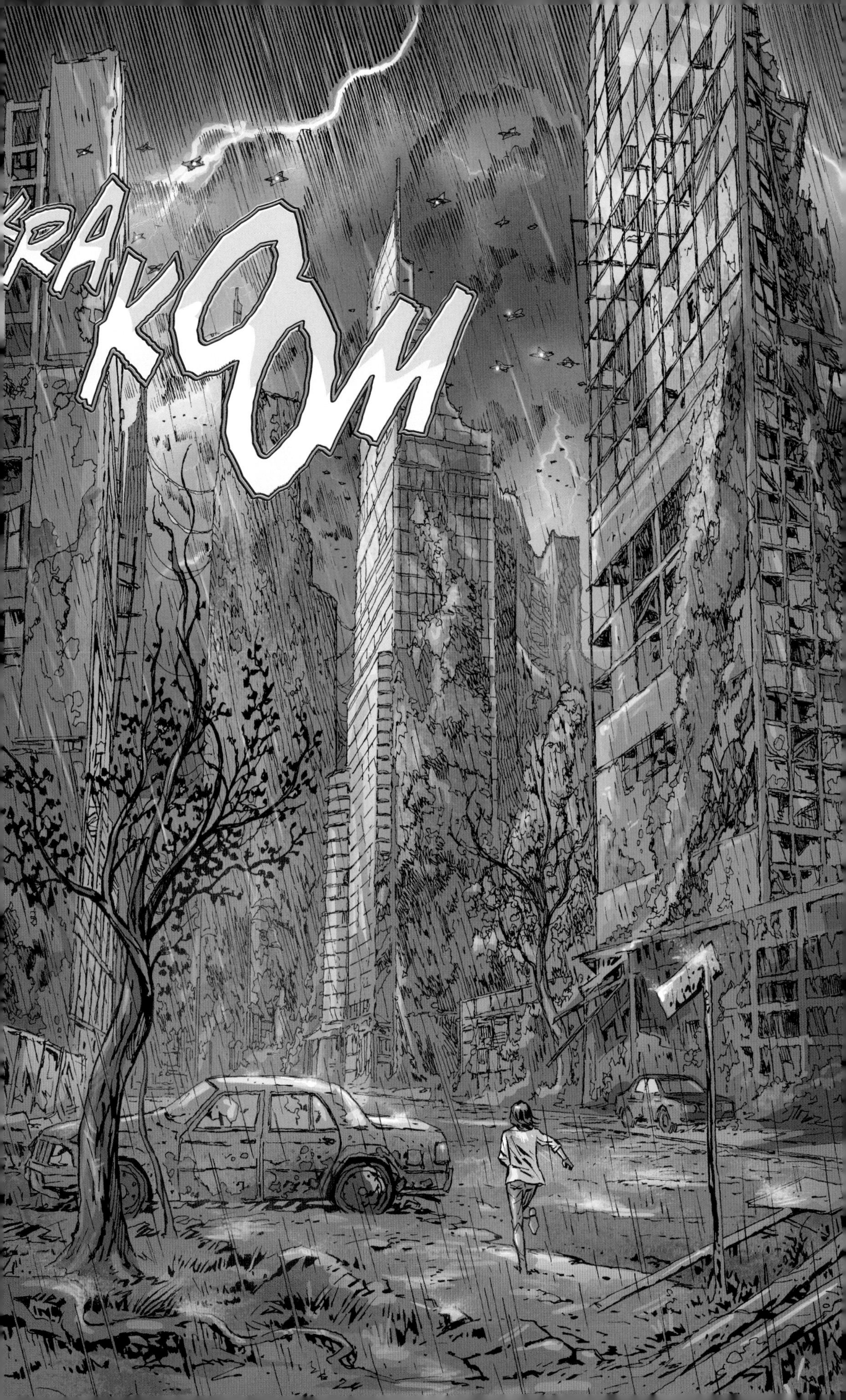
KRAKOOM

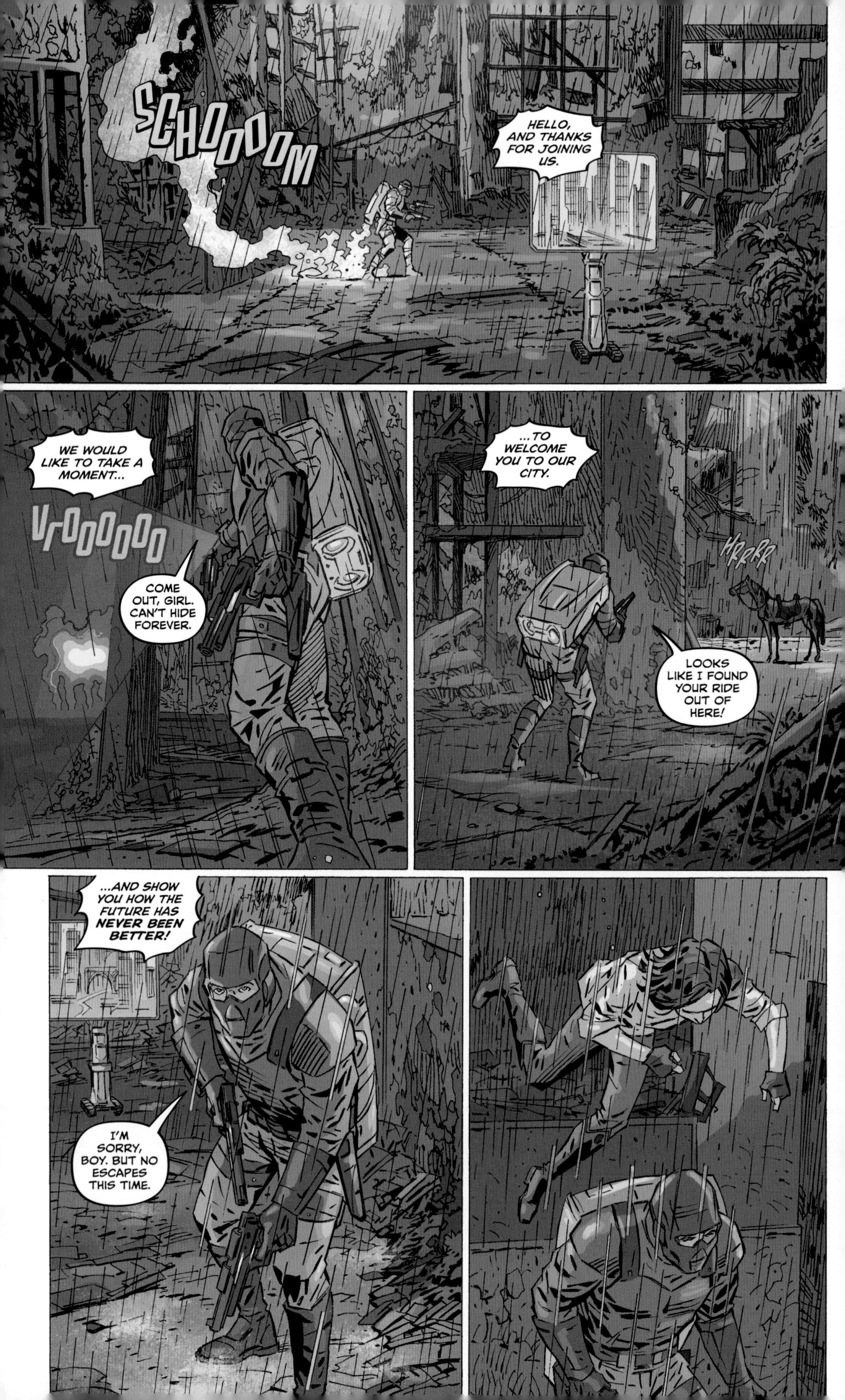
SCHOOOOM
HELLO, AND THANKS FOR JOINING US.
WE WOULD LIKE TO TAKE A MOMENT...
VrOOOOOO
COME OUT, GIRL. CAN'T HIDE FOREVER.
...TO WELCOME YOU TO OUR CITY.
HRRRR
LOOKS LIKE I FOUND YOUR RIDE OUT OF HERE!
...AND SHOW YOU HOW THE FUTURE HAS **NEVER BEEN BETTER!**
I'M SORRY, BOY. BUT NO ESCAPES THIS TIME.

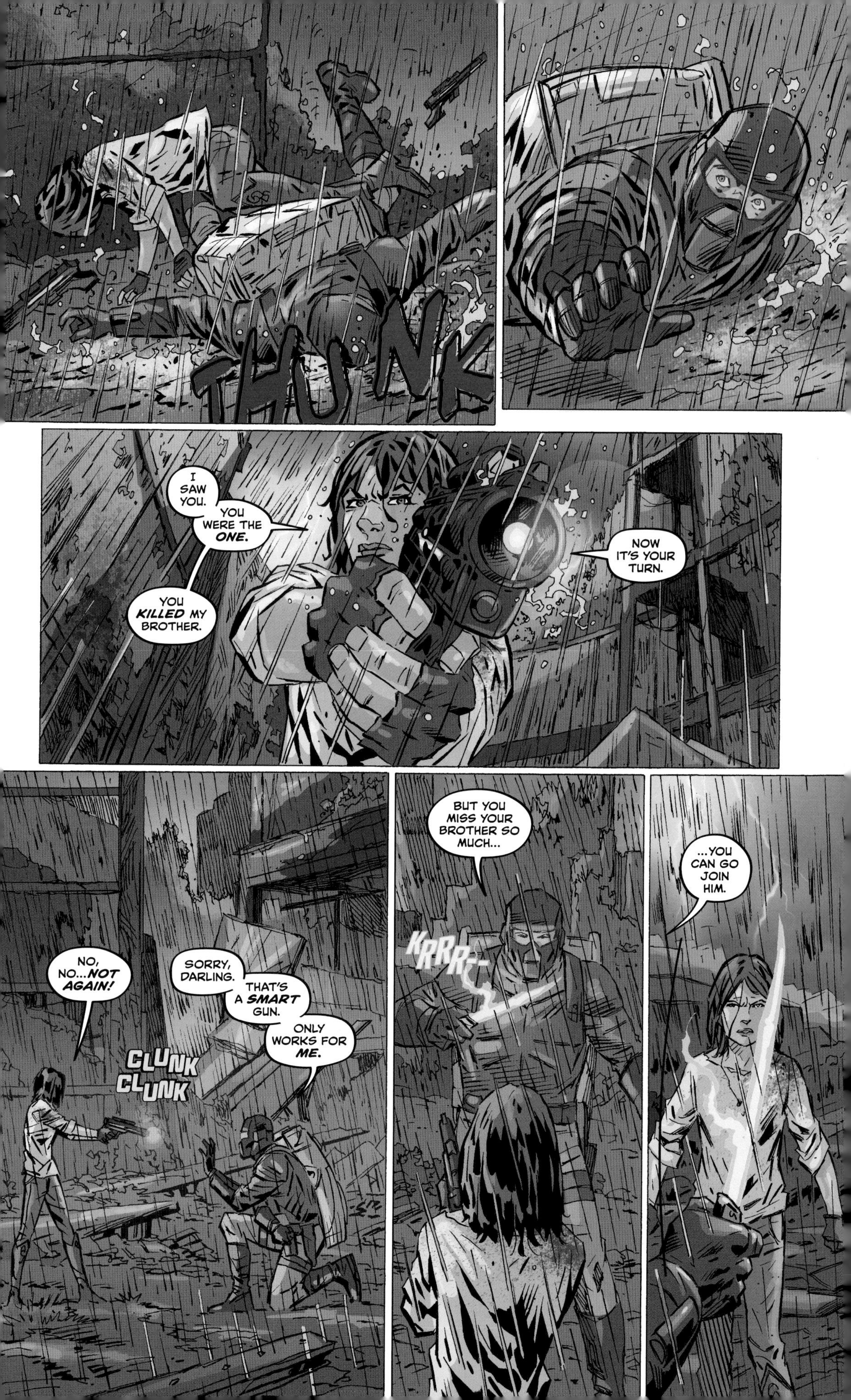
THUNK
I SAW YOU.
YOU WERE THE ONE.
YOU KILLED MY BROTHER.
NOW IT'S YOUR TURN.
NO, NO...NOT AGAIN!
CLUNK
CLUNK
SORRY, DARLING.
THAT'S A SMART GUN.
ONLY WORKS FOR ME.
BUT YOU MISS YOUR BROTHER SO MUCH...
KRRR--
...YOU CAN GO JOIN HIM.

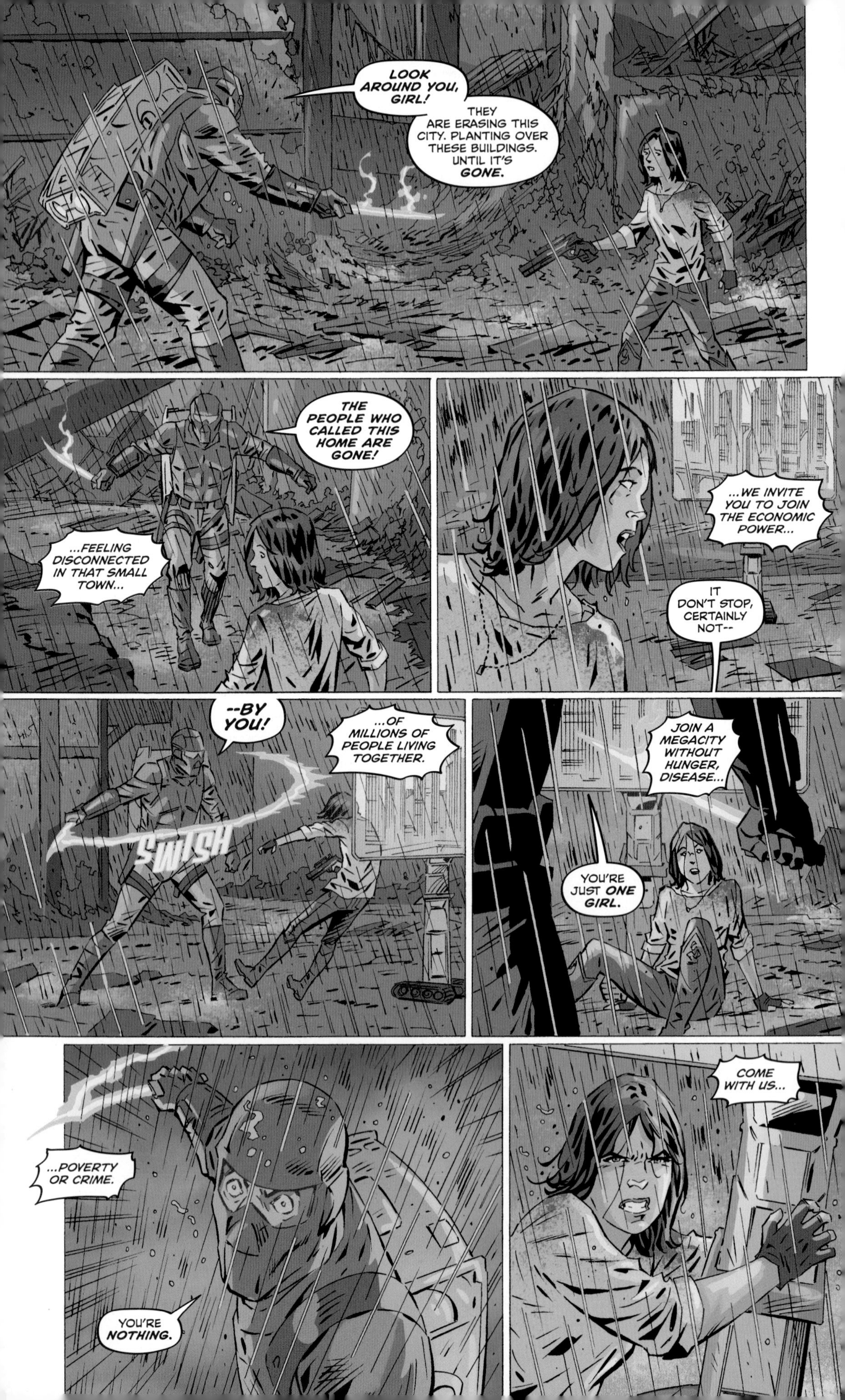
LOOK AROUND YOU, GIRL!
THEY ARE ERASING THIS CITY. PLANTING OVER THESE BUILDINGS. UNTIL IT'S GONE.
THE PEOPLE WHO CALLED THIS HOME ARE GONE!
...FEELING DISCONNECTED IN THAT SMALL TOWN...
...WE INVITE YOU TO JOIN THE ECONOMIC POWER...
IT DON'T STOP, CERTAINLY NOT--
--BY YOU!
...OF MILLIONS OF PEOPLE LIVING TOGETHER.
SWISH
JOIN A MEGACITY WITHOUT HUNGER, DISEASE...
YOU'RE JUST ONE GIRL.
...POVERTY OR CRIME.
YOU'RE NOTHING.
COME WITH US...

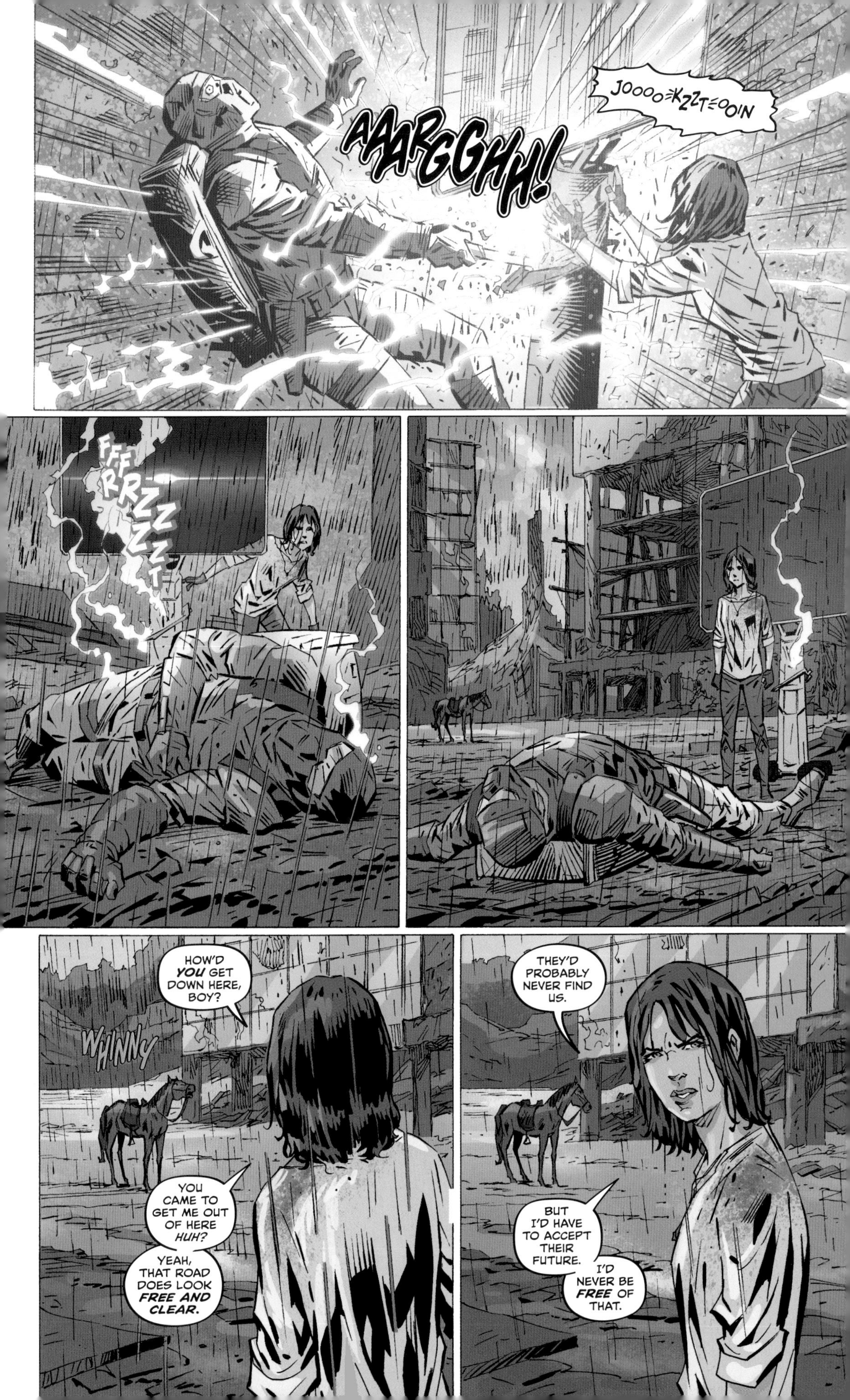
AAARGGHH!
JOOOOKZZTOOIN
FFFRRZZZZZT
HOW'D *YOU* GET DOWN HERE, BOY?
WHINNY
YOU CAME TO GET ME OUT OF HERE *HUH?*
YEAH, THAT ROAD DOES LOOK ***FREE AND CLEAR.***
THEY'D PROBABLY NEVER FIND US.
BUT I'D HAVE TO ACCEPT THEIR FUTURE.
I'D NEVER BE ***FREE*** OF THAT.

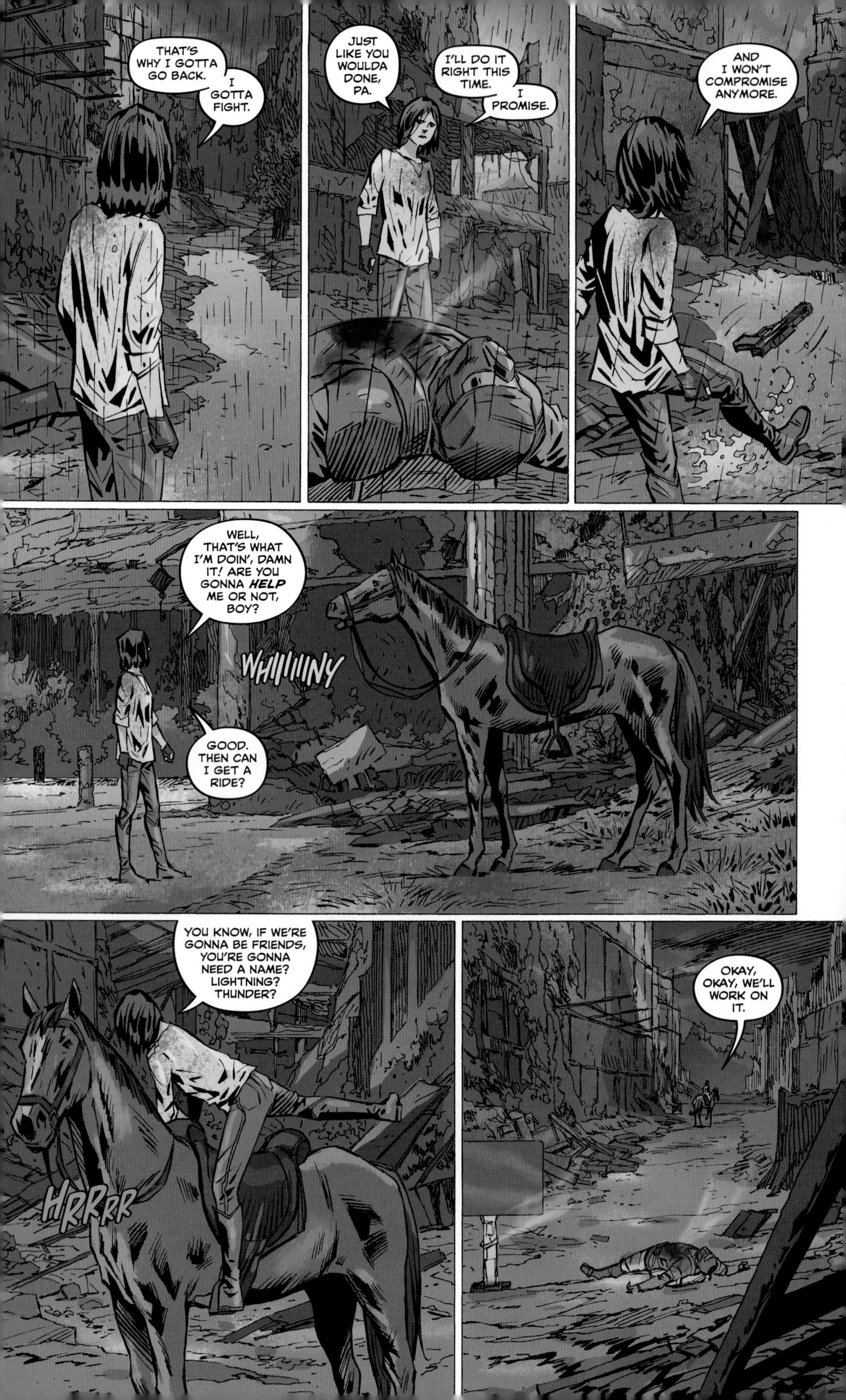
THAT'S WHY I GOTTA GO BACK.
I GOTTA FIGHT.
JUST LIKE YOU WOULDA DONE, PA.
I'LL DO IT RIGHT THIS TIME.
I PROMISE.
AND I WON'T COMPROMISE ANYMORE.
WELL, THAT'S WHAT I'M DOIN', DAMN IT! ARE YOU GONNA HELP ME OR NOT, BOY?
WHIIIIINY
GOOD. THEN CAN I GET A RIDE?
YOU KNOW, IF WE'RE GONNA BE FRIENDS, YOU'RE GONNA NEED A NAME? LIGHTNING? THUNDER?
HRRRR
OKAY, OKAY, WE'LL WORK ON IT.

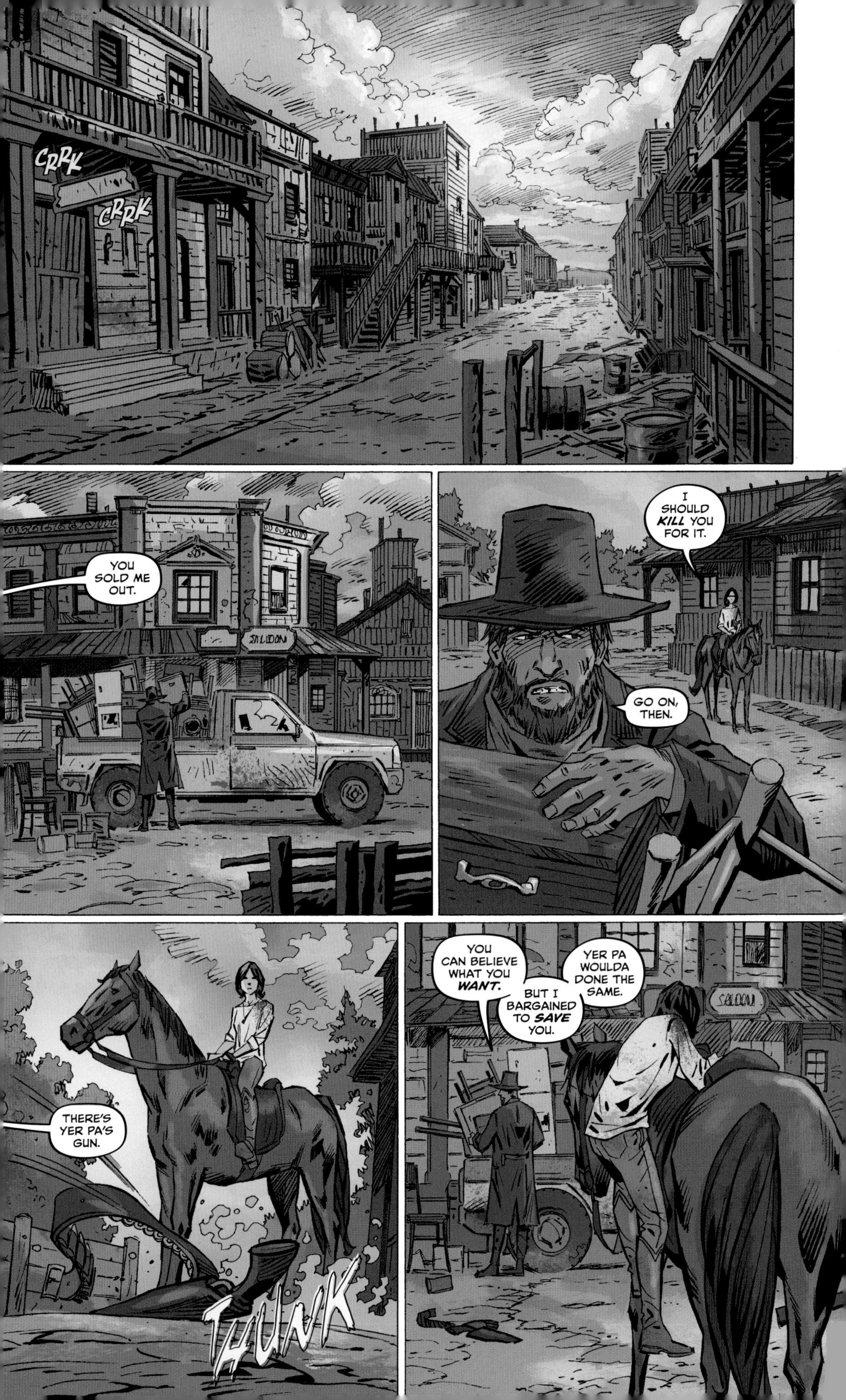
CRRK
CRRK
YOU SOLD ME OUT.
I SHOULD KILL YOU FOR IT.
GO ON, THEN.
THERE'S YER PA'S GUN.
THUNK
YOU CAN BELIEVE WHAT YOU WANT.
BUT I BARGAINED TO SAVE YOU.
YER PA WOULDA DONE THE SAME.
SALOON

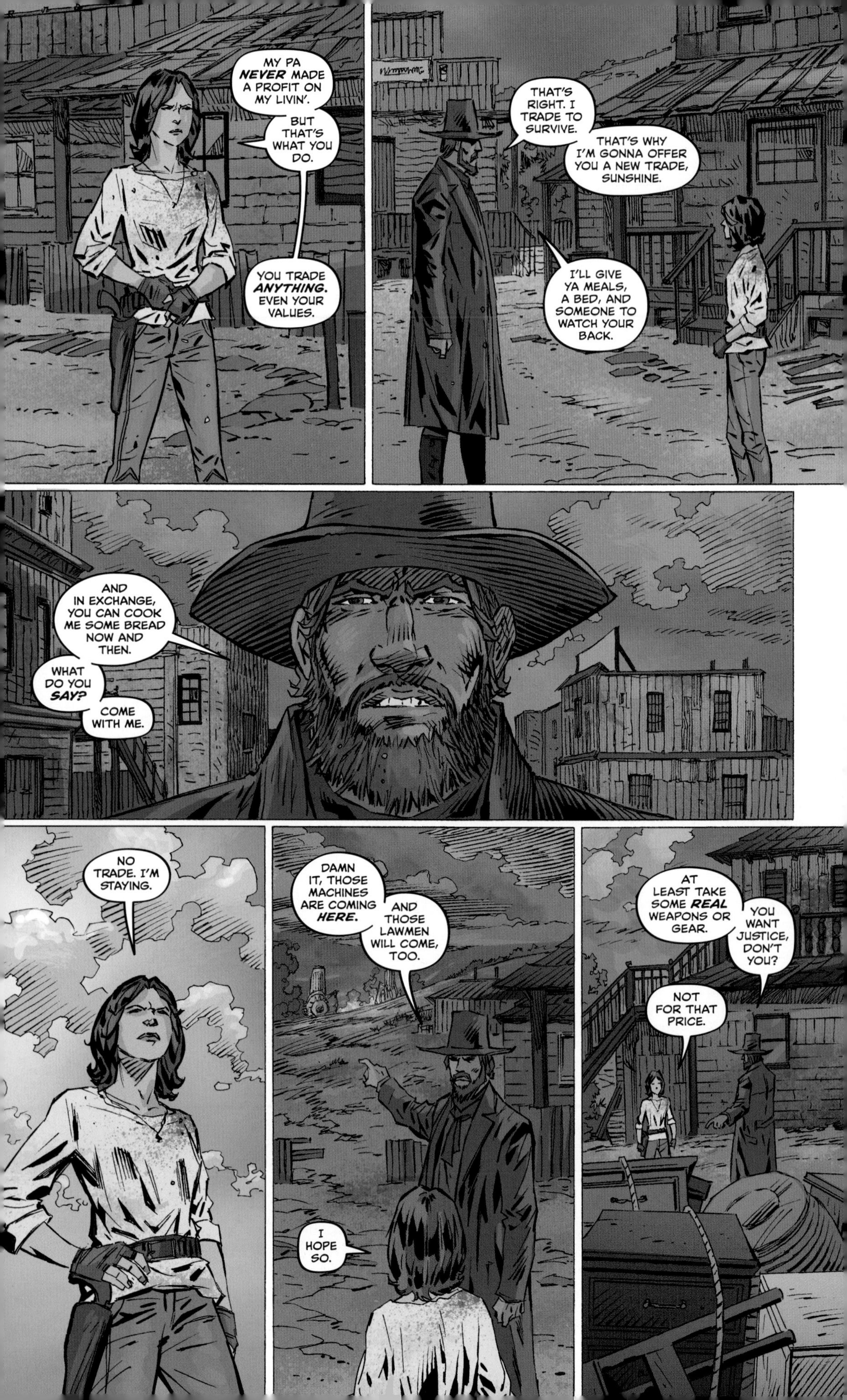
MY PA NEVER MADE A PROFIT ON MY LIVIN'.
BUT THAT'S WHAT YOU DO.
YOU TRADE ANYTHING. EVEN YOUR VALUES.
THAT'S RIGHT. I TRADE TO SURVIVE.
THAT'S WHY I'M GONNA OFFER YOU A NEW TRADE, SUNSHINE.
I'LL GIVE YA MEALS, A BED, AND SOMEONE TO WATCH YOUR BACK.
AND IN EXCHANGE, YOU CAN COOK ME SOME BREAD NOW AND THEN.
WHAT DO YOU SAY?
COME WITH ME.
NO TRADE. I'M STAYING.
DAMN IT, THOSE MACHINES ARE COMING HERE.
AND THOSE LAWMEN WILL COME, TOO.
I HOPE SO.
AT LEAST TAKE SOME REAL WEAPONS OR GEAR.
YOU WANT JUSTICE, DON'T YOU?
NOT FOR THAT PRICE.

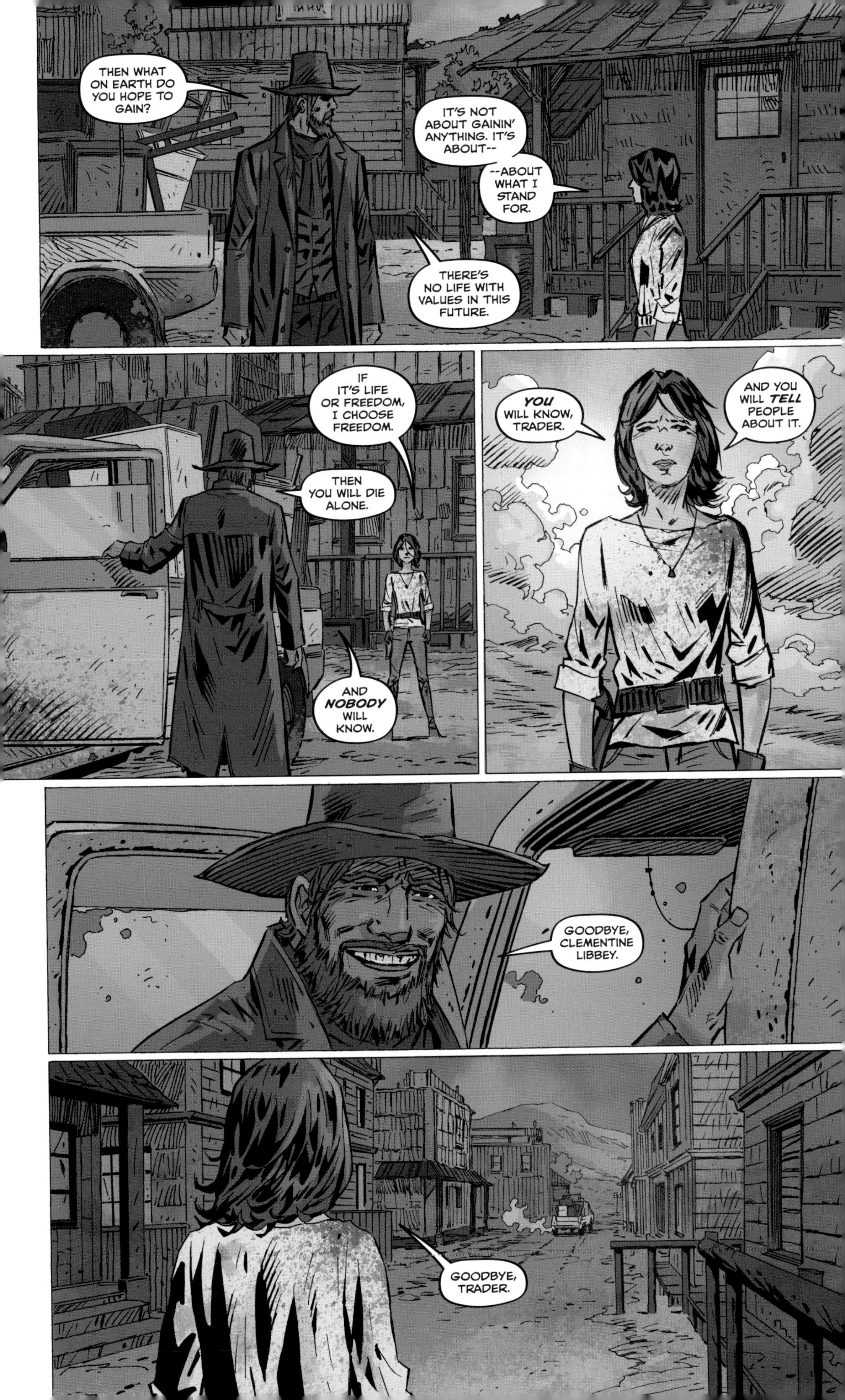
THEN WHAT ON EARTH DO YOU HOPE TO GAIN?
IT'S NOT ABOUT GAININ' ANYTHING. IT'S ABOUT--
--ABOUT WHAT I STAND FOR.
THERE'S NO LIFE WITH VALUES IN THIS FUTURE.
IF IT'S LIFE OR FREEDOM, I CHOOSE FREEDOM.
THEN YOU WILL DIE ALONE.
AND NOBODY WILL KNOW.
YOU WILL KNOW, TRADER.
AND YOU WILL TELL PEOPLE ABOUT IT.
GOODBYE, CLEMENTINE LIBBEY.
GOODBYE, TRADER.

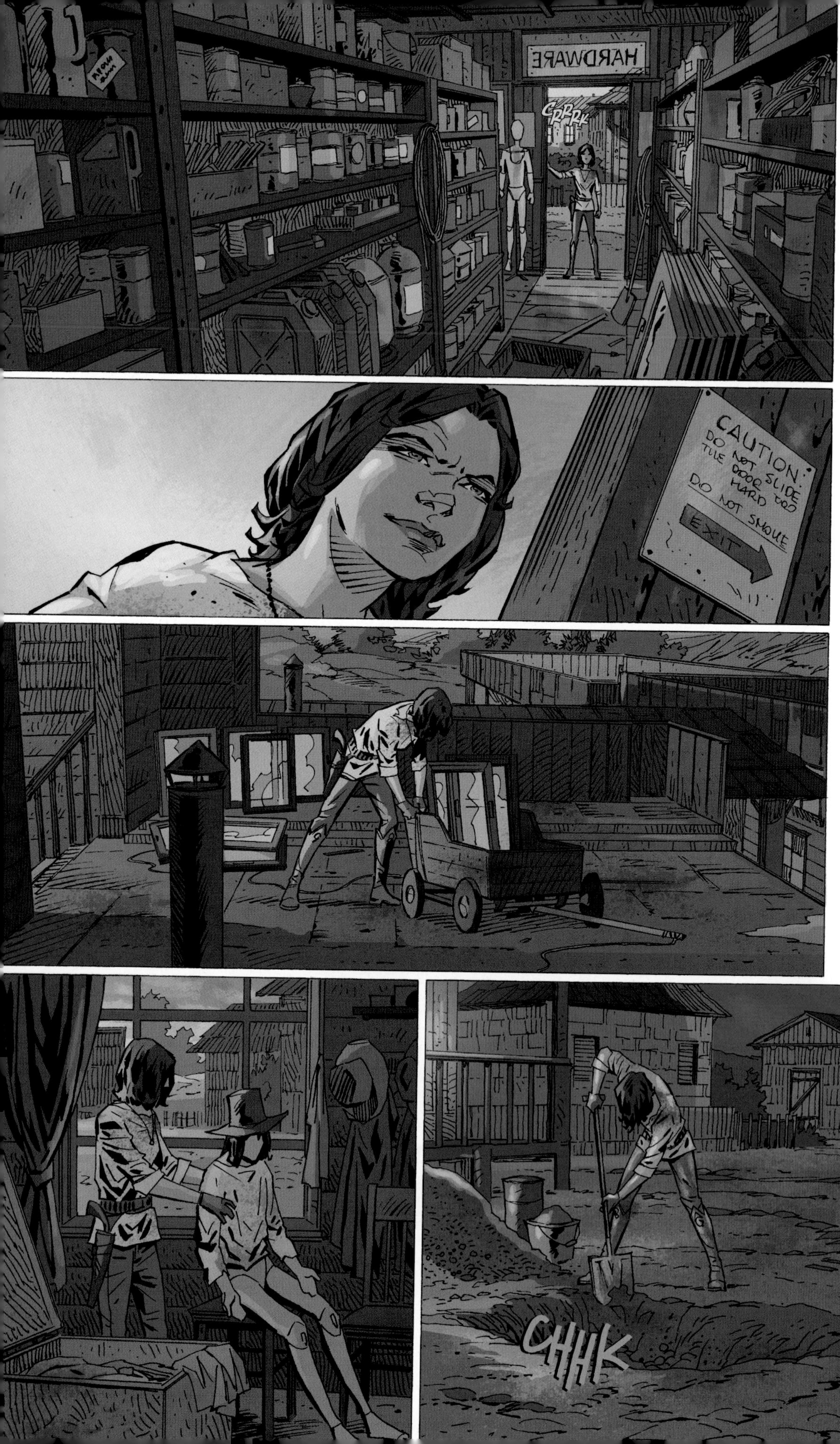
HARDWARE
CRRRK
CAUTION
DO NOT SLIDE
THE DOOR TOO
HARD
DO NOT SMOKE
EXIT
CHHK

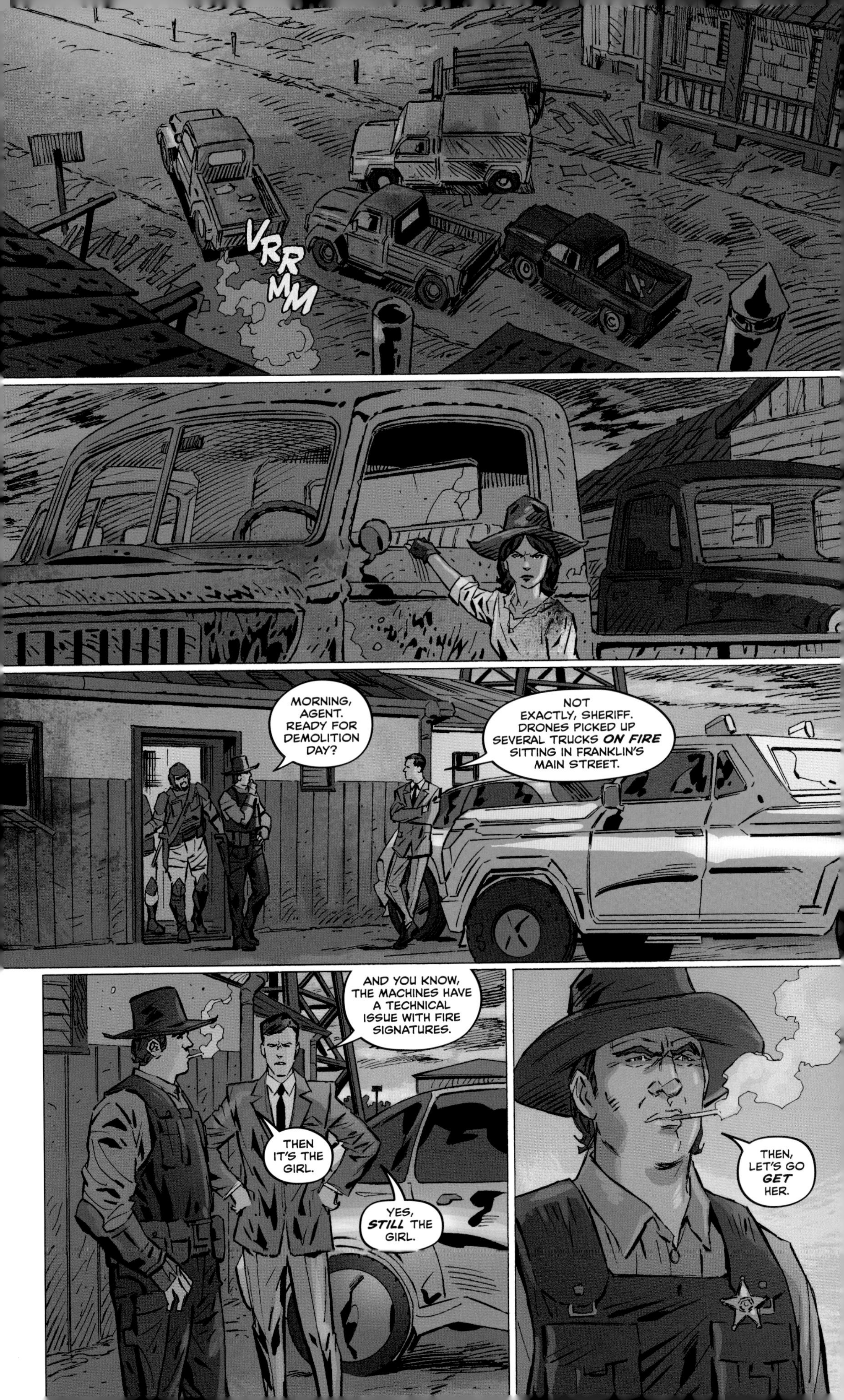
VRRMM
MORNING, AGENT. READY FOR DEMOLITION DAY?
NOT EXACTLY, SHERIFF. DRONES PICKED UP SEVERAL TRUCKS ON FIRE SITTING IN FRANKLIN'S MAIN STREET.
AND YOU KNOW, THE MACHINES HAVE A TECHNICAL ISSUE WITH FIRE SIGNATURES.
THEN IT'S THE GIRL.
YES, STILL THE GIRL.
THEN, LET'S GO GET HER.

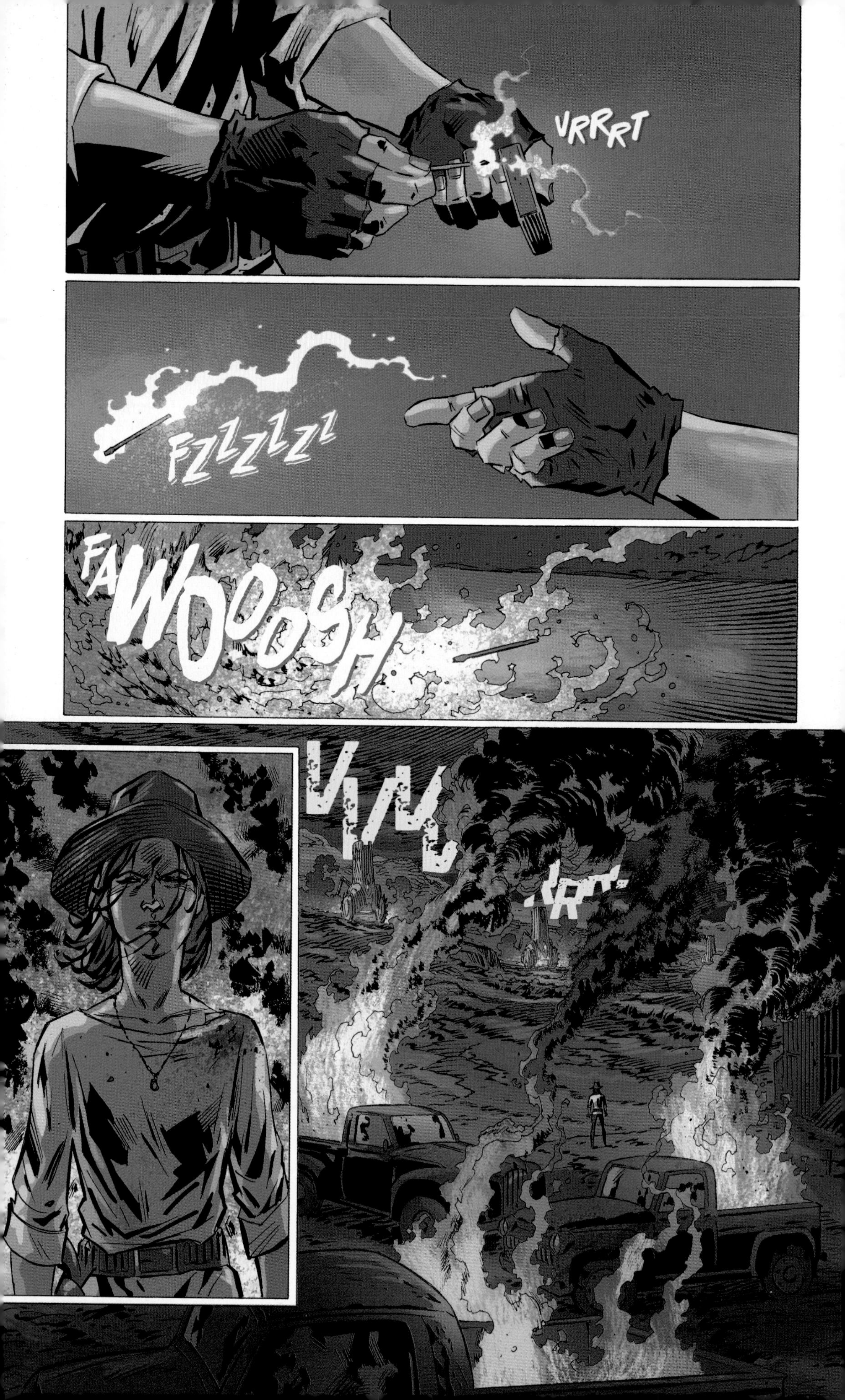
VRRRT
FZZZZZZ
FAWOOOSH

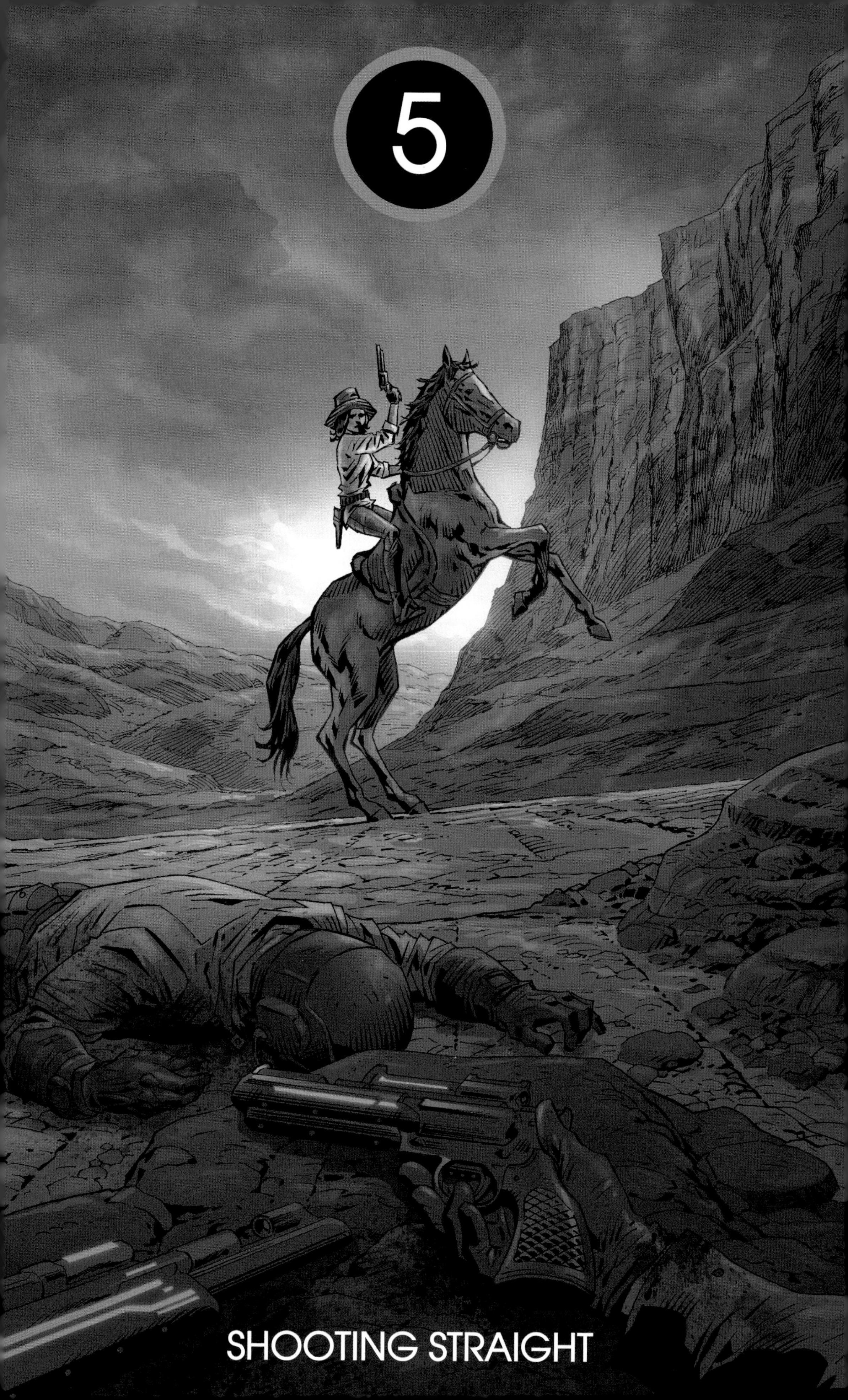
5
SHOOTING STRAIGHT

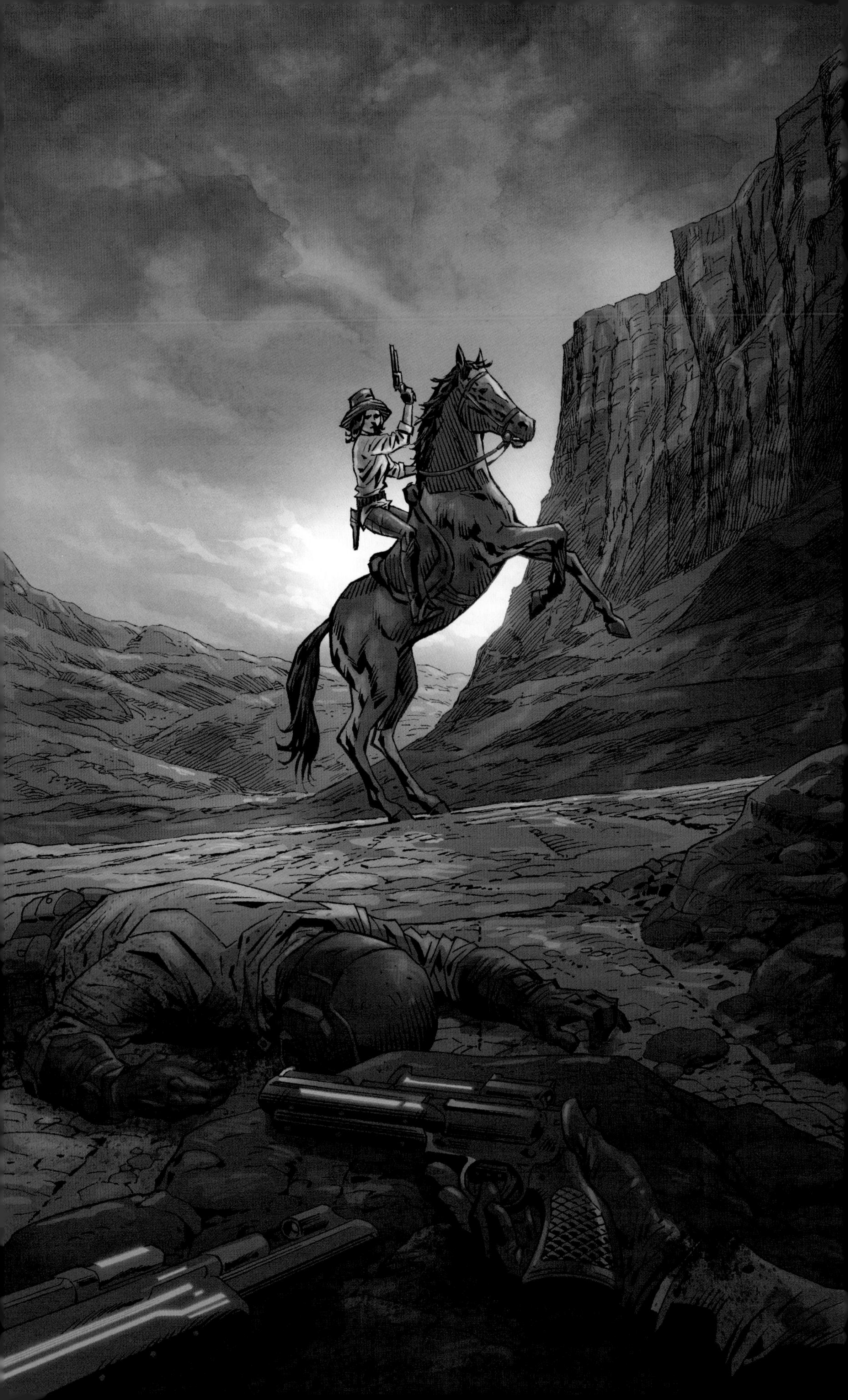

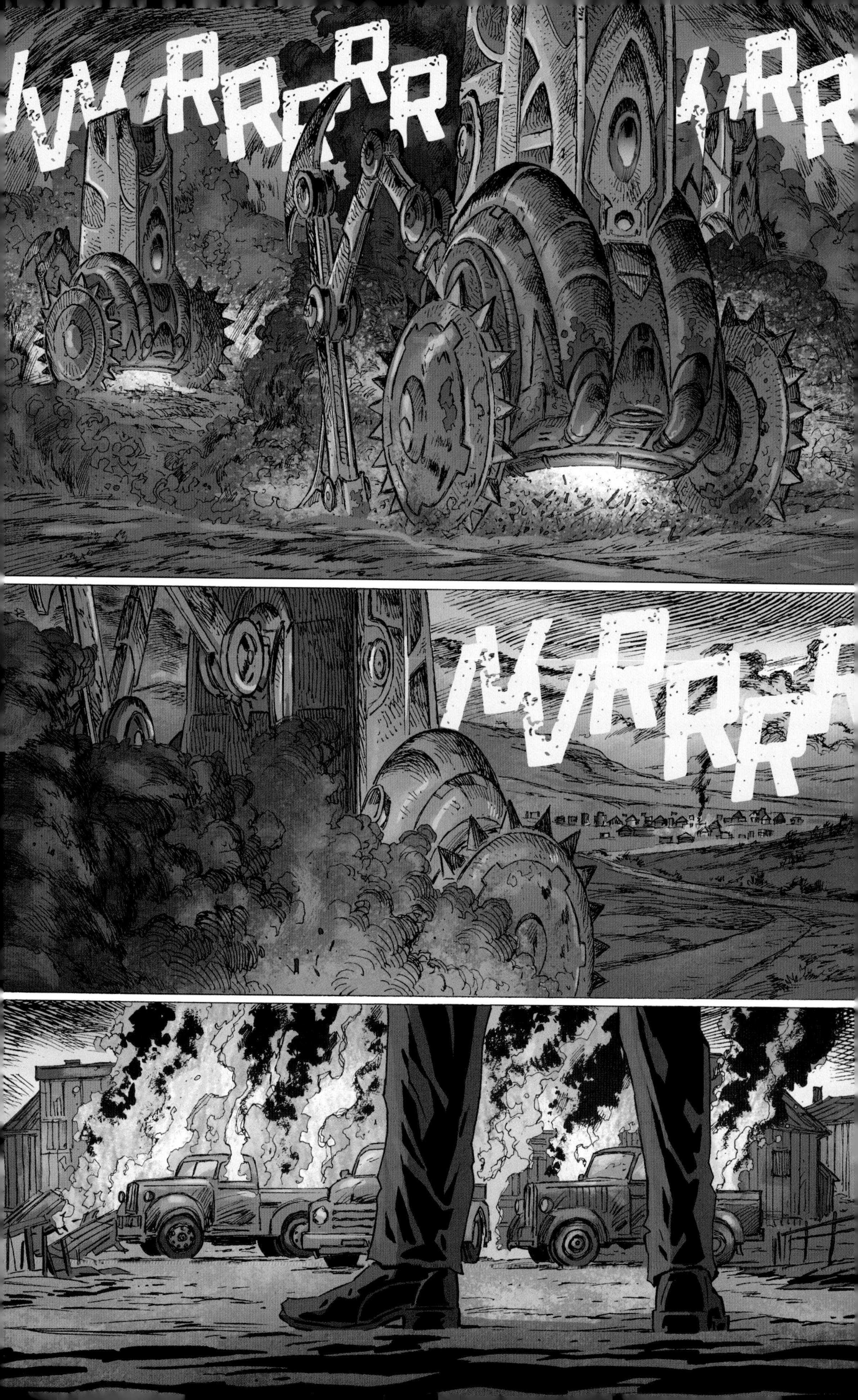
WRRRRR
WRRR
WRRRRR

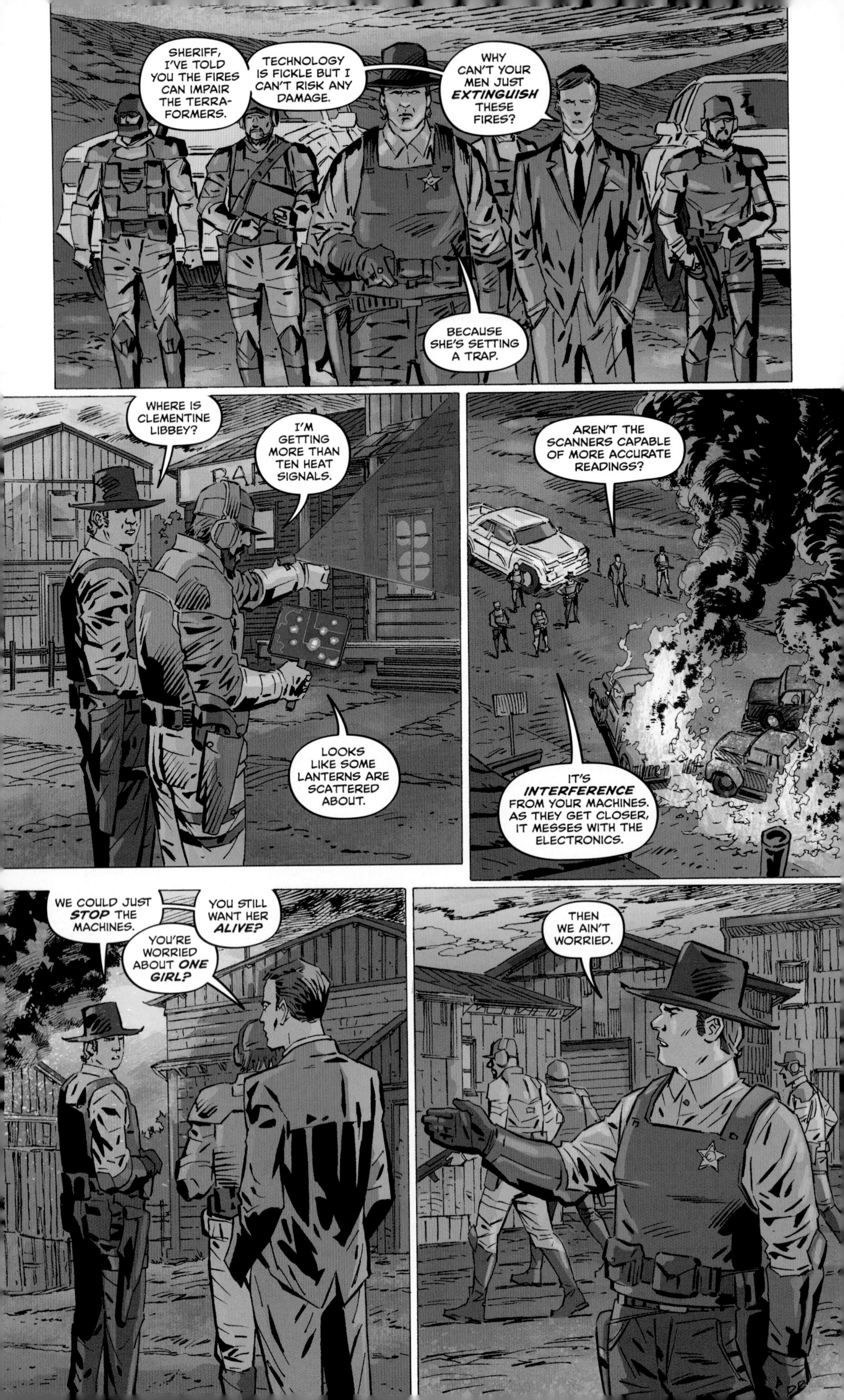
SHERIFF, I'VE TOLD YOU THE FIRES CAN IMPAIR THE TERRA-FORMERS.
TECHNOLOGY IS FICKLE BUT I CAN'T RISK ANY DAMAGE.
WHY CAN'T YOUR MEN JUST **EXTINGUISH** THESE FIRES?
BECAUSE SHE'S SETTING A TRAP.
WHERE IS CLEMENTINE LIBBEY?
I'M GETTING MORE THAN TEN HEAT SIGNALS.
LOOKS LIKE SOME LANTERNS ARE SCATTERED ABOUT.
AREN'T THE SCANNERS CAPABLE OF MORE ACCURATE READINGS?
IT'S **INTERFERENCE** FROM YOUR MACHINES. AS THEY GET CLOSER, IT MESSES WITH THE ELECTRONICS.
WE COULD JUST **STOP** THE MACHINES.
YOU STILL WANT HER **ALIVE?**
YOU'RE WORRIED ABOUT **ONE GIRL?**
THEN WE AIN'T WORRIED.

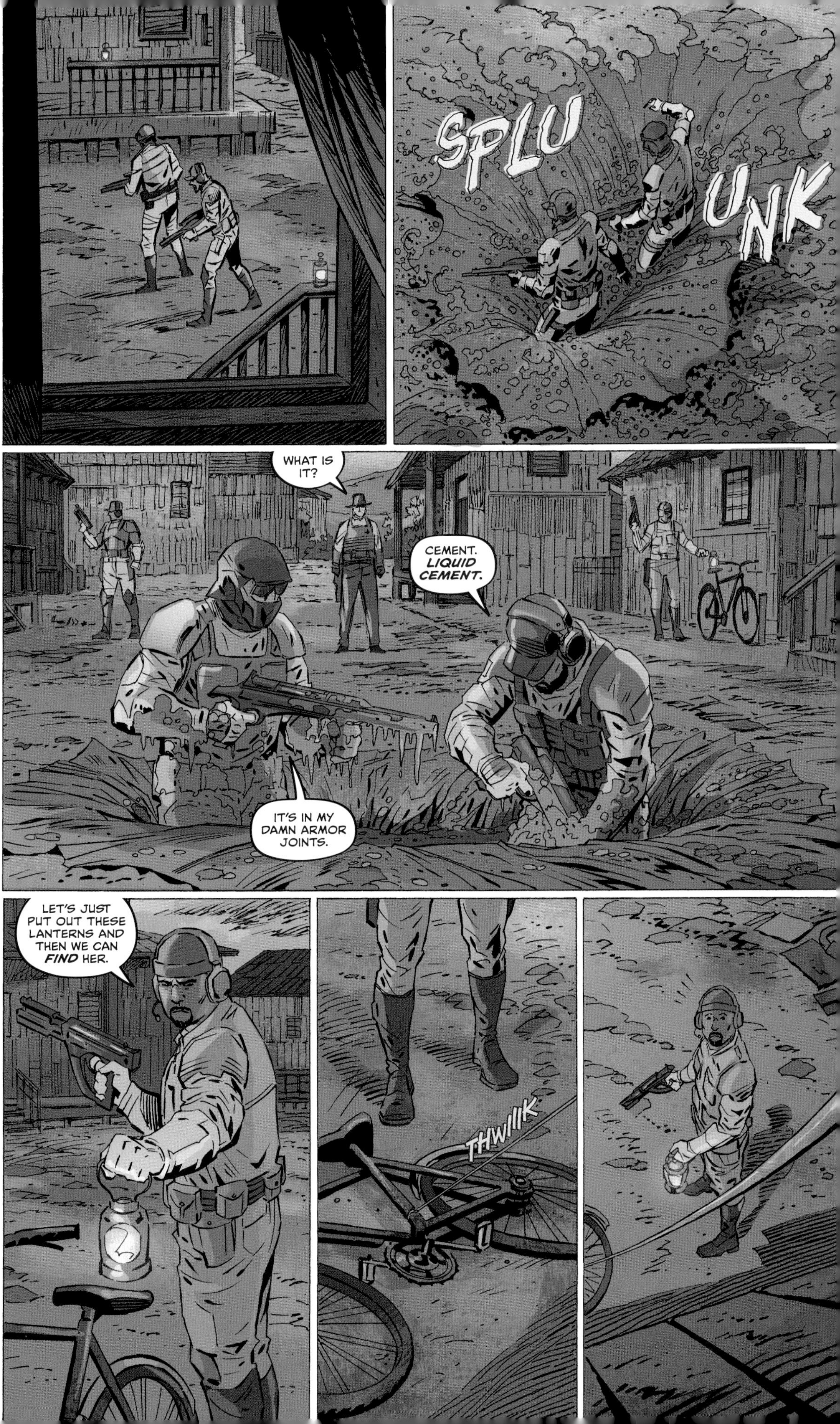
SPLU
UNK
WHAT IS IT?
CEMENT. LIQUID CEMENT.
IT'S IN MY DAMN ARMOR JOINTS.
LET'S JUST PUT OUT THESE LANTERNS AND THEN WE CAN FIND HER.
THWIIIK

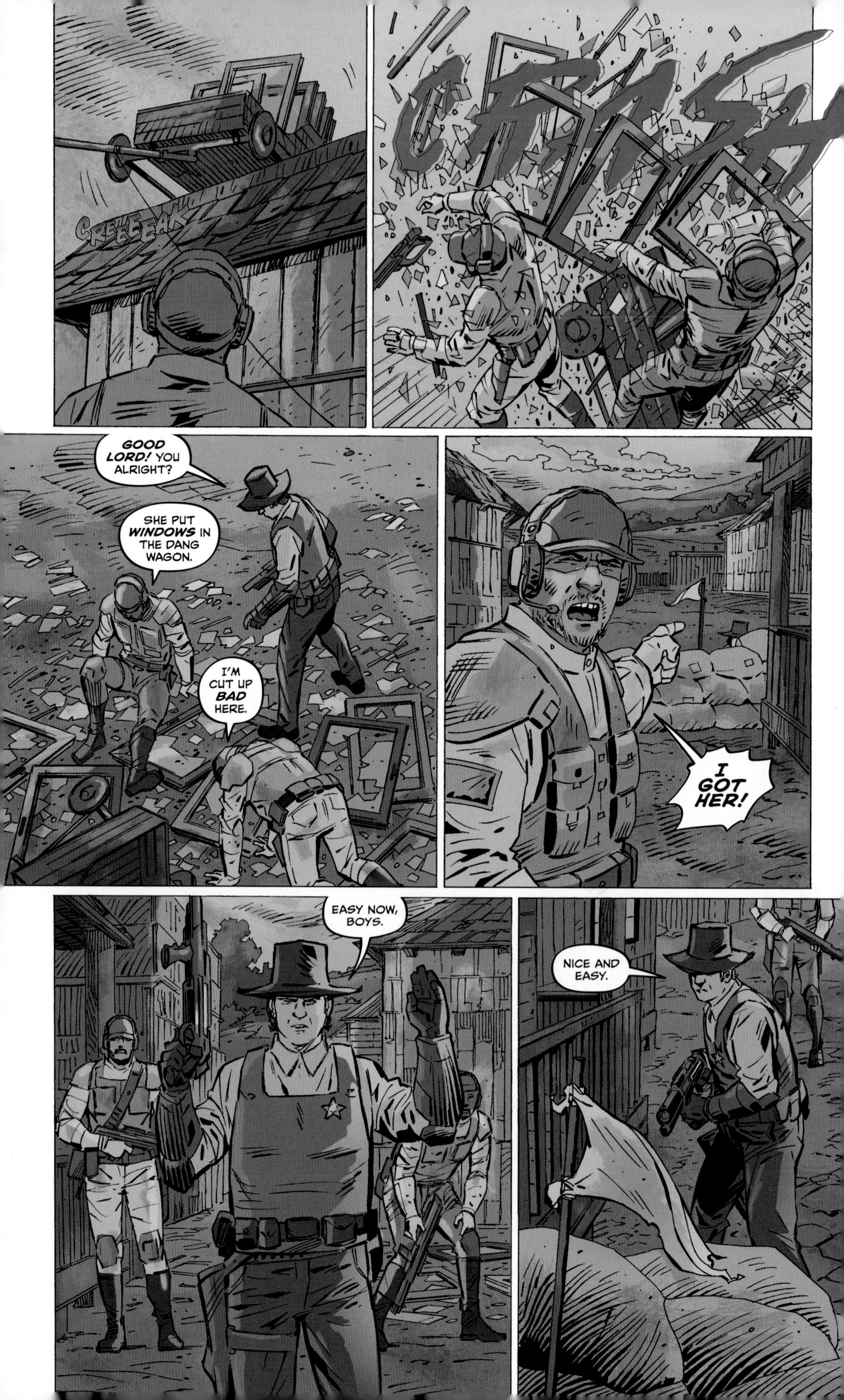
CREEEEAK
CRASH
GOOD LORD! YOU ALRIGHT?
SHE PUT WINDOWS IN THE DANG WAGON.
I'M CUT UP BAD HERE.
I GOT HER!
EASY NOW, BOYS.
NICE AND EASY.

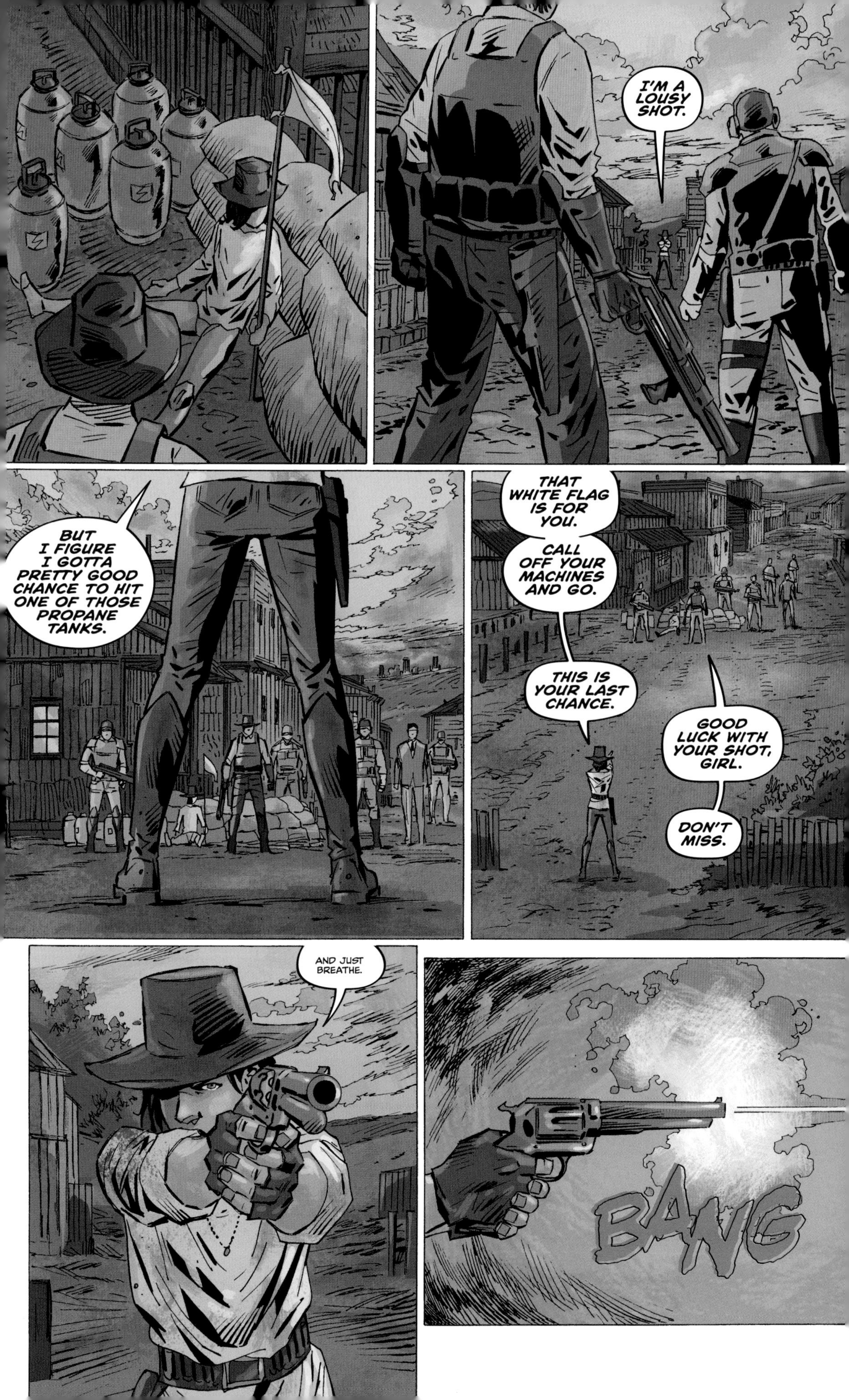
I'M A LOUSY SHOT.
BUT I FIGURE I GOTTA PRETTY GOOD CHANCE TO HIT ONE OF THOSE PROPANE TANKS.
THAT WHITE FLAG IS FOR YOU.
CALL OFF YOUR MACHINES AND GO.
THIS IS YOUR LAST CHANCE.
GOOD LUCK WITH YOUR SHOT, GIRL.
DON'T MISS.
AND JUST BREATHE.
BANG

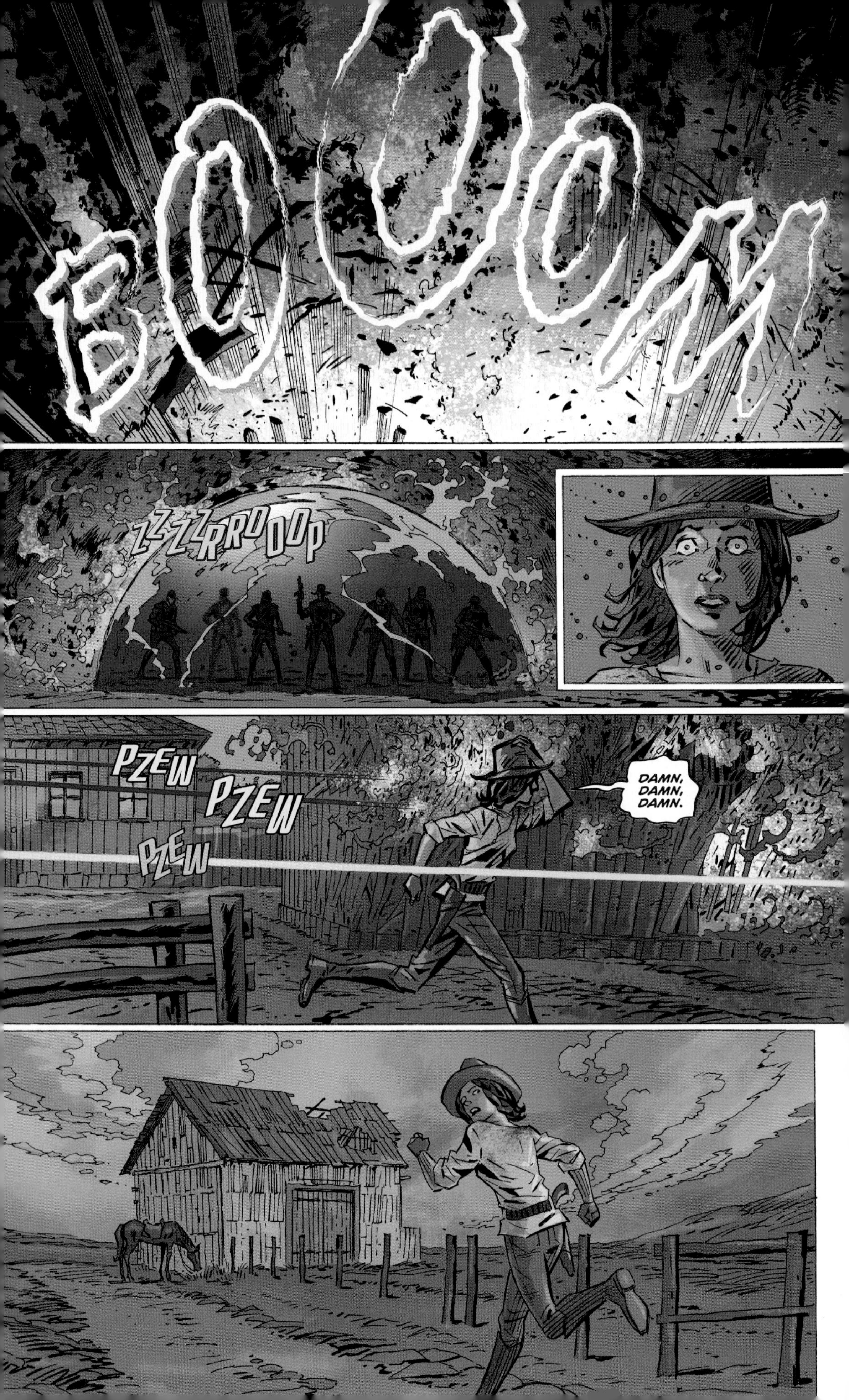
BOOOOM
ZZZZRROOOOP
PZEW
PZEW
PZEW
DAMN, DAMN, DAMN.

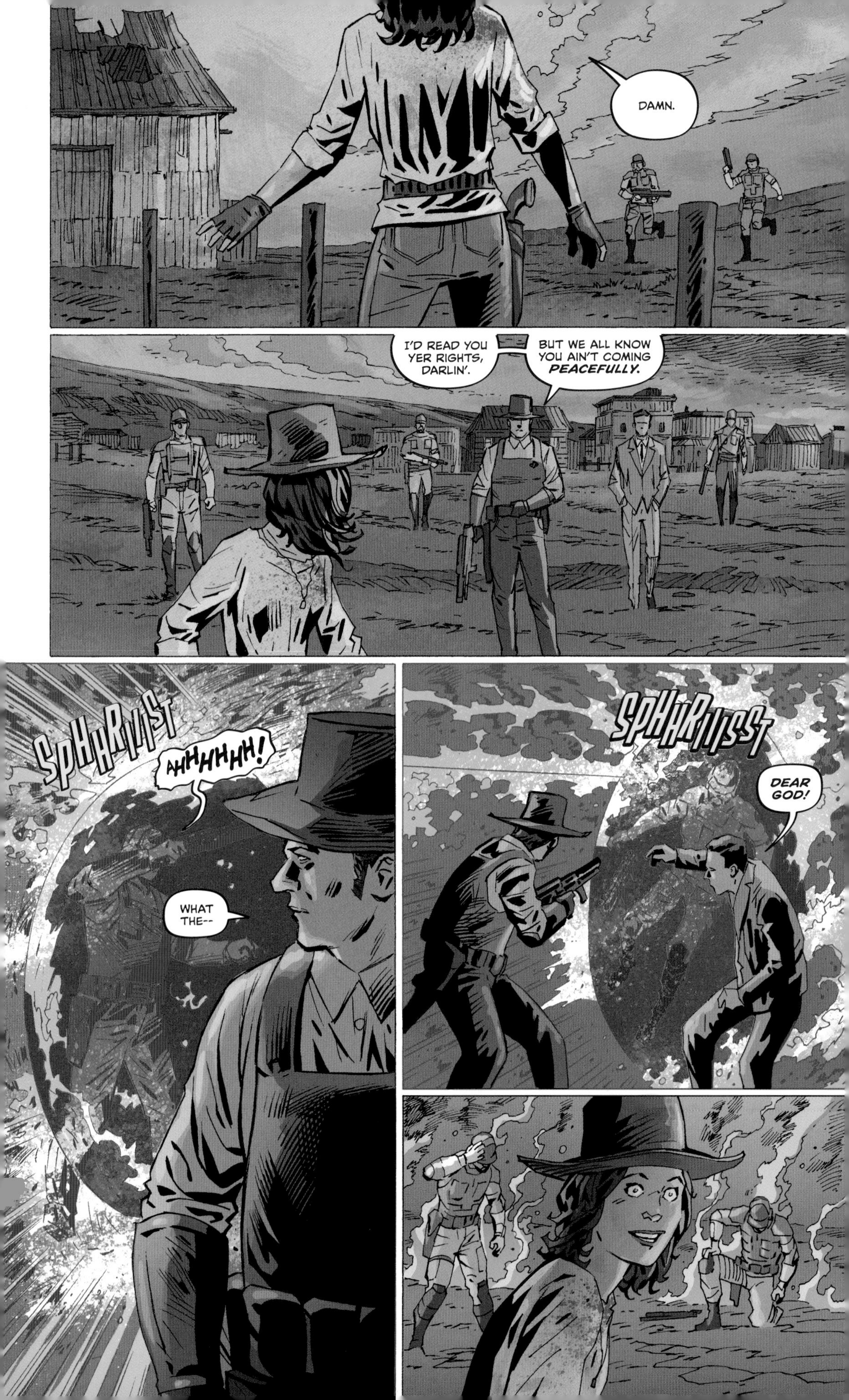
DAMN.
I'D READ YOU YER RIGHTS, DARLIN'.
BUT WE ALL KNOW YOU AIN'T COMING *PEACEFULLY.*
SPHHRIIISST
AHHHHHH!
WHAT THE--
SPHHRIIISSST
DEAR GOD!

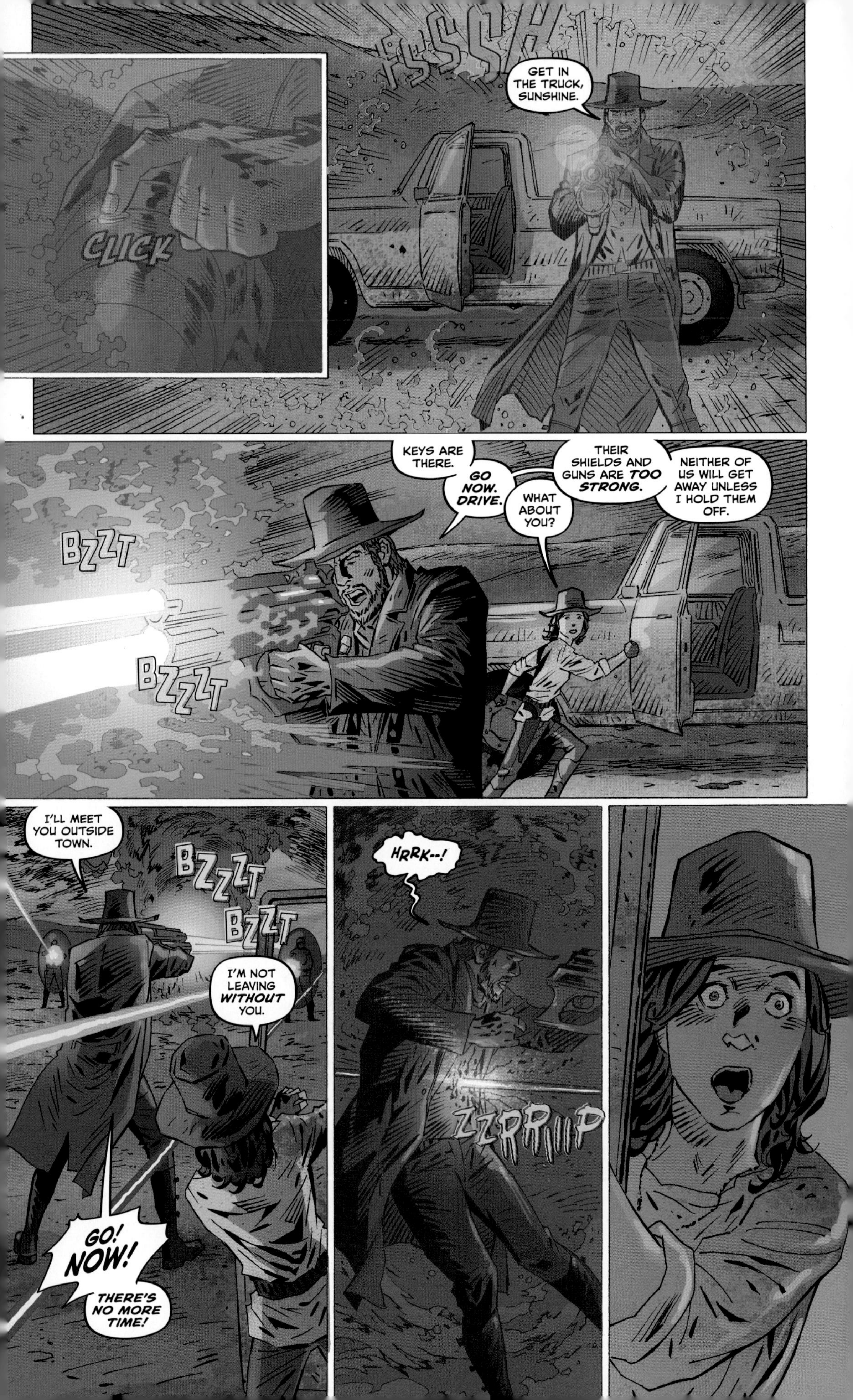
FSSSH
CLICK
GET IN THE TRUCK, SUNSHINE.
BZZT
BZZZT
KEYS ARE THERE. GO NOW. DRIVE.
WHAT ABOUT YOU?
THEIR SHIELDS AND GUNS ARE TOO STRONG.
NEITHER OF US WILL GET AWAY UNLESS I HOLD THEM OFF.
I'LL MEET YOU OUTSIDE TOWN.
BZZZT
BZZT
I'M NOT LEAVING WITHOUT YOU.
GO! NOW!
THERE'S NO MORE TIME!
HRRK--!
ZZRRIIIP

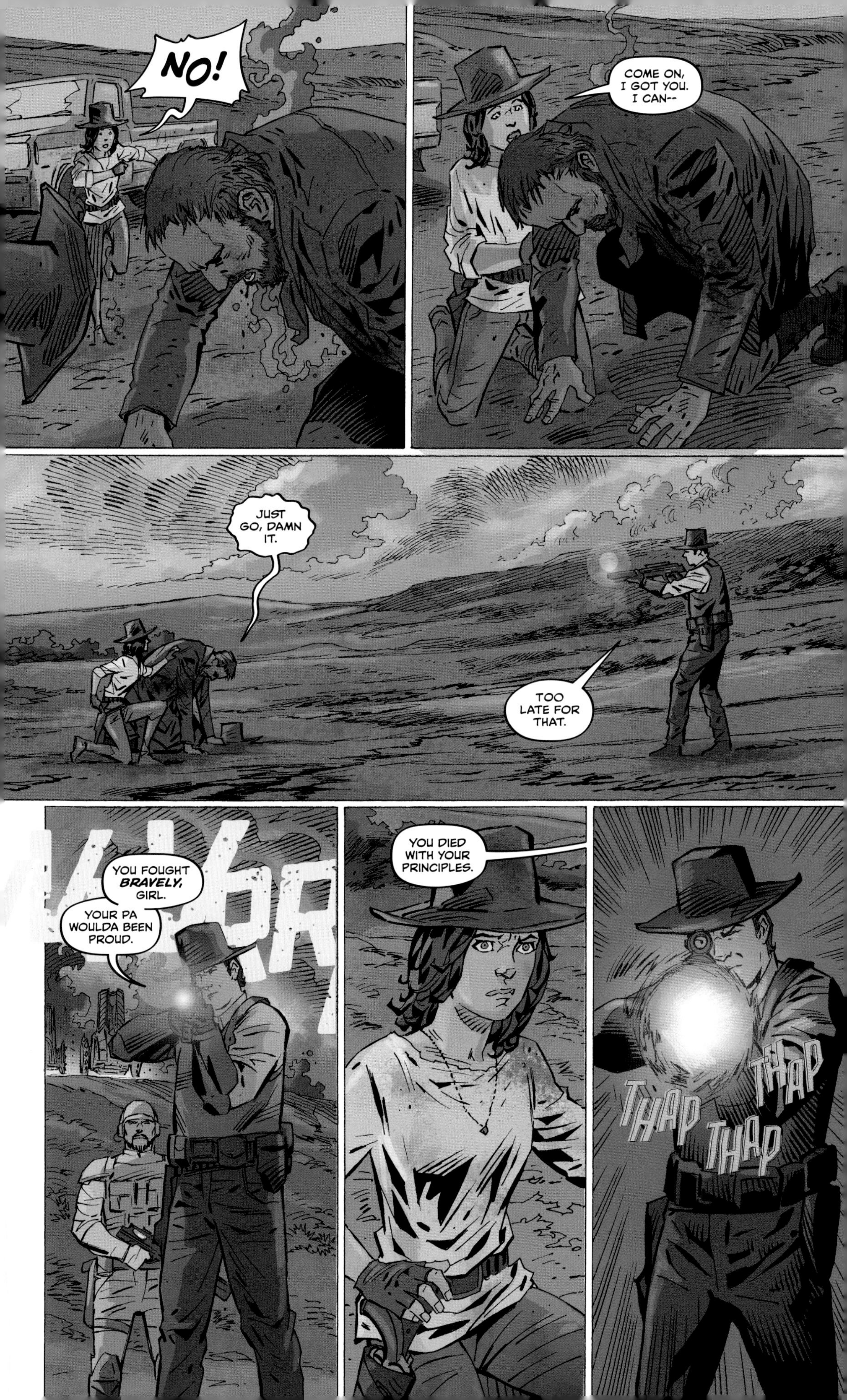
NO!
COME ON, I GOT YOU. I CAN--
JUST GO, DAMN IT.
TOO LATE FOR THAT.
YOU FOUGHT BRAVELY, GIRL.
YOUR PA WOULDA BEEN PROUD.
YOU DIED WITH YOUR PRINCIPLES.
THAP THAP THAP

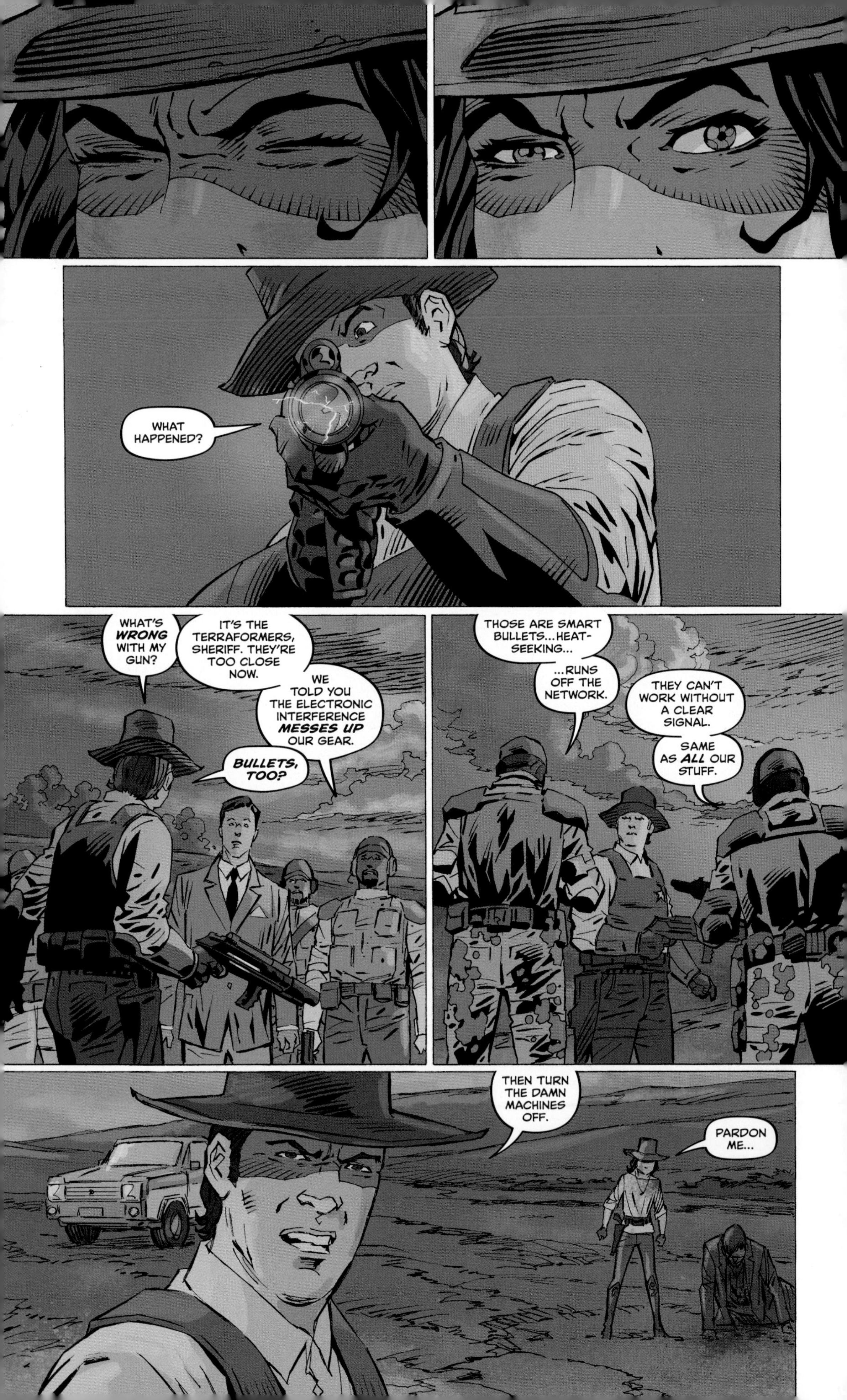
WHAT HAPPENED?
WHAT'S **WRONG** WITH MY GUN?
IT'S THE TERRAFORMERS, SHERIFF. THEY'RE TOO CLOSE NOW.
WE TOLD YOU THE ELECTRONIC INTERFERENCE **MESSES UP** OUR GEAR.
BULLETS, TOO?
THOSE ARE SMART BULLETS...HEAT-SEEKING...
...RUNS OFF THE NETWORK.
THEY CAN'T WORK WITHOUT A CLEAR SIGNAL.
SAME AS **ALL** OUR STUFF.
THEN TURN THE DAMN MACHINES OFF.
PARDON ME...

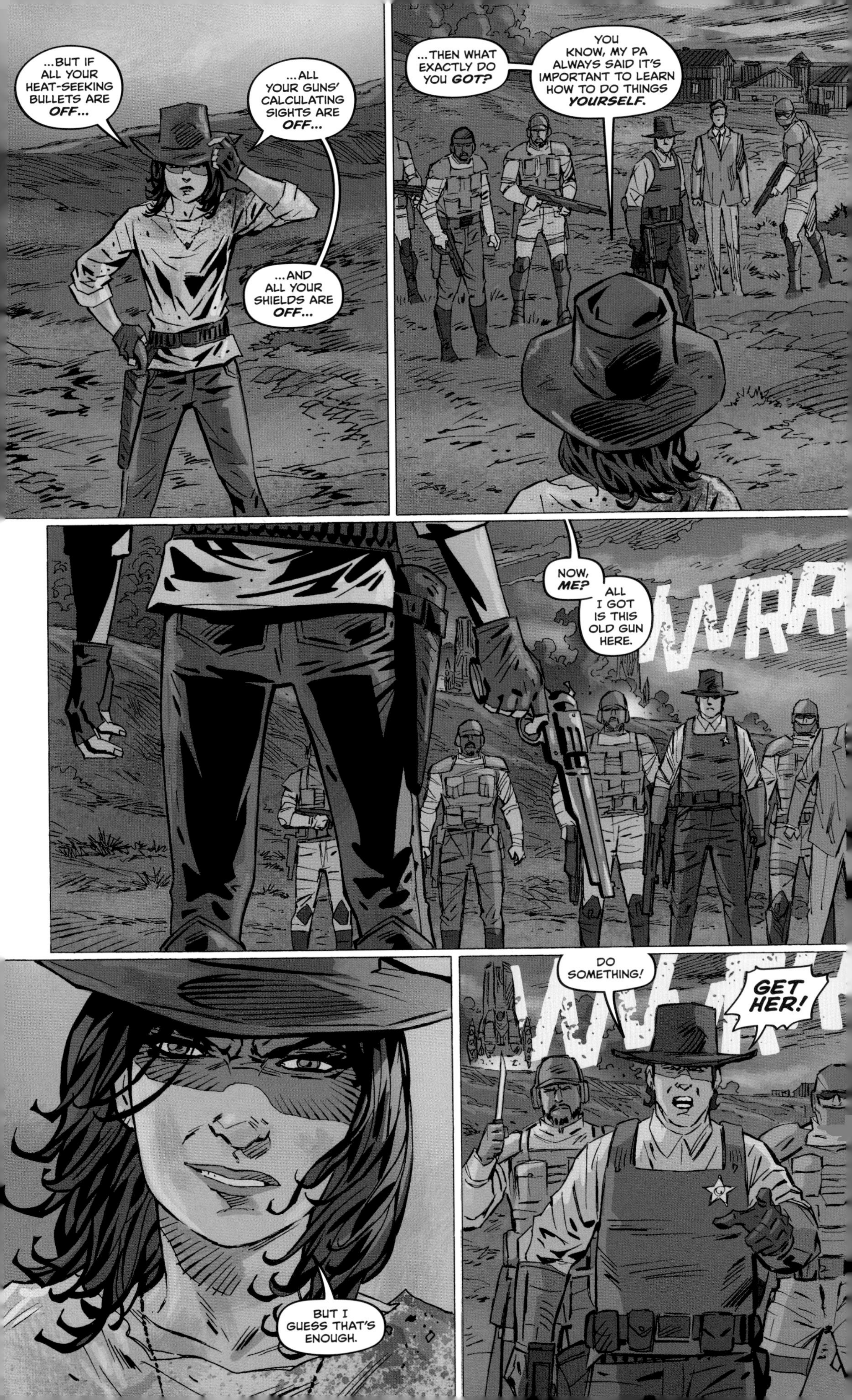

...BUT IF ALL YOUR HEAT-SEEKING BULLETS ARE *OFF*...
...ALL YOUR GUNS' CALCULATING SIGHTS ARE *OFF*...
...AND ALL YOUR SHIELDS ARE *OFF*...
...THEN WHAT EXACTLY DO YOU *GOT?*
YOU KNOW, MY PA ALWAYS SAID IT'S IMPORTANT TO LEARN HOW TO DO THINGS *YOURSELF.*
NOW, *ME?*
ALL I GOT IS THIS OLD GUN HERE.
WRR
BUT I GUESS THAT'S ENOUGH.
DO SOMETHING!
GET HER!

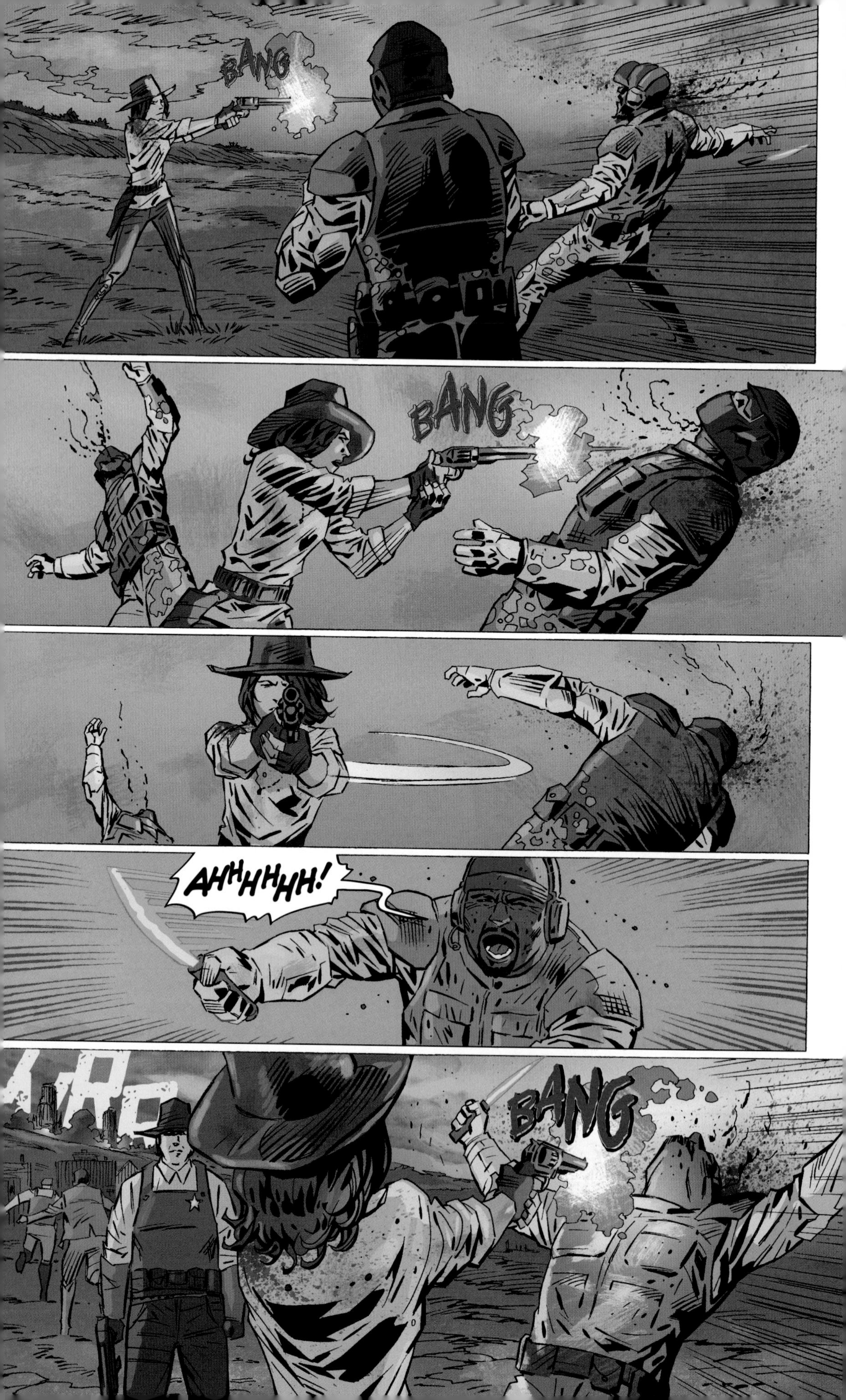
BANG
BANG
AHHHHHH!
BANG

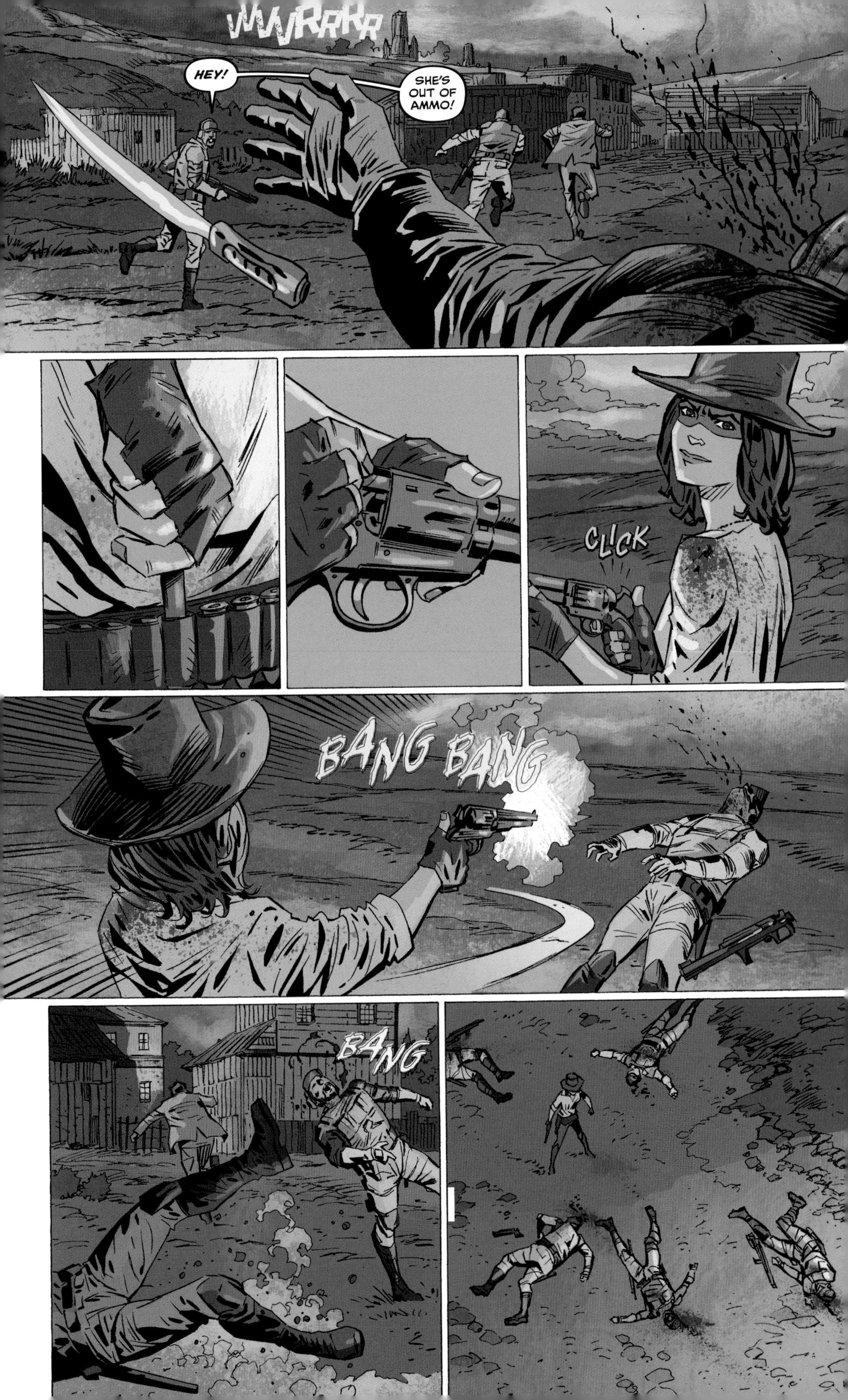
WWRRKR
HEY!
SHE'S OUT OF AMMO!
CLICK
BANG BANG
BANG

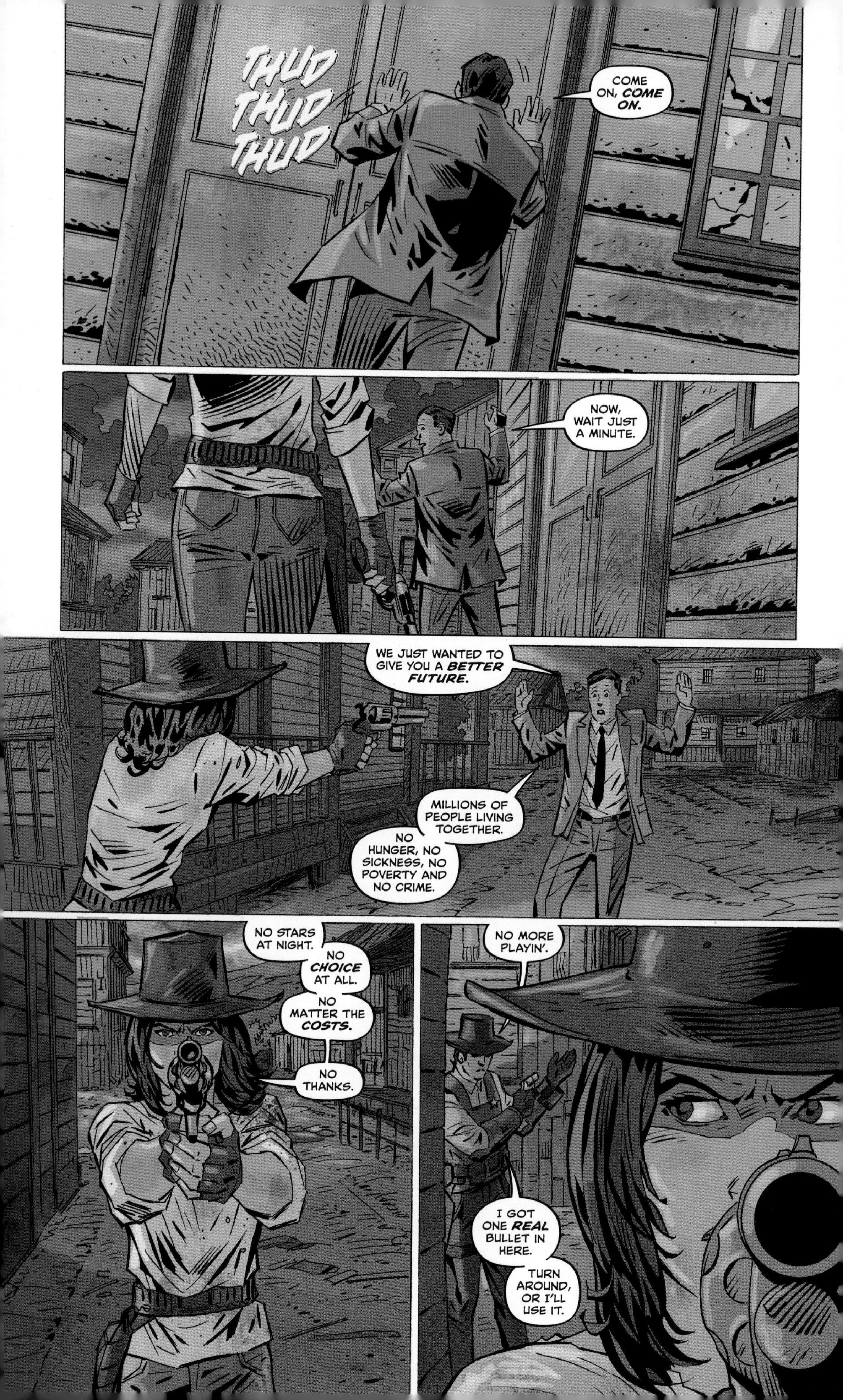
THUD THUD THUD
COME ON, COME ON.
NOW, WAIT JUST A MINUTE.
WE JUST WANTED TO GIVE YOU A BETTER FUTURE.
MILLIONS OF PEOPLE LIVING TOGETHER.
NO HUNGER, NO SICKNESS, NO POVERTY AND NO CRIME.
NO STARS AT NIGHT.
NO CHOICE AT ALL.
NO MATTER THE COSTS.
NO THANKS.
NO MORE PLAYIN'.
I GOT ONE REAL BULLET IN HERE.
TURN AROUND, OR I'LL USE IT.

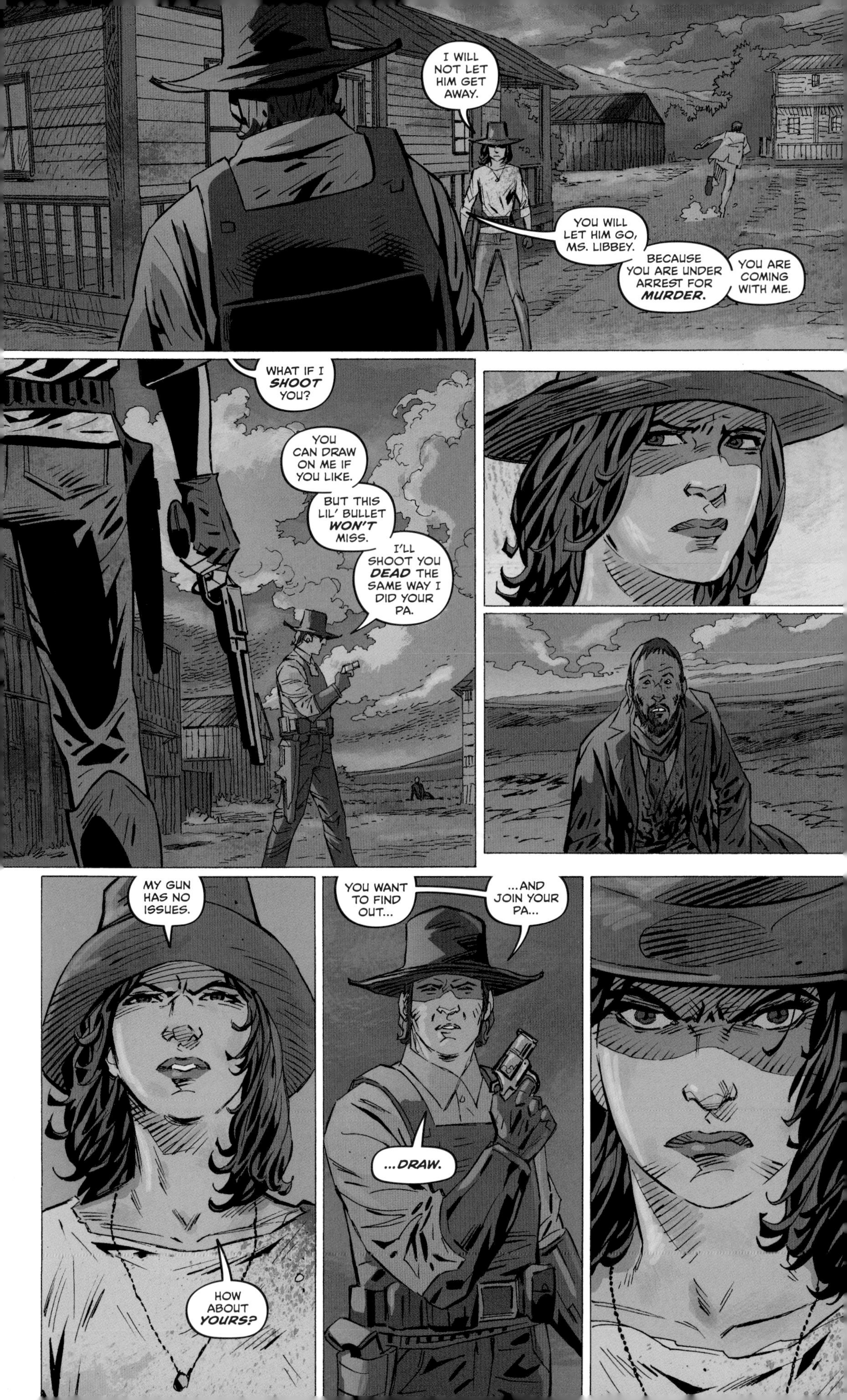
I WILL NOT LET HIM GET AWAY.
YOU WILL LET HIM GO, MS. LIBBEY.
BECAUSE YOU ARE UNDER ARREST FOR MURDER.
YOU ARE COMING WITH ME.
WHAT IF I SHOOT YOU?
YOU CAN DRAW ON ME IF YOU LIKE.
BUT THIS LIL' BULLET WON'T MISS.
I'LL SHOOT YOU DEAD THE SAME WAY I DID YOUR PA.
MY GUN HAS NO ISSUES.
HOW ABOUT YOURS?
YOU WANT TO FIND OUT...
...AND JOIN YOUR PA...
...DRAW.

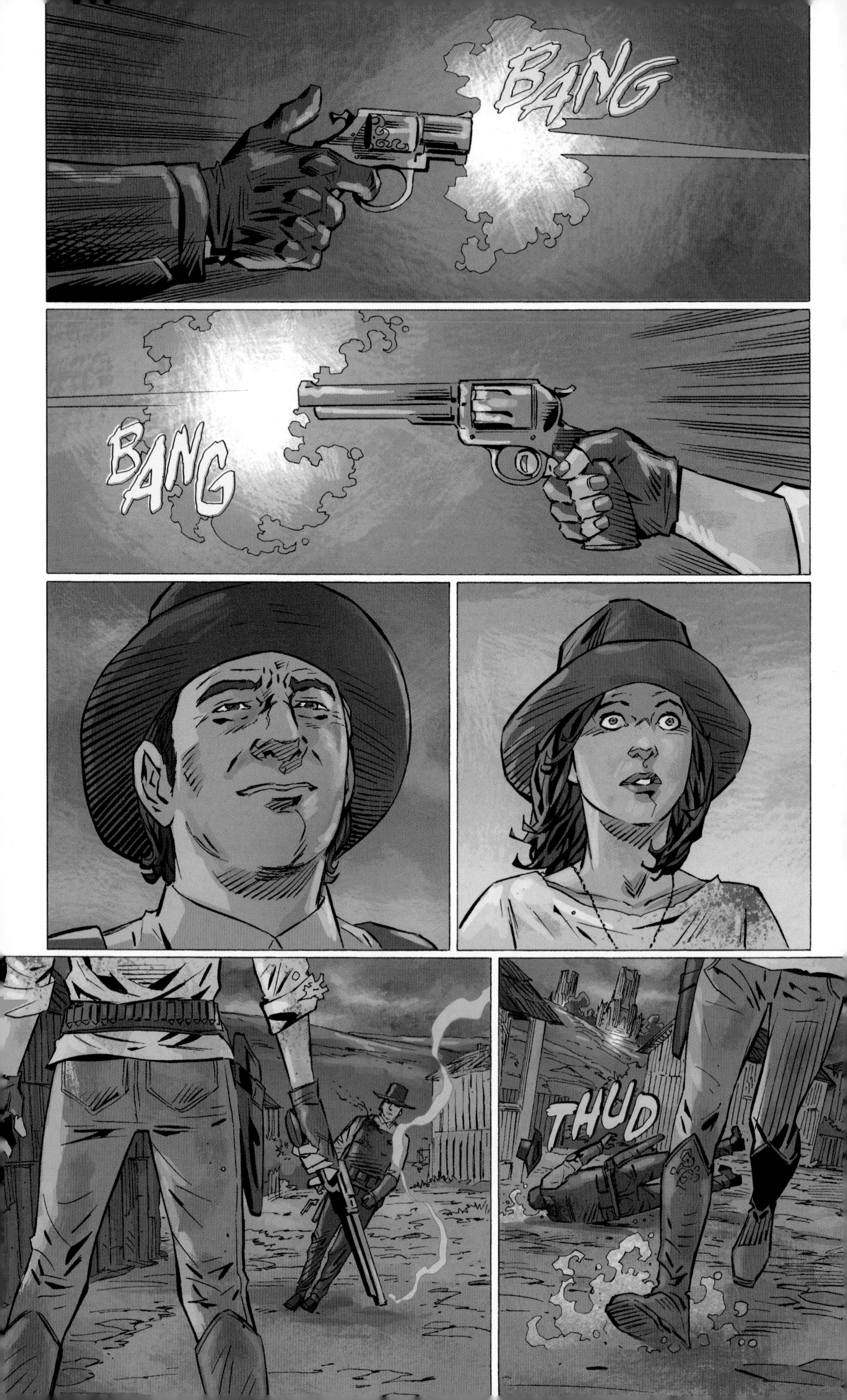
BANG
BANG
THUD

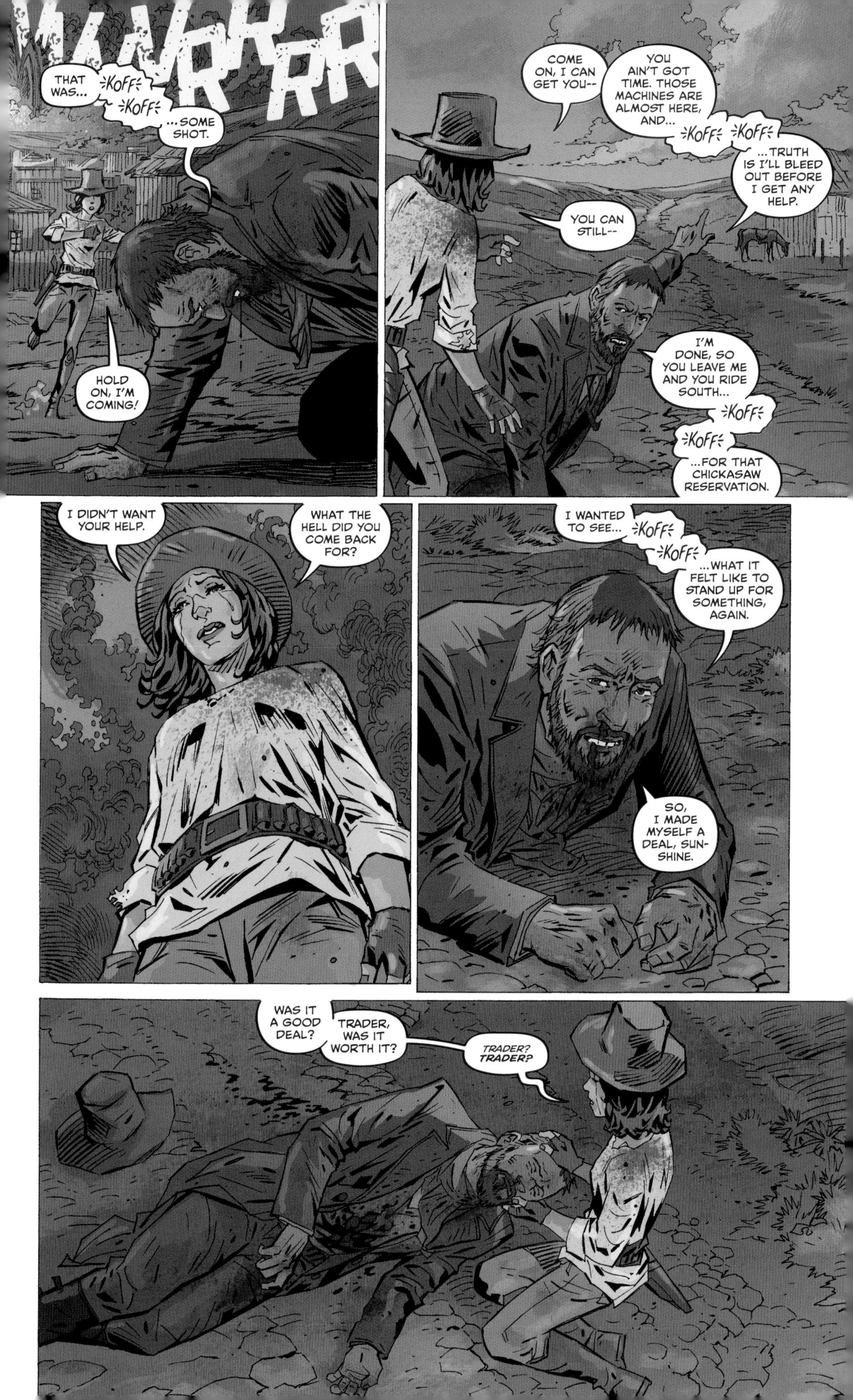
WNRRRR
THAT WAS... KOFF KOFF ...SOME SHOT.
HOLD ON, I'M COMING!
COME ON, I CAN GET YOU--
YOU AIN'T GOT TIME. THOSE MACHINES ARE ALMOST HERE, AND... KOFF KOFF
...TRUTH IS I'LL BLEED OUT BEFORE I GET ANY HELP.
YOU CAN STILL--
I'M DONE, SO YOU LEAVE ME AND YOU RIDE SOUTH... KOFF KOFF
...FOR THAT CHICKASAW RESERVATION.
I DIDN'T WANT YOUR HELP.
WHAT THE HELL DID YOU COME BACK FOR?
I WANTED TO SEE... KOFF KOFF
...WHAT IT FELT LIKE TO STAND UP FOR SOMETHING, AGAIN.
SO, I MADE MYSELF A DEAL, SUNSHINE.
WAS IT A GOOD DEAL?
TRADER, WAS IT WORTH IT?
TRADER? TRADER?

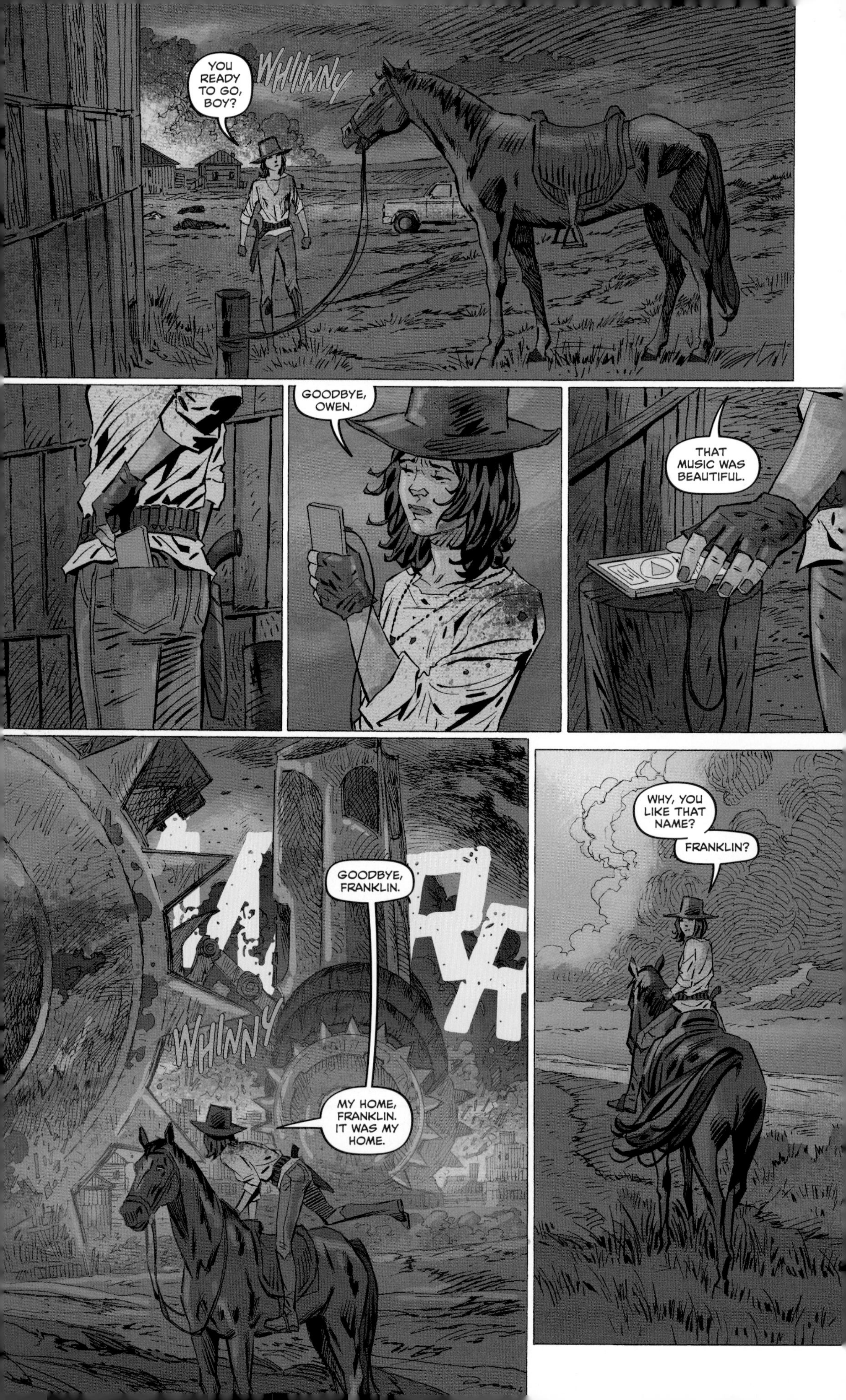
YOU READY TO GO, BOY?
WHIINNY
GOODBYE, OWEN.
THAT MUSIC WAS BEAUTIFUL.
GOODBYE, FRANKLIN.
WHINNY
MY HOME, FRANKLIN. IT WAS MY HOME.
WHY, YOU LIKE THAT NAME?
FRANKLIN?

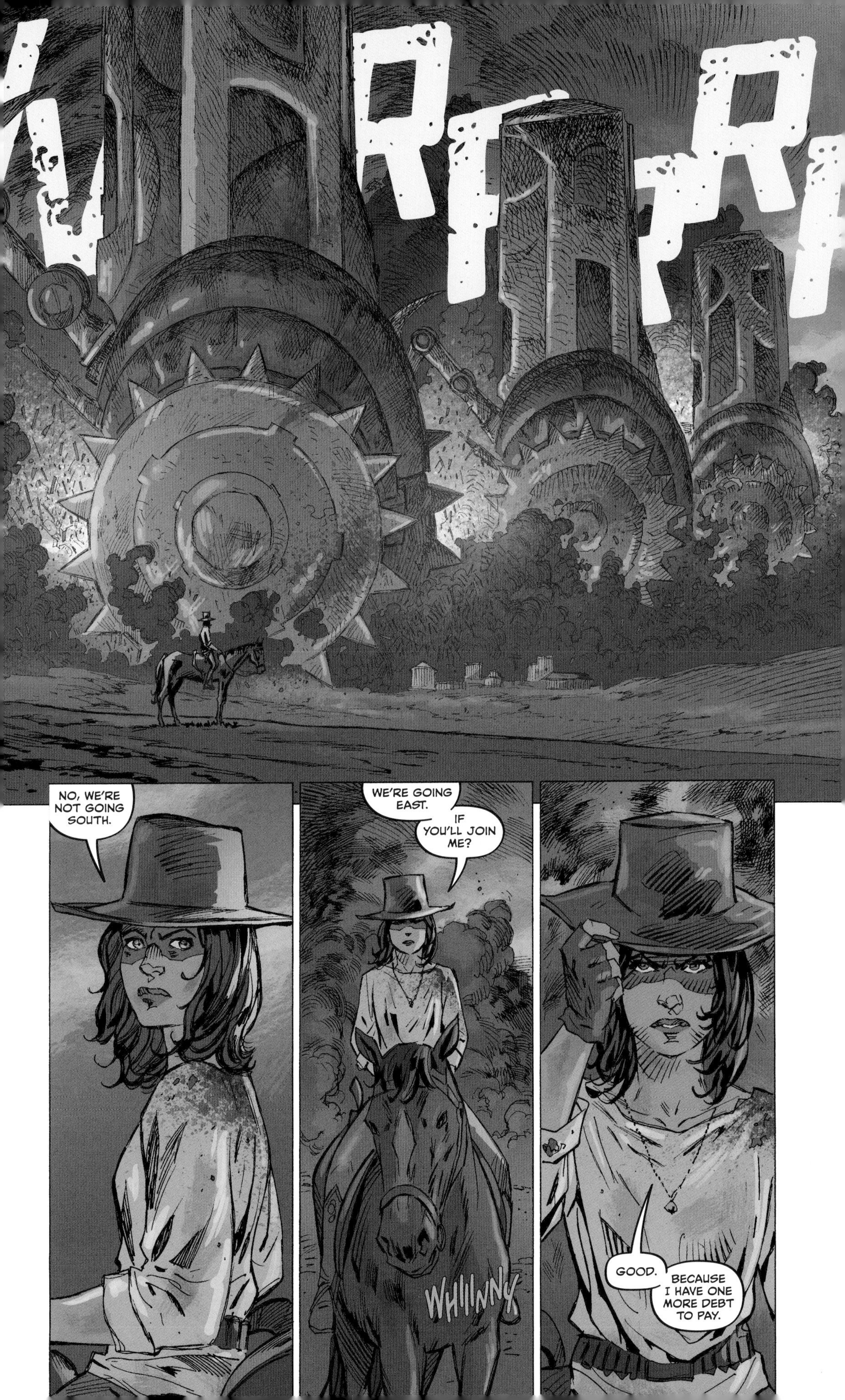

WRRRR
NO, WE'RE NOT GOING SOUTH.
WE'RE GOING EAST.
IF YOU'LL JOIN ME?
WHIIINNY
GOOD.
BECAUSE I HAVE ONE MORE DEBT TO PAY.

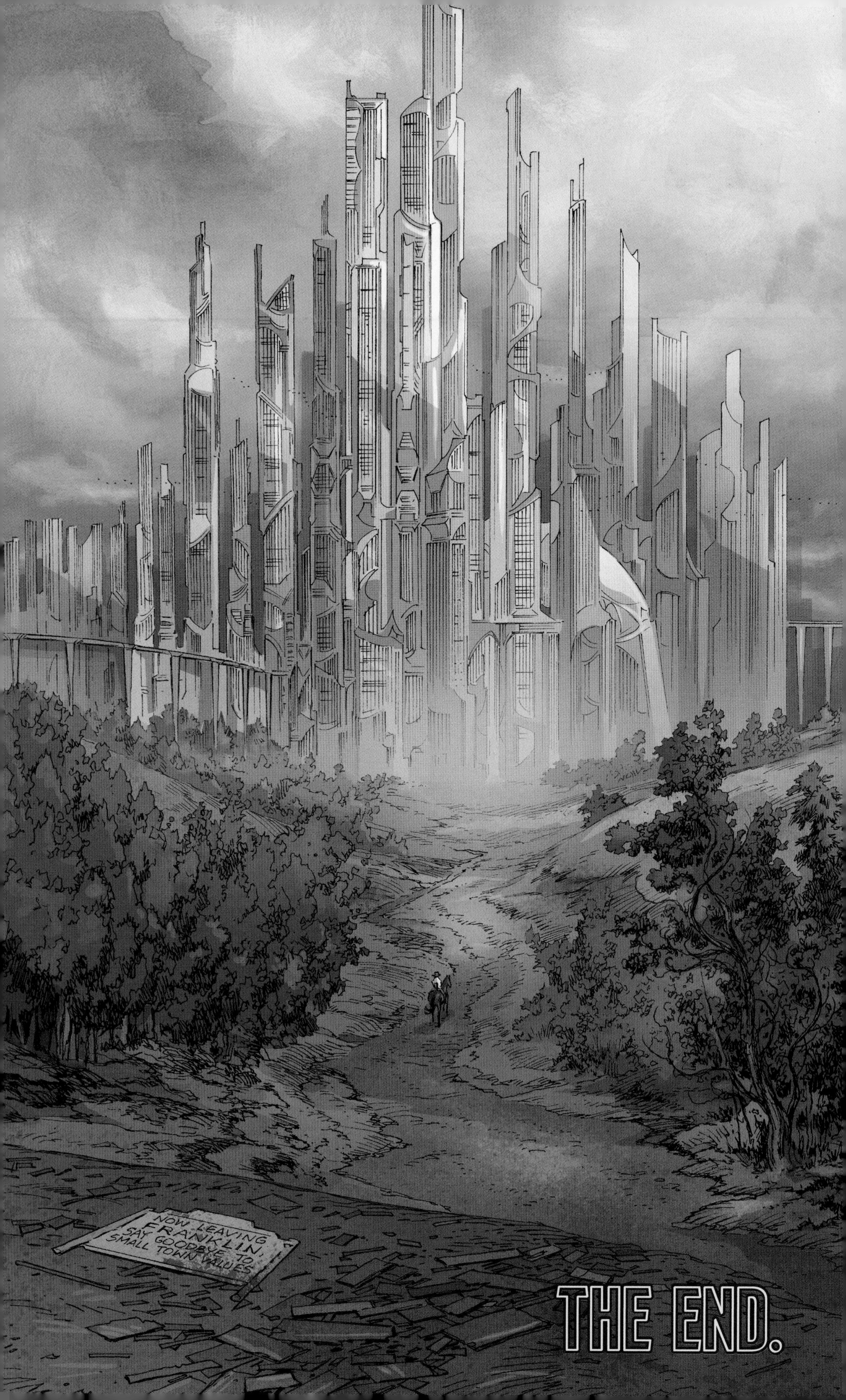
NOW LEAVING
FRANKLIN.
SAY GOODBYE TO
SMALL TOWN VALUES
THE END.

JOIN THE FUTURE

C L O S I N G   R E M A R K S

A few years ago, I read several articles about an ongoing trend in rural America, in which many residents were moving to suburban and metropolitan areas. I actually grew up during my pre-adolescent years in a small town in Iowa—Spielbergian cornfields and all. Reading about the decline of small towns made me curious about a future where that decline might hit rock bottom.

Could the American small town vanish?

It was a question apolitical in nature, dismissing the notion that small towns belong to red states or political parties, rather exploring the intimate and self-sufficient nature of small towns in a fast-approaching future that offers technological dependence and such a large sprawling population that human connection is optional, not required. And in that theme, in the style of a classic Western set in the future, with sci-fi laser guns to boot, our little series was born.

I was thrilled when AfterShock Comics immediately saw the daring vision, and agreed to do it. Editors Mike Marts and Christina Harrington helped mold the revenge story to further test the ideals and willpower of our young heroine. For art, I recently fell in love with Piotr Kowalski and Brad Simpson's epic landscapes and world-building, so I was beyond thrilled when they were available and excited to join our team. (Get it, JOIN our team?)

It was a challenging artistic mission to create two different worlds: a bright and clean futuristic city side-by-side with a dirty (but warm) Western town. Piotr and Brad delivered ten times over what you see in this book, a majestic portrait of a futuristic American countryside.

Hassan Otsmane-Elhaou is a powerhouse letterer with a consistent ability to elevate words into vivid pops and cleverly-paced moments. So, we were all ecstatic when he JOINED our adventure. (Sorry, I can't help myself with the "join" wordplay. I'll stop. Won't do it again.)

Let me tell you, it's a dream to make a book at AfterShock. The design work is crisp and beautiful, the marketing is carefully crafted and powerful and the passion to make great comics drives every decision. We poured our hearts into this book. And despite a dramatic hook, a big world, some heady themes, grand visuals and cool genre mash-up, well, the story was always centered on a girl.

A girl with grit. A girl facing a fast-moving future. A girl dealing with terrible tragedy. A girl who refuses to give up and inspires hope in us all. We strived to create a protagonist that had empathy for others, a complexity in her struggle and a drive to fight until the end. In some ways, she transforms from adolescence to adulthood before our very eyes.

The following backmatter showcases some letters written from the world of JOIN THE FUTURE, as well as some character sketches and comments from artist Piotr Kowalski. We hope you enjoy a look at the world-building and the process, and that you enjoyed our little yarn.

Thanks for JOINING us! (Couldn't resist!)

ZACK KAPLAN
October 2020

Issue 1
BRANDON PETERSON
Incentive Cover

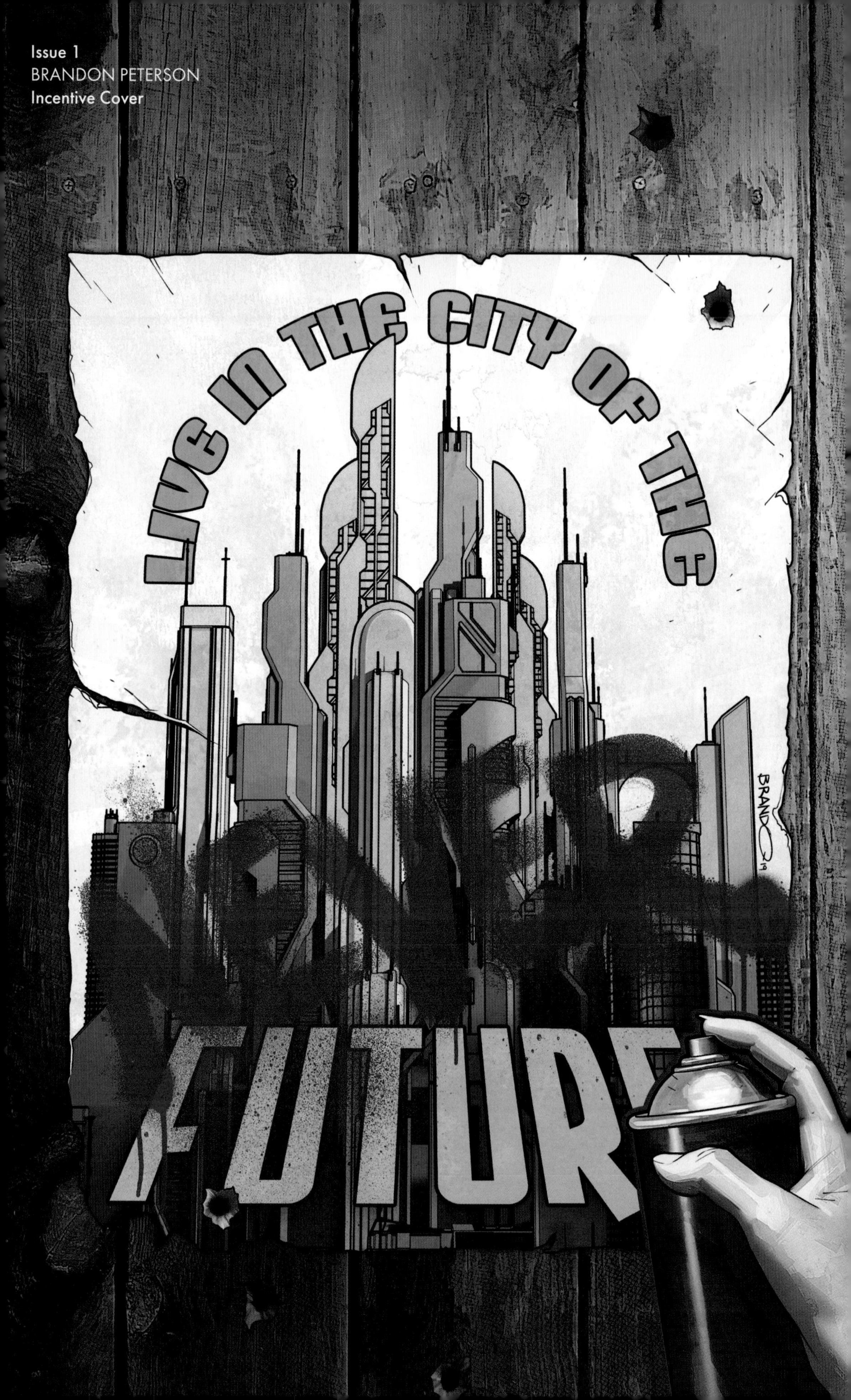

LIVE IN THE CITY OF THE
FUTURE
BRANDO 19

Issue 1

NATASHA ALTERICI

Knowhere Comics & Gaming Exclusive Variant Cover

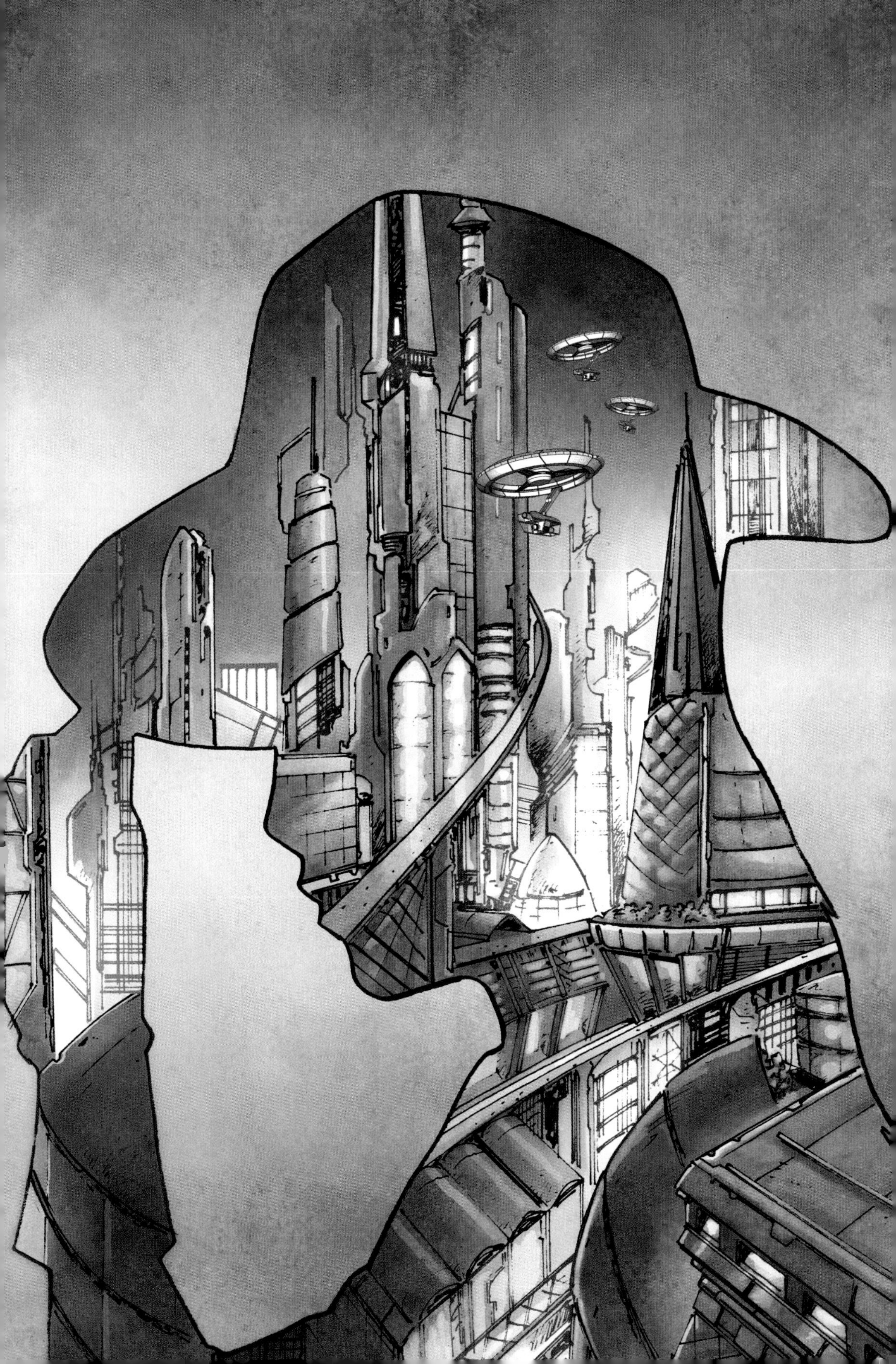

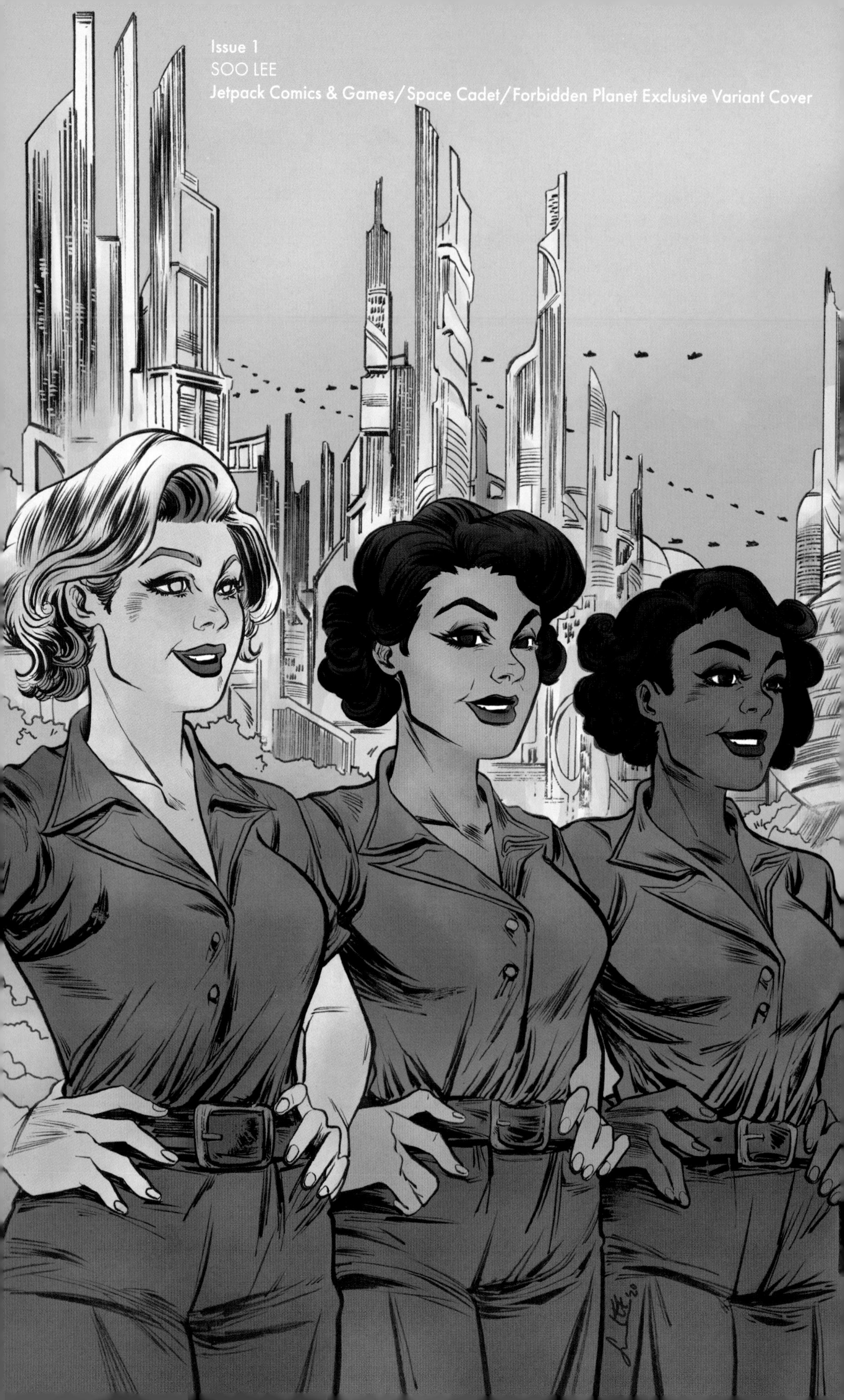

Issue 1
SOO LEE
Jetpack Comics & Games/Space Cadet/Forbidden Planet Exclusive Variant Cover

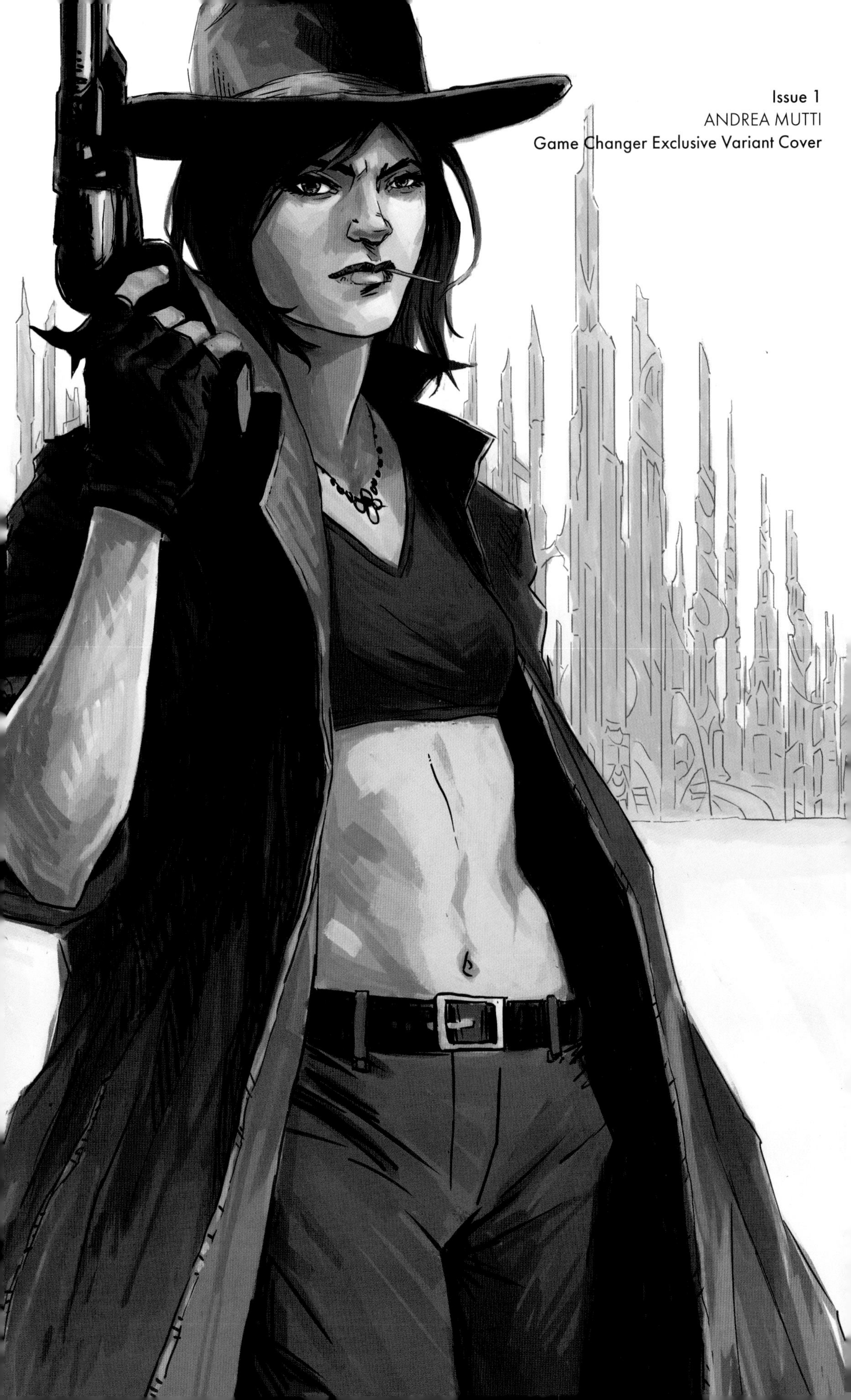

Issue 1
ANDREA MUTTI
Game Changer Exclusive Variant Cover

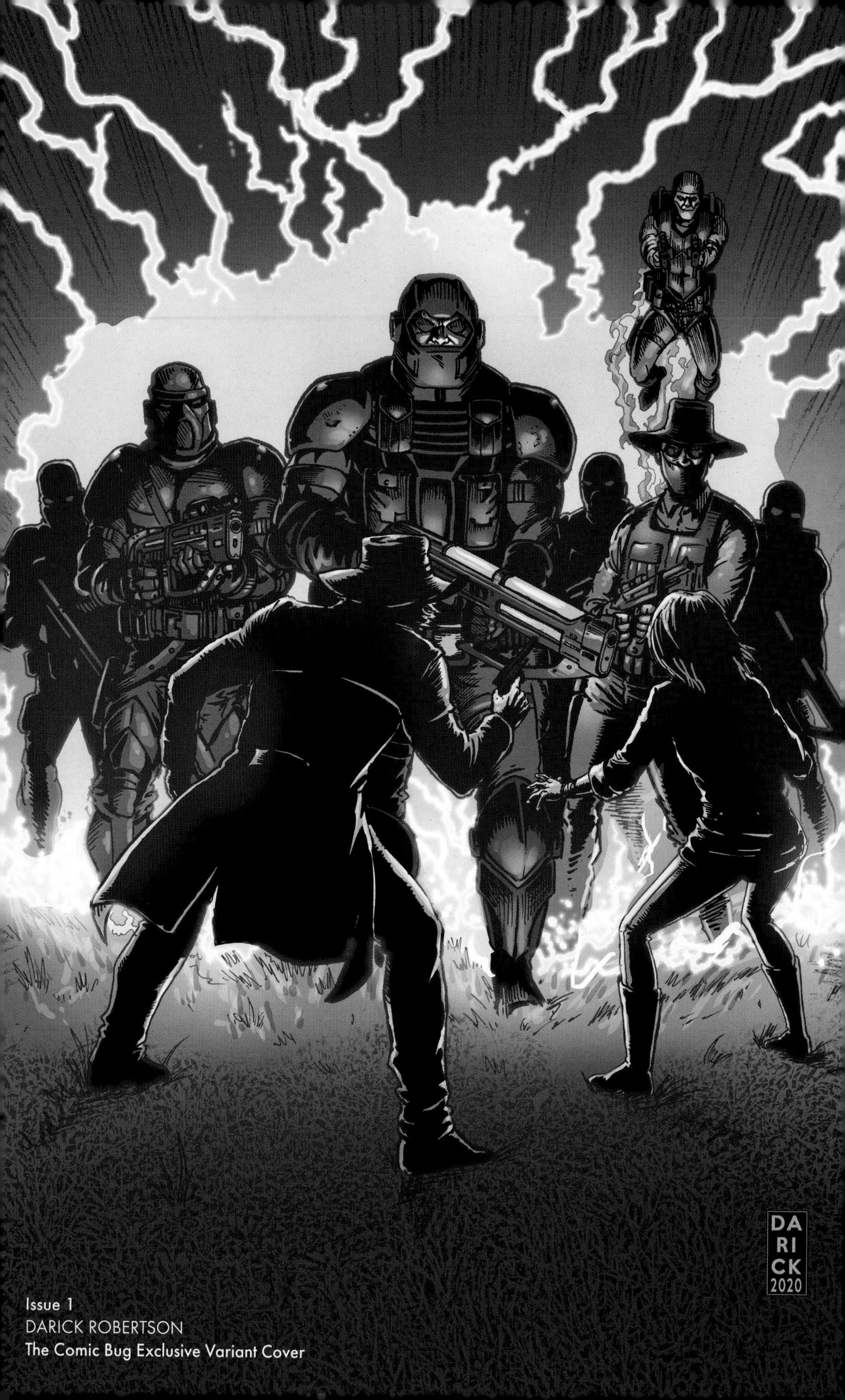
DA
RI
CK
2020

Issue 1
DARICK ROBERTSON
The Comic Bug Exclusive Variant Cover

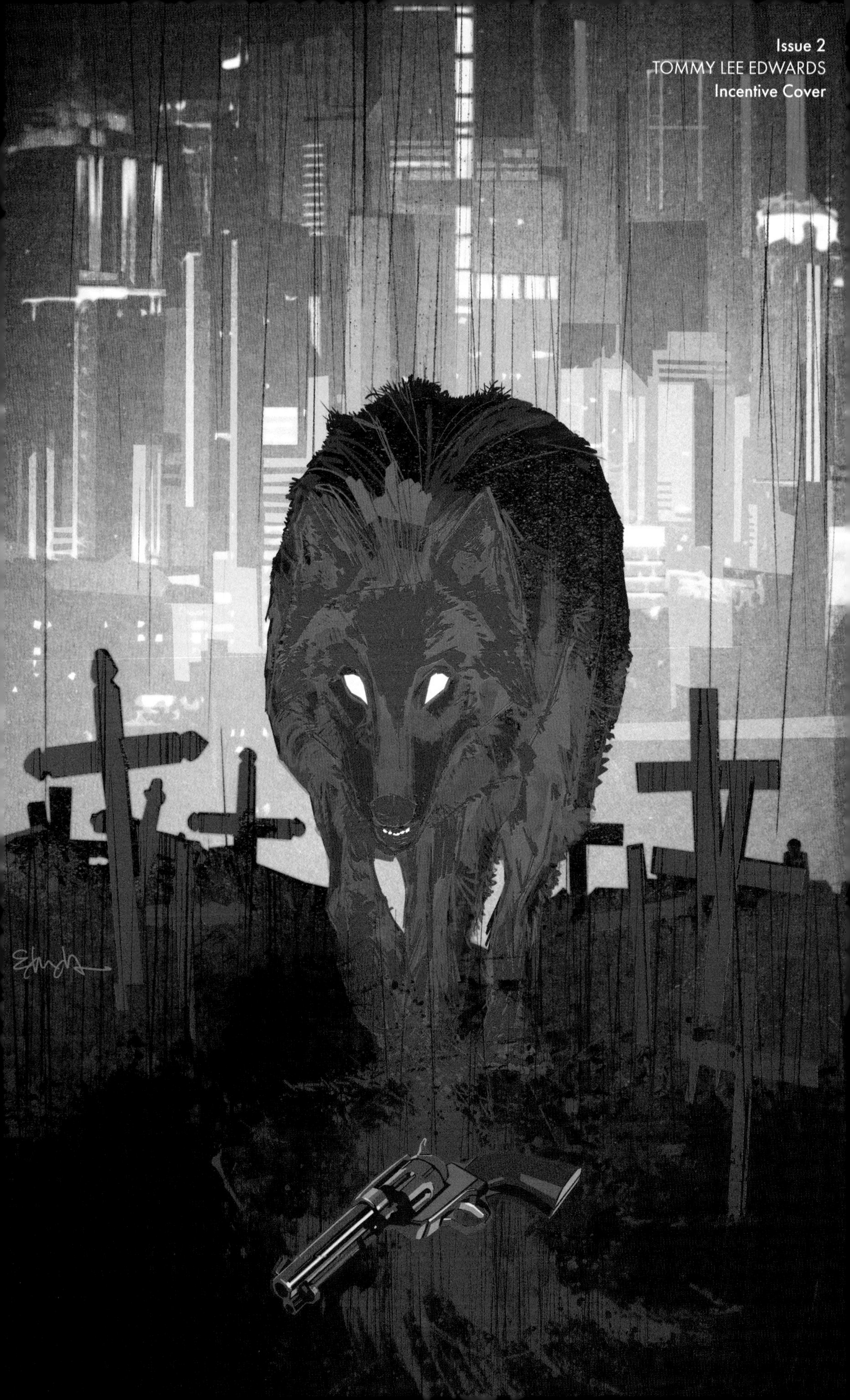

Issue 2
TOMMY LEE EDWARDS
Incentive Cover

LETTERS FROM THE PAST

Before abandoned towns are terraformed into natural preserve, they are scavenged by traders and merchants, who then travel the countryside and sell their discoveries. Most of these gatherers deal only in items of utility, but a few save trinkets and nostalgic memories from the past. Collected here are letters and journal entries left behind in the ruins of small town, USA.

Dear Maria,

I'm looking at the stars as I write this and I'm thinking of you.

This will be the last time I write you from Arlington. In the morn, my family is moving to the city. I think you know, but my pa is quite the doctor, and they told him he could have whatever he wanted if he came. They gave us a fancy house in one of the towers, and my pa gets his own elevator right to a car that drives him to the hospital. He can even sleep while he goes to work.

My ma didn't wanna go, but I'm excited. I'm gonna be one of those virtual gamers I heard so much about. If you're good enough, they pay you to play all day, and all you gotta do is support some drinks and shoes and let them take videos of you. They put me in school, but I don't need to learn much. I'll finally get online and then I can do anything. It's the city. Anything is possible.

I will miss meeting you at the lake, but I hope that one day your family will come around, too, and you will come to the city and we can be together there. You were my first kiss and I will never forget you and our time looking at the stars. I hear they use drones to simulate star watching in the city, but that don't make much sense to me. I think you and the stars will be the only things I miss.

I'd write you again, but I don't think they allow paper in the city. It's all done with computers, and I don't know how letters get out to these parts. My ma says they used to deliver letters once, but I guess they stopped that. Don't forget me and please come find me in the city one day.

Goodbye and with love,
Aaron

Sammy,

I won't ask for your help, again. You and your siblings have made their choice and now I will make mine. My whole life, people have left me and left Old Washington. I didn't mind it because that was their choice. But this selling off of the municipality, all this legal nonsense, telling me I have to go live somewhere else now, I don't understand a bit of it.

My father's father was born here, and his father, and your father and I were both born in this town just five miles apart. We sat in school together. Your father worked with my father and my brothers in one of the largest car plants in the Midwest. They built over five million cars during their time there, back when cars brought us together. Back when they connected us. Your pa and my brothers worked every day breaking their backs so you and your siblings could go to those city colleges and have a better future.

When you and your brother and sister moved away, we managed here. We managed when you didn't come back in over ten years, and we managed without your empty video chats. We managed when the car plant closed, and we managed when our trucking company was replaced by these computer driving trucks, and we managed when they told us to build windmills and then they decided our mills weren't advanced enough, so they'd just leave us, too.

I watched as my brothers passed on, and then your father. I watched as you all left, one by one. But I won't go. When they come, I'll be dead, and the Paulson's have agreed to bury me next to your father. And they can tear up this town, but I'll still be here with the roots. Tell your children they were from Washington, and that their grandmother is still there.

Your mother,

Peggy Jean

SUPERION GASOLINE
A CROMWELL COMPANY

9.22.59

My son, Isaac,

I'm near the 191, on the border of Wyoming and Idaho, and I was able to purchase this actual paper and an ink pen from a nearby store to write you this letter. I remember my father writing me letters when I went to college; it's old-fashioned but I couldn't resist.

We've just transformed our largest recovery, over four-thousand square feet of recycled land into a beautiful natural preserve, and I've named it Isaac's Gully. We've upgraded our water design feature, and I'm thrilled to say the machines, along with our coordinated drone force, now can create waterfalls over ten feet tall. It was one thing to work in the flat lands of Kansas, but here in the mountains, the entire terraforming team is in awe. I'm sending you a 3-D virtual scene so you can see for yourself the before, with these dilapidated, decaying half-abandoned towns, and the after, with these picturesque tree lines and our engineered water features.

I hear from your mother that you working with a team of classmates and AI avatars to deliver new genome coding. That is fantastic! Everyone needs drugs specially tailored for them, and working with super AI will prepare you for great jobs in the future.

I won't be back in October, but I will return for the holidays. Take care of your sister and listen to your mother.

Love,
your father

Date, 2/29/55

Lee,

I'm sending this note through a friend, a trader in these parts, and I hope to God you get it in time.

I got caught up in some bad news here. I was approached by some men from Fordham who had a plan about hitting the trucks. They knew I was always the first one on the scene when they break down and they wanted my help. You never did get my new job, but it wasn't terrible work for a former mechanic.

These self-driving trucks break down like any other, and I would show up, assess the nature of the breakdown and make sure the right drone repair was ordered onto the scene.

The boys suggested when the truck with valuable medicine breaks down, I request the drone repair that takes the longest. Unfortunately, after a few times, the authorities caught wind, and they sent the law in. Fancy law, with guns I never seen before. I tried to deal my way out, but it didn't go well, and now I'm holed up in Watter's End Tavern off the 44.

If the law don't find me, the Fordham boys might. I need wheels out of here.

Please come get me.

Bring your gun and bring help.

Your brother, James

JOIN THE FUTURE™

JOIN THE FUTURE is the second Western comic series I have done in my life. I did the first one for my European publisher, and when I finished it, I wasn't really keen on revisiting the Old Wild West.

I have never been a big Western fan, neither in comics nor in movies. A few years went by and then Zack [Kaplan] sent me his script. When I read it, I knew right away that JOIN THE FUTURE would be my second chance to plunge into the Wild West.

But this time it would be totally different—Zack provided me with a story that blended genres, added a new commentary to the familiar struggle between the Old World and the New World and threw a seemingly helpless individual right into a grinding machine of an oppressive system. I absolutely loved it.

I like comics that give me opportunity to create my own movie with good actors, with carefully designed sets, with conscientiously-chosen clothes and props.

I also like scripts that allow me to design "fluid" layouts which are necessary for smooth visual narration.

JOIN THE FUTURE gave me all that—plus, it gave me a very interesting protagonist in Clementine Libbey, a teenage girl who was given a choice: sign her life to the modern, overwhelming polis or die.

Everything was taken from Clementine—she was captured, but managed to escape, found an unexpected friend and eventually was given a chance to face the murderer of her father.

"Without a doubt, it is a captivating, emotional journey. And a comic book I hope readers enjoyed reading as much as I did drawing it.

PIOTR KOWALSKI

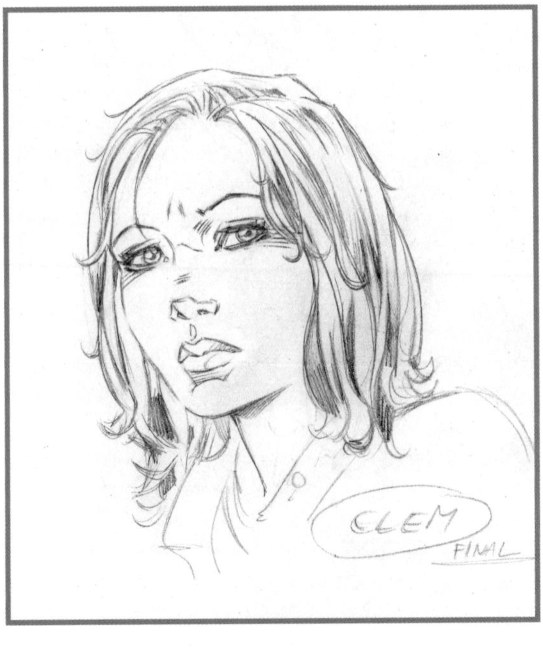
CLEM
FINAL

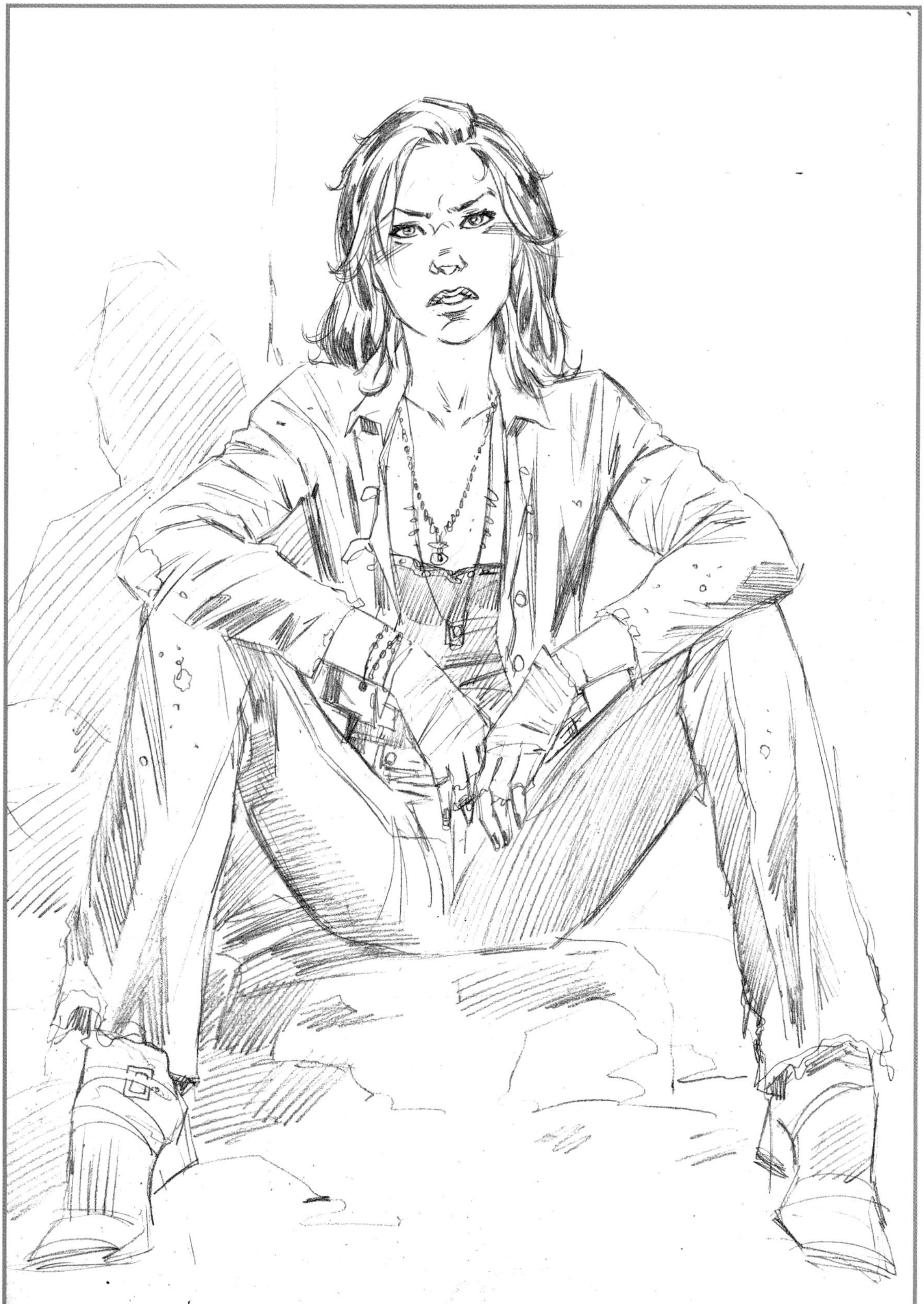

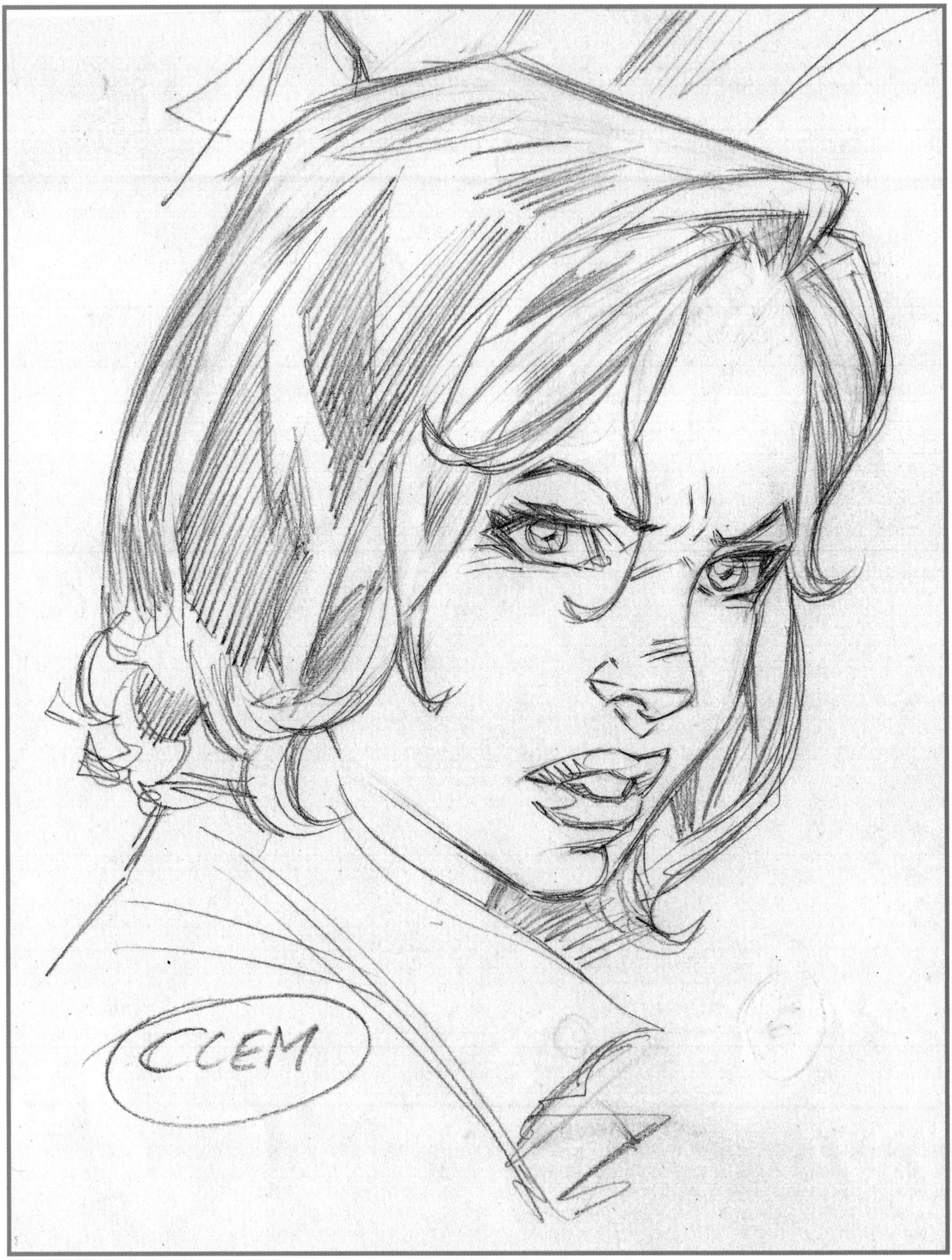
CCEM

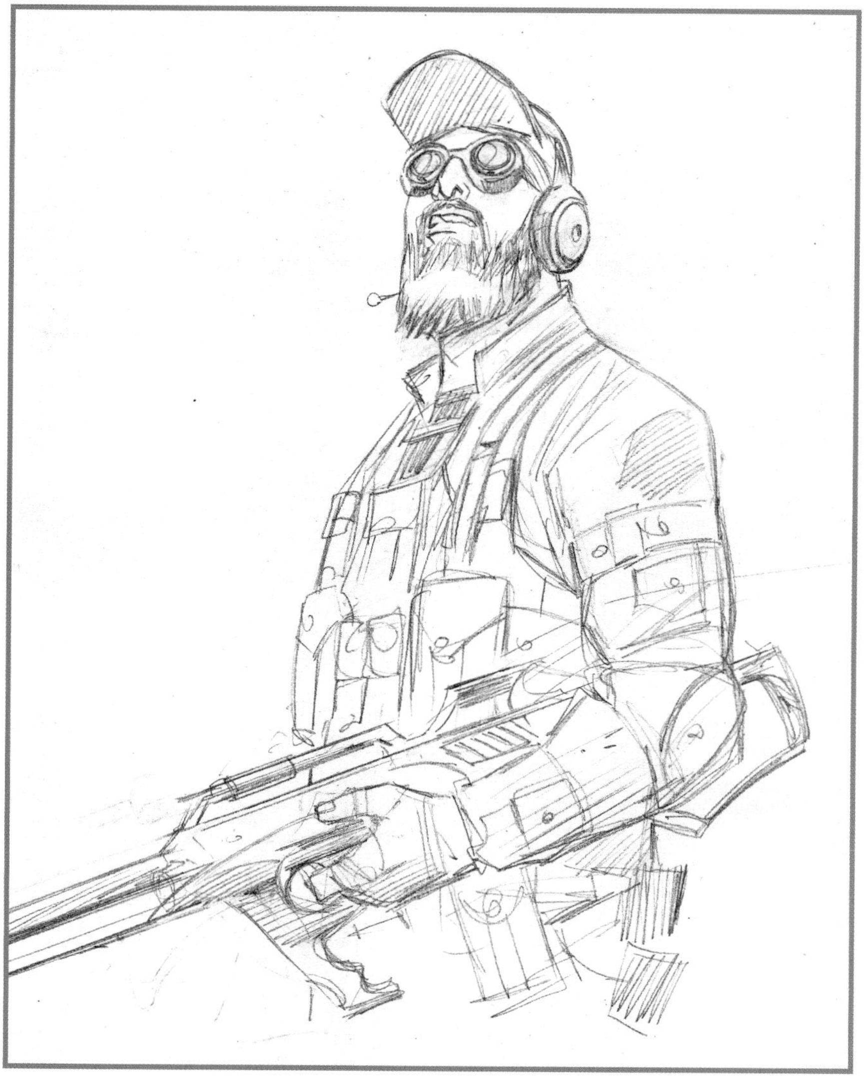

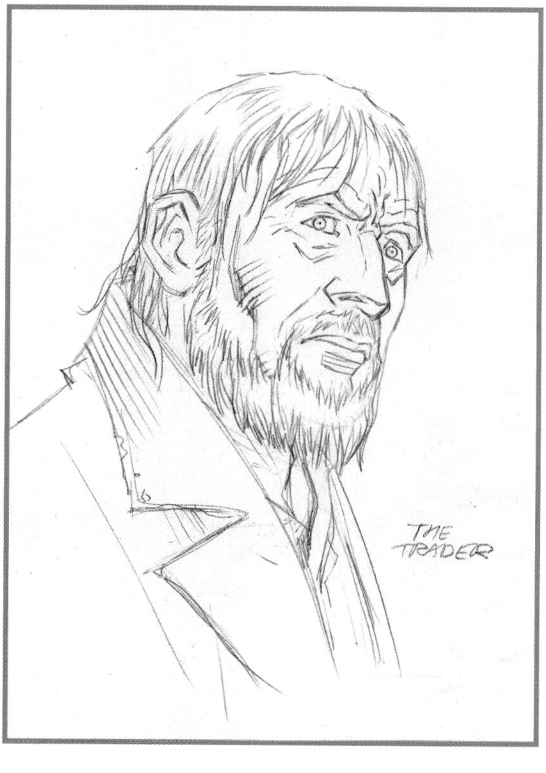
THE TRADER

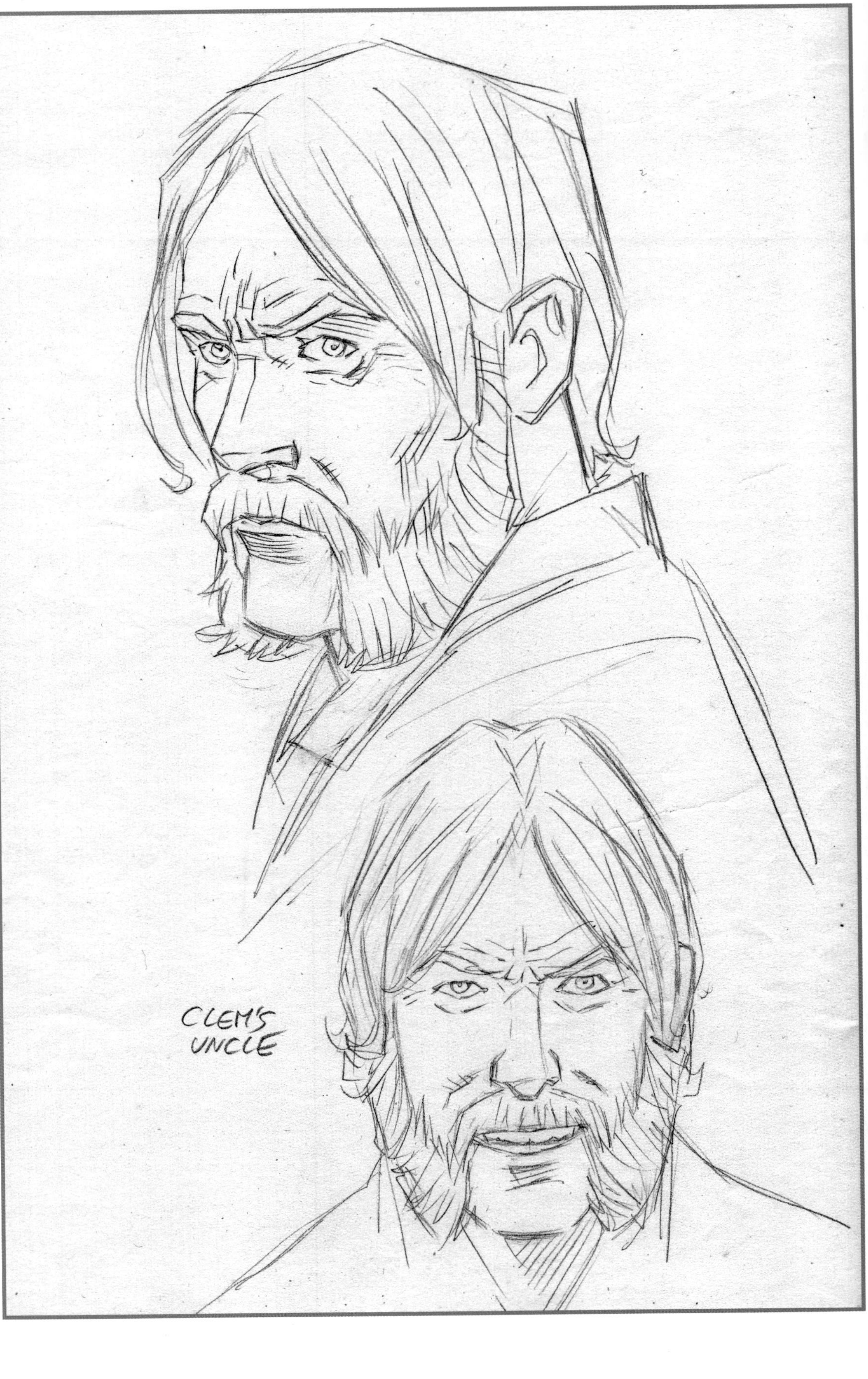
CLEM'S
UNCLE